LIVING WITH ENVIRONMENTAL CHANGE

Climate change is a lived experience of changes in the environment, often destroying conventional forms of subsistence and production, creating new patterns of movement and connection, and transforming people's imagined future.

This book explores how people across the world think about environmental change and how they act upon the perception of past, present and future opportunities. Drawing on the ethnographic fieldwork of expert authors, it sheds new light on the human experience of and social response to climate change by taking us from the Arctic to the Pacific, from the Southeast Indian Coastal zone to the West African dry-lands and deserts, as well as to Peruvian mountain communities and cities.

Divided into four thematic parts – Water, Technology, Landscape, Time – this book uses rich photographic material to accompany the short texts and reflections in order to bring to life the human ingenuity and social responsibility of people in the face of new uncertainties. In an era of melting glaciers, drying lands, and rising seas, it shows how it is part and parcel of human life to take responsibility for the social community and take creative action on the basis of a localized understanding of the environment.

This highly original contribution to the anthropological study of climate change is a must-read for all those wanting to understand better what climate change means on the ground and interested in a sustainable future for the Earth.

KIRSTEN HASTRUP is Professor at the Department of Anthropology, University of Copenhagen, Denmark.

CECILIE RUBOW is Associate Professor at Department of Anthropology, University of Copenhagen, Denmark.

Is it possible to understand climate change through scientific theories, data and models? Hastrup and Rubow in this important book show why the answer is a decisive 'no'. Drawing upon a rich and diverse array of sites around the world, Living with Environmental Change: Waterworlds *offers dozens of compelling portraits of what climate change means to different people living in different places. This impressive collection of short essays shows why the anthropological study of climate change is at least as important as its scientific study. Rather than something to be feared, climate change is becoming part of the way in which humans and their cultures continually respond to the future and thereby re-shape it.*

MIKE HULME
King's College London, UK

A unique contribution to the understanding of climate change as it appears to people all over the world. Using the framework of water, technology, landscape and time it is a bold attempt to summarise a lot of human interest, experience and theory. It should be appreciated by anyone interested in the topic and not just by specialists.

JONATHAN PAUL MARSHALL
University of Technology Sydney, Australia

The Waterworlds team has produced a book that 'shows rather than tells' how communities experience climate change at a local level. By highlighting narratives from different parts of the world, they illuminate the complex pressures that emerge as shifts in climate initiate changes in social and material environments, as well as the creative adaptations that people are making in confronting these challenges.

VERONICA STRANG
Durham University, UK

LIVING WITH ENVIRONMENTAL CHANGE

Waterworlds

Edited by
Kirsten Hastrup
& Cecilie Rubow

LONDON AND NEW YORK

First published 2014
by Routledge
2 Park Square, Milton Park, Abingdon, Oxon, OX14 4RN

and by Routledge
711 Third Avenue, New York, NY 10017

Routledge is an imprint of the Taylor & Francis Group, an informa business

© 2014 Kirsten Hastrup and Cecilie Rubow

British Library Cataloguing in Publication Data
A catalogue record for this book is available from the British Library

Library of Congress Cataloging-in-Publication Data
Living with environmental change : waterworlds / edited by Kirsten
Hastrup, Cecilie Rubow.
    pages cm
Includes bibliographical references and index.
1. Water–Environmental aspects. 2. Climatic changes.
3. Global environmental change. I. Hastrup, Kirsten.
    GB661.2.L58 2014
    333.91–dc23
    2013040606

ISBN13: 978-0-415-74667-0 (hbk)
ISBN13: 978-1-315-79746-5 (ebk)

Typeset by Alex Lazarou

CONTENTS

P. X   CONTRIBUTORS

P. XIV   PREFACE &
ACKNOWLEDGEMENTS

P. 2   INTRODUCTION

P. 10   PORTRAITS

P. 18   PART ONE
WATER

P. 86   PART TWO
TECHNOLOGY

P. 152   PART THREE
LANDSCAPE

P. 220   PART FOUR
TIME

P. 286   BIBLIOGRAPHY

P. 294   FURTHER READING

PART ONE
WATER

PART TWO
TECHNOLOGY

P. 20 Introduction
Kirsten Hastrup

P. 28 Narwhals and Navigators on the
Arctic Sea Kirsten Hastrup

P. 32 Ephemeral Tsunamis, Emotional
Waves, and Enduring Islands
Maria Louise B. Robertson

P. 36 Seawater to the Mountain Top:
The Hydrological Cycle in Chivay,
Peru Astrid B. Stensrud

P. 40 Bursting Bodies of Water
Mattias Borg Rasmussen

P. 44 When It Rains and the River Grows
Astrid O. Andersen

P. 48 The Elusive Pleasure of Rain in the
Sahel Jonas O. Nielsen

P. 52 Dams: Management Versus Luck
Mette Fog Olwig

P. 56 Water as Power and Destroyer
Frank Sejersen

P. 60 New Opportunities Turning into
Disaster Anette Reenberg

P. 64 Coastal Gardens and Their Magic
Frida Hastrup

P. 68 The Sprawled Way of Detergents
Cecilie Rubow

P. 72 Droughts: Complex Social
Phenomena Christian Vium

P. 76 Water Quantity Vs Water Quality
Laura Vang Rasmussen

P. 80 Fixed and Fluid Waters: Mirroring
the Arctic and the Pacific
Kirsten Hastrup
and Maria Louise B. Robertson

P. 88 Introduction
Cecilie Rubow

P. 94 Sea Level and Coastal Protection
Cecilie Rubow

P. 98 Urbanizing Water in a Context of
Scarcity Christian Vium

P. 102 A Job Machine Powered by Water
Frank Sejersen

P. 106 Life in the Shadow of a Water Tower
Astrid O. Andersen

P. 110 Waste and Water: Connected and
Mixed Maria Louise B. Robertson

P. 114 Inverted Watering Strategies in
Senegal Anette Reenberg

P. 118 Cobs as Technological Solutions
Mette Fog Olwig

P. 122 The Imagined Water Pump
Jonas Ø. Nielsen

P. 126 Unpredictable Side Effects of
New Technologies
Laura Vang Rasmussen

P. 130 Scalable and Fluid Sprinklers
Astrid B. Stensrud

P. 134 Dry Technologies and
Community Bureaucracies
Mattias Borg Rasmussen

P. 138 A Life Jacket Story
Frida Hastrup

P. 142 Unpacking the Dog Sledge
Kirsten Hastrup

P. 146 Water Technologies: Mirroring
Great Expectations in Greenland
and Ghana
Mette Fog Olwig and Frank Sejersen

PART THREE
LANDSCAPE

PART FOUR
TIME

P. 154   Introduction
Kirsten Hastrup

P. 162   Hualca Hualca: Mountain Lord and
Life Source   Astrid B. Stensrud

P. 166   Knowing Landscapes of Water in
Kiribati   Maria Louise B. Robertson

P. 170   Borders at Sea   Frida Hastrup

P. 174   Making Urban Landscapes: People,
Water, Materials   Astrid O. Andersen

P. 178   Dreams, Water and the Remodelling
of Place   Frank Sejersen

P. 182   Strategic Thinking:
Changeable Usages of the Nigerian
Landscape   Anette Reenberg

P. 186   Landscapes of Droughts and Floods
on the Desert Margins
Laura Vang Rasmussen

P. 190   A Landscape of Ice
Kirsten Hastrup

P. 194   Walking Along Water
Mattias Borg Rasmussen

P. 198   Old Water, Gardens and Prophetic
Powers in the Sahel   Jonas Ø. Nielsen

P. 202   Can You See Climate Change in a
Changing Environment?   Cecilie Rubow

P. 206   Mental Topographies
Mette Fog Olwig

P. 210   Nomadic Landscapes and Ephemeral
Resources   Christian Vium

P. 214   Icons of Climate Change: Mirroring
the Sahel and the Andes   Astrid O.
Andersen and Jonas Ø. Nielsen

P. 222   Introduction
Cecilie Rubow

P. 228   Glacial Time
Kirsten Hastrup

P. 232   Seasons, Timings, and the Rhythms
of Life   Mattias Borg Rasmussen

P. 236   Flexible Trajectories: Nomadic Pastoral
Mobility Patterns   Christian Vium

P. 240   Still Life on the Shore   Frida Hastrup

P. 244   Appraising Change: A Question
of Baseline   Anette Reenberg

P. 248   Litres Per Second: Measuring the
Water Flow   Astrid B. Stensrud

P. 252   New Scenarios and Unstable
Temporalities   Cecilie Rubow

P. 256   Facing Reality: Managing/Imagining
the Time Left on an Atoll
Maria Louise B. Robertson

P. 260   Anticipating Futures and the Rhythms
of Water   Frank Sejersen

P. 264   Slow Versus Fast Changes in Sahelian
Land Use Systems
Laura Vang Rasmussen

P. 268   Three Calendars and the Test of Time
in Northern Sahel   Jonas Ø. Nielsen

P. 272   'Packages' with Disparate Time
Horizons   Mette Fog Olwig

P. 276   Urban Talks about Climate and Weather
Astrid O. Andersen

P. 280   Times of Climate Change in Religion
and Ethics: Mirroring the Andes
and the Pacific   Cecilie Rubow and
Mattias Borg Rasmussen

CONTRIBUTORS

ASTRID O. ANDERSEN joined the *Waterworlds* team in 2010 as a PhD fellow at the University of Copenhagen. She carried out fieldwork in Arequipa in arid Southern Peru, exploring how water is enacted in multiple ways along the urban waterscape. Andersen examined how water is simultaneously produced as scarce and abundant, in the course of discursive and material practices by actors with different interests, aspirations, desires and needs. Her analytical approach combines theories of political ecology, science and technology studies and political anthropology to argue that water, knowledge and power are intrinsically connected, and to show how climate change occurs and is experienced as a part of daily life in particular sites and situations, where local and global processes get entangled and perforate concrete topographies, generating new human and non-human relations.

FRIDA HASTRUP was a postdoctoral fellow in the *Waterworlds* programme (2009–2012). She has conducted fieldwork in Tamil Nadu, India, focusing primarily on people's environmental concerns along the southern Bay of Bengal, ranging from the Asian tsunami, cyclones and soil erosion to climate change. Her research explores the collaborative and contingent ways in which the coastal zone in a district of Tamil Nadu is put together by different actors – fishermen, marine biologists, development workers, government officers, cultural heritage advocates and anthropologists to name but some – all of whom are engaged in the shared project of making a liveable world by the water's edge. She is currently Assistant Professor at the Saxo Institute, Ethnology Section, University of Copenhagen.

KIRSTEN HASTRUP is Professor of Anthropology at the University of Copenhagen. She received an ERC Advanced Grant in 2008, enabling the collaborative research project *Waterworlds* to take off in 2009. She has worked intensively with the entwinement of the long-term natural and social histories in Iceland, from the warm Middle Ages, through the Little Ice Age, and until the present; this work has been published by Oxford University Press in three monographs. In more recent years, she has worked with a hunting community in High Arctic Greenland, facing unpredictable environmental changes. Through successive periods of fieldwork, she has followed the development and studied how people gradually reorient themselves and appropriate new opportunities.

JONAS ØSTERGAARD NIELSEN has a MA in anthropology and a PhD in geography from the University of Copenhagen. He joined the *Waterworlds* team in 2010 as a postdoctoral fellow. His research has focused on how climate change is understood and adapted to in a small village in Northern Burkina Faso, with particular interest in questions of causal relations. He has explored how and if climate change can be untangled as a driver of change when decisions taken in the study village are entangled in and perforated by local, national and global connections and disconnections of both socio-economic and environmental character. He has also been involved in understanding and advancing the concept of adaptation and how and if it is possible to use this concept without losing sight of human agency and imagination. He is currently a Junior Professor at Humboldt University, Berlin.

METTE FOG OLWIG is Assistant Professor in International Development Studies at Roskilde University, Denmark. She did her PhD in Geography while affiliated with *Waterworlds*. Her research applied a multi-sited, multi-level perspective on the social dimensions of climate change and development. Within the context of the unusually severe northern Ghanaian floods of 2007, she examined changes in development policy and practice taking place in times of climate change anxiety, and how these changes influence local lives and livelihood possibilities. She investigated, first, conceptualizations of climate change among donors by examining their use of key terms applied in policy and analysis, most notably 'resilience', second, how local development practitioners in northern Ghana approach and implement these concepts, in particular, 'vulnerability'; and, third, how the concepts have shaped recipients' perceptions of their own opportunities and abilities.

MATTIAS BORG RASMUSSEN is an anthropologist and a post-doctoral fellow in the Department of Food and Resource Economics at the University of Copenhagen. In December 2012, he defended his doctoral dissertation entitled 'Prisms of Water: Abandonment and the Art of Being Governed in the Peruvian Andes' – in which the different entanglements between environmental change and local political forms are scrutinized. Based on long-term fieldwork in highland Peru, he has explored questions of environmental change, local resource governance and state–citizen relations in poor peasant communities. Interested in how the changing flows of water influence life in the high Andes in the context of climate change, Mattias traced how flows of water are located within different physical, historical and political landscapes. His current research is on territorial governance, peasant politics and nature conservation in a highland area adjacent to the Huascarán National Park in Peru's Cordillera Blanca mountain range.

LAURA VANG RASMUSSEN has a PhD in geography from the Department of Geosciences and Natural Resource Management, University of Copenhagen. Her research has focused on land use changes in the Sahelian drylands of Africa. Of particular interest has been the analysis of different drivers of change across various temporal as well as spatial scales and their impacts on local land use decisions. Her PhD research was part of the interdisciplinary DANIDA-funded research programme LASYRE (LAnd SYstem REsilience) and affiliated with *Waterworlds*. In particular, the focus on Sahelian villagers' use of the land and how that may be affected by climate in these harsh environments is closely linked with one of the main research aims in *Waterworlds*: to enhance the general understanding of living in an environment at risk. He is now Professor at the Humboldt University in Berlin.

ANETTE REENBERG is Professor of Geography, University of Copenhagen. She has been involved in *Waterworlds* as a senior researcher, primarily engaged with the drylands pillar of the project. She has almost 30 years of field experience in human–environmental interactions in the Sahelian region in West Africa, notably in Burkina Faso and Niger. Since the 1980s she has been exploring a range of perspectives related to sustainability and resilience of the land use systems in the Sahel. These include issues of desertification, sustainable natural resource management, climate adaptation and globalization. Lately, she has led a project involving African colleagues on the triple exposure of land use systems to globalization, climate variations and population pressure, which complement her work in *Waterworlds* (see www.lasyresa-hel.ku.dk).

MARIA LOUISE BØNNELYKKE ROBERTSON is a PhD fellow in the Department of Anthropology at the University of Copenhagen, . Her research is affiliated with *Waterworlds* Research Centre where studies of local social responses to environmental disasters related to water are carried out. Maria Louise is an environmental anthropologist with a multidisciplinary profile, and she has collaborated with engineers, natural scientist, and designers in solving problems in the private and the public sector. Her PhD is an ethnographic study of the environmental change faced by the islanders of the island nation Kiribati in the Central Pacific, where climate change, sea level rise and freshwater scarcity present an imminent threat. In her studies she pays special attention to how technological interventions (both local and within development work) attempting to address the challenges posed by climate change are always embedded in social worlds and have social implications.

CECILIE RUBOW is Associate Professor in the Department of Anthropology, University of Copenhagen. As a senior researcher in the research centre *Waterworlds*, she has focused on social and metaphysical aspects of environmental change in coastal areas in the Cook Islands. In particular, she has been working with questions of climate projections, changing sea level and cyclones in the nexus between climate sciences, governmental agencies, various types of expert knowledge and local residents on the main island of Rarotonga. In the *Waterworlds* team, she has also worked with nature ethics, Christian eco-theology, and the intersections between technology and metaphysics. Before the present engagement with environmental change in the Pacific, she had published widely on religion and everyday theology in Denmark. Presently, she is reorienting her research interests to the Danish field again in diverse intersections between environmental change and cultural metaphysics.

FRANK SEJERSEN is Associate Professor in the Eskimology and Arctic Studies Section, Department of Cross-Cultural and Regional Studies, at the University of Copenhagen. His principal areas of research are environmental governance, resource use, self-determination policies, climate change, local knowledge, as well as cultural, economic and societal changes. As part of the *Waterworlds* research project, he studied how Greenlanders navigate in a world where they try to maintain livelihoods but also push for further economic development and self-determination. Among other things, the project investigates how local users perceive and cope with the establishment of a new water regime based on large-scale hydro-electricity production made possible by the melting ice. The process of hyper-industrialization is compared to other Arctic regions, where institutions take different scales into account when formulating adaptation strategies.

ASTRID BREDHOLT STENSRUD has a PhD in social anthropology from the University of Oslo. She carried out extensive fieldwork in the Southern Peruvian Andes from 2001 to 2011. Her PhD dissertation analyses entrepreneurial activities and animistic practices in a working-class neighbourhood in Cusco, Peru, and explores how values and relations among persons, things and places are negotiated. From 2010 till 2012, she worked as a postdoctoral fellow in the research project 'From Ice to Stone', affiliated with *Waterworlds*, at the Department of Anthropology, University of Copenhagen. Here she studied perceptions of and responses to climate change, water practices and water management in Chivay and other villages of Colca Valley. She currently holds a post-doctoral position in the Department of Social Anthropology, University of Oslo, Norway, as part of the research project 'Overheating: the three crises of globalization'.

CHRISTIAN VIUM was a PhD fellow in the Department of Anthropology, University of Copenhagen and member of the *Waterworlds* Research Centre on Climate Change. He was awarded his PhD in December 2013. Working on water scarcity in the Islamic Republic of Mauritania, Christian is particularly preoccupied with anthropological investigations of how nomadic pastoralists creatively mitigate the convergence of extreme water scarcity and increasing political instability. Working predominantly among nomadic pastoralists in remote parts of the south-eastern frontier provinces as well as among sedentary nomads on the fringes of the capital city, Nouakchott, he has done recurrent ethnographic fieldwork in the country since 2001 on issues such as rural–urban migration, urbanization, urban restructuring and renewal, droughts and political insecurity. Photography and film are an integral part of Vium's methodological and analytical approach. He has recently received a post-doctoral fellowship at the University of Aarhus, Denmark, to work on the project 'Camera as Cultural Critique'.

PREFACE & ACKNOWLEDGEMENTS

This book is the outcome of a collaborative research project, investigating how people in various regions of the globe live with manifest environmental changes. The collaboration within the group of anthropologists and geographers, who have contributed to the book, is one thing. The more important collaborative relation has been with the people in the different fields, the NGOs, the officials, and the experts who have readily shared their thoughts and knowledge with us. Their contribution to the work is gratefully acknowledged, and we hope this book may find its way to many of them.

While all of the projects have been carried out in regions or places that have been more or less openly designated hotspots of climate change, we have let the particular situations and local concerns shape the arguments. While climate scientists repeatedly stress that there is a huge difference between weather events and climate, the latter being based on the *average* temperature, precipitation, etc. over a long period of time, in everyday life there is not such a firm distinction. People living with, sometimes dramatic, change in their immediate environment may or may not understand it in terms of climate change, and for the social scientist, their views are what matters most. Humans do not live by 'averages' but by sensations, memories, events, practices, immediate concerns, available vocabularies, and aspirations for the future. The baseline is neither the beginnings of the planetary system, nor the invention of mega-scale computer simulations of climate development. The baseline for identifying change is everyday experience and personal recollection, while the interpretation draws on all available sources. Even within such a relatively short timespan, the people populating the following pages have a strong perception of changes in their environment, and give voice to no small uncertainty about the future in their current landscapes. This again may be further nourished by scientific reports of all kinds.

What we have found is that in spite of the uncertainties, our protagonists' views on the future are not predominantly dressed as horror stories or scenarios of catastrophe, but rather of strategic thinking and hope. There is a surplus of reflection and ideas, of the will to redress whatever goes wrong, and of technological inventiveness. Sociality itself generates this, because people pool their knowledge and engage in collective thinking that keeps despair at bay. Social communities are flexible and creative, and all while their land seems to change beyond recognition, they invest their efforts in a future, which thereby is already taking shape. It is not a matter of simple adaptation, it is a creative response to circumstances. People take responsibility for their own lives and for the future of the community, even where 'climate scenarios' seem adverse to their aspirations.

In the process of working on this book, we have incurred some debts, beyond the principal debt mentioned above. Henny Pedersen once again contributed with her skills of organization, notably of seminars and writing retreats for the group of authors, but also of travels to the field and keeping track of expenditures. In an important phase of collating and streamlining the manuscript, Martin Arvad Nicolaisen provided valuable help. Graphic designer Troels Faber made us see how ours dreams about a richly illustrated book could be realized, and thus co-shaped our thoughts. Khanam Virjee of Earthscan in turn trusted the project enough to bring it forward for production; Helen Bell and the entire production team kindly and skilfully oversaw the process. We thank them all for their vital contribution.

At a more comprehensive level, we thank the European Research Council (ERC) for the Advanced Grant, which made the collaborative research project *Waterworlds* possible in the first place, and the Danish Research Council for Culture and Communication and the Research Council for Development Research, funding additional junior research positions that became affiliated with *Waterworlds*.

WATERWORLDS

LIVING WITH ENVIRONMENTAL CHANGE

Kirsten Hastrup & Cecilie Rubow

INTRODUCTION

This book is about people who experience dramatic
changes to their environment. They are dramatic,
because these changes have as yet unknown
repercussions in the social communities and demand
both attention and effort lest they shall be downright
destructive. At a time when climate change has become
a prominent object of interest in the international
community and among scientists responding to the
call for more knowledge, it is worth remembering
that for most people, climate change is specific. It is a
concrete experience of changes in the environment, of
opening or closing opportunities for making a living,
creating or destroying conventional forms of subsistence
and production, inducing migration or technological
innovation, and stretching or bending the imagined
futures.

In the concrete experience, climate change is specific, yet it unfolds in composite waterworlds.

In 2009, a collaborative anthropological research project called *Waterworlds* was established around three major water-related challenges: the melting ice, the rising seas, and the drying lands. Focusing on the social responses to these changes made it possible to study and compare widely different societies and environments without losing sight of more general patterns. All of the chapters are based on recent fieldwork in places that were already on the map of climate scientists as facing serious environmental challenges. The studies took place in Arctic Greenland and Andean Peru, two sites where the melting ice is a major issue; in Mauretania, Burkina Faso, Ghana and Niger in West Africa, generally known for drought and drying lands, but also occasionally hit by flooding; finally, in the Cook Islands and Kiribati in the Pacific, and on the Indian coast, regions that are under threat from rising seas and coastal degradation. Wherever we worked, water was somehow in focus, either because it took a new form, such as ice turning to water, or because there was too little or too much of it, or it became too violent.

The central tenet of the book is the power of water to make or unmake social worlds; it does not work on its own, however, because people respond to it and refashion their life according to their understanding of water's course and force. They respond by using particular technologies to channel it away, to harness it, or to secure clean drinking water, and in some sense even their knowledge can be seen as a kind of technology, by which they control the flow or the absence of water. All social communities are located in particular landscapes, to which people relate in different ways; landscapes are socialized and incorporated into the human world of resources and imagination, to the extent that social habits are also spatial habits, which is one reason why environmental changes are often experienced as deeply unsettling. The destabilization of known landscapes again affects the sense of continuity with the past, and of the possible future; in other words, environmental changes affect the sense of time and history. This line of argument underpins the structure of the book, which is organized into four parts: Water, Technology, Landscape, and Time, each foregrounding their aspect of the composite experience of change. We shall introduce these four parts separately and in more depth, as they appear.

Here we need to present the specific organization of the book in many shorter chapters, which are perhaps best seen as portraits of particular situations, of certain landscapes, of individual reflections, of ingenious solutions to local challenges, and of the multiple ways in which people respond to the perceived environmental challenges. The texts are accompanied by an abundance of pictures taken in the field and giving body and flesh to the words. There is a high degree of realism and precision in the chapters that, hopefully, conveys a direct sense of what it means to actually live with the kind of unease that people face in the wake of climate change.

In the international community, the dominant image of climate change is provided by the natural sciences while ours derives from the social sciences. This shifts the focus from an understanding of the natural processes at play in the long term, to the ways in which they are mixed up with social processes in the shorter term, where the future of a particular community is questioned. While the chapters move between continents, communities, and waters at short intervals, we have the larger ambition of providing a truly general understanding of what living with massive environmental changes means. Thus, while the ethnographic narratives tell their own particular stories, in conjunction they aspire to convey a universal message of the human potential to carve out new futures even in seriously troubling times.

THE EXPERIENCE OF CLIMATE CHANGE

At present, people all over the world are noticing changes in their environment, ranging from peculiarities in the daily experience of weather and wind to major calamities, such as hurricanes, flooding, depletion of freshwater resources, coastal erosion or drought. Even with gradual changes, the well-known rhythms of days and seasons may suddenly seem out of order, and people begin to respond to the irregularities by devising new strategies at the level of everyday activities. At this level, the changes are still perceived to lie within the horizon of the manageable, but with time even small and almost imperceptible moves will have remade society and opened up a new history.

In time, new towns may grow up, spreading their fingers along roads and waterways, cities may turn into mega-cities with influx from rural areas, where agriculture may no longer be possible, and stretch the city's water resources to their limit, or forests may appear as the result of the slow process of trees having multiplied and imperceptibly matured in landscapes that were earlier barren. Some rivers start to overflow from unexpected amounts of rain, while others are becoming disturbingly dry for months. Whether long- or short-term changes, they potentially affect people's perceptions of the world deeply. More sudden and violent irregularities may cause massive uncertainties about the future.

With the prominent international debate on global climate change, almost any kind of environmental change experienced by people in so many ways will be interpreted as a sign of an irreversible change in nature itself, causing more than a little concern. Yet, we should still remember that for people all over the world, climate change is not something abstract, the result of a particular way of modelling, or a political demand for prediction. It is a lived reality. The changes are felt, embraced, feared and prepared for, they string together, and connect what used to be separate. Their impingement on lived experience induces humans to respond, first by seeking to understand them and assess their range, and then to anticipate their future course so as to prepare to meet the new world.

From an anthropological perspective, environmental changes cannot be kept apart from social life in general, or isolated as changes-in-themselves. People *live* with them in a comprehensive way. One of the major claims of this book is precisely this: climate change never comes alone, because it is enfolded in lived actualities. In consequence, the social responses to climate change are not simply a matter of adapting to new temperatures or changing winds, but of altering a composite way of life, encompassing modes of cultivation, ways of house

Even changes perceived to lie within the horizon of the manageable potentially open up an entirely new history.

construction, means of water regulation, modes of thinking and of anticipating nature, and much more. If rain does not fall, if whales do not turn up, or if the harvest of mangoes and minerals increases, then social life has already changed, and a new history is in the making. Social and natural phenomena are deeply entangled.

Changes that are continuing, whether at a slow or a fast pace, are extremely difficult to picture and to hold still for observation and disentanglement. Yet, this is exactly what scientists are attempting in our times by ingenious devices for measurement and modelling, observation and systematic comparison. In some cases, past and present land use patterns are compared and the relative degradation of the soil is measured; in other cases, degrees of pollution are identified and the boundary for toleration is established. In yet other projects, the sea levels of various epochs are extracted from complex sets of geological data. Thus, all kinds of environmental changes may be measured and described, and will feed into the general, global knowledge about past and present environmental states. Yet, central to any scientific interest, even at the most abstract level, are those changes that people live with on the ground. The scientists are concerned humans themselves, and their research energies are directed to social and political challenges. Conversely, only if the scientific knowledge captures actual experiences will the general message about climate change take root.

THE SCIENCES OF CLIMATE CHANGE

At the present time, the changes related to the humanly induced warming possibly constitute the most intensely studied scientific field: books, journals, reports, White Papers, and policy briefs relating to climate change abound, their arguments based on the newest scientific knowledge. In the present book, all such work, and all of the accompanying facts, theories, projections, and discussions of findings are of course important elements in the overall argument and are part of the background knowledge for all the ethnographic fields. Yet, our intention is not to single out climate change as such, but to show how it appears as entangled with all sorts of social or cultural phenomena, permeating the everyday and becoming part of a compound historical and environmental process.

With such composite processes, science often works by way of singularizing its constituents. To singularize is to reduce the actual complexity of a deeply entangled historical-natural-social-political-technological reality in order to identify the constituent phenomena, to establish particular causal relations, and to find a means of acting and new ways of navigating. To singularize in this sense is what scientists must do, when they establish facts, stabilize trends, theorize about feedback mechanisms, and make projections about future changes. It is an on-going work carried out in extremely detailed and necessarily selective processes where certain questions are asked, some methods are chosen and assorted data are interpreted in various established ways. Yet, given the complex and virtually boundless implications of climate change, presently it is impossible to pin down the future changes, climatic and social, for a singular community or coast, a singular massif of ice or a mountain top, a singular type of flora or a piece of cultivable land, or for the singular town or nation.

At the same time, people do live in particular places, and perforce must seek to understand the local implications of the changes, because they matter to them and to the future of their community or their way of life. This means that they seek a particular rather than a general understanding, and this shows us how knowledge is always *located*. If the melt water from a glacier is drying up, it may be pertinent to identify the cause of this and suggest particular avenues of action that will of necessity have to take the various uses of the run-off into consideration. Whether the water is normally used for drinking, for making hydropower, or for irrigation, makes a huge difference to the sense of the 'problem'; the societal consequences and means of intervention will be perceived in particular ways, and even 'the causes' seen to produce the problem will probably also be differentiated. In this way, climate change is constantly singularized, and understood as located; at the same time the perceived changes multiply – each place has its own concerns. It is not surprising, therefore, that people neither agree about the facts nor the causes, with new singularized findings constantly coming to the fore amid many different concerns. Controversies are arising, and scenarios are constantly revised at all levels.

For many good reasons, 'climate change' has become a science-driven social phenomenon, in the sense that the sciences have shaped the societal awareness about large-scale interactions between the oceans, the atmosphere, and the landmass. It began with hard sciences as atmospheric physics, but now the field of climate science has extended across dozens and dozens of disciplines. The reports from the Intergovernmental Panel on Climate Change (IPCC) and other large research agencies, where knowledge from a multiplicity of scientific fields is coordinated and summarized, are extremely important vehicles for the general understanding of the large patterns of climate change and the seriousness of the climate crisis for nations all over the world. Even if these reports and findings are not perfect, they are the best we have in terms of robust, collaborative knowledge, gathered and reviewed by the finest standards. On the strength of this knowledge, the situation seems painfully plain: The world is confronted by an unprecedented crisis, deeply affected by and affecting human life.

Geologists are debating whether we are now living in 'the Anthropocene', a new geological era succeeding the Holocene. The Holocene has so far been the name of the period after the last glacial period, to which we have become accustomed. It has been a period in which agriculture was invented (or became possible), and which has seen human society change through various technological and scientific revolutions until the modern age of immense global challenges. Now, the term the Anthropocene has been suggested for the present era, where the human imprint on the globe deeply affects its future, and where we can no longer speak of a self-generating *natural* world, beyond human impact. Whether we agree with the term or not, is less important than to learn from it: the future of the globe is deeply intertwined with human history and with the human capacity for reflection and remaking their world.

The climatic irregularities produce new kinds of uncertainty, even in regions that have always been characterized by weather variability.

This is an important impetus for the present book, based upon fieldwork in a number of locations and communities across the world in which climate change is manifestly part of the lived changes. In the field, however, we have not started our investigations by singularizing climate change as a phenomenon in itself, or querying it. Our field of study as anthropologists and geographers is the lived world, the world lived by people amid a myriad of other living beings, of artefacts, and elements – rocks, stones, sand, water, winds, and sun rays – that change together. Evidently, in conversations about all kinds of social matters, climate change has frequently popped up, and sometimes been foregrounded and discussed at length. But on the whole, we have studied it as an implicit, rather than as a main topic, to be able to sense it as part of the lived world, and to hear what our conversational partners say about it themselves.

This does not imply that we are somehow exempt from any bias or pre-formed concern. Even anthropologists and geographers must make choices, and in the field we have started by identifying situations where changes in the environment are prominent and talked about locally. We insist, however, that environmental changes are not natural phenomena occurring *around* people, outside of their lives, whether in their gardens, along the coasts, or up the hill. Throughout the pages of this book, change is seen as a natural-social phenomenon happening in the midst of the human world. Thus, climate change – in itself a scientific and thus a social abstraction – is not happening in the untamed, vast or crowded outdoors. It takes place in lived worlds. Further, the increasingly robust and detailed knowledge about climate change is not only *received* (differently) by different publics, but processed with a view to located social realities. Knowledge *happens*; it changes when used in particular settings.

WATERWORLDS: COLLABORATIVE KNOWLEDGE

The social sciences are increasingly joining the hard sciences in the attempts to understand climate change. Some even speak of 'the human turn' in the study of climate change, and this present volume may be seen as an example of this, by turning towards people who actually live in hotspots of change and reflect upon it on their own account. Even on the smallest islands in the great oceans, on the rim of the ice, and in the high mountains, people are increasingly becoming aware of the current climatic challenges; they may be global when seen in a particular scientific perspective, but they are embedded in located life-worlds. All over the world, the reports from the IPCC, the media, the governmental, and the non-governmental organizations are read, retold, criticized, sung, and painted – integrating scientific knowledge into daily lives, social habits, and new ventures in multiple ways.

Our particular way of turning towards the human dimensions of climate change grows out of the anthropological tradition. This is a discipline devoted to the *anthropos*, the human being and the human condition. When we take a human turn in the study of climate change we build on a long tradition of studies of people's engagement and interaction with the environment in which they live. As already mentioned, we start by unpacking the water-related

Climate change is entangled with all sorts of social or cultural phenomena and permeates everyday life.

changes in all our fields. Due to the central position of water in social life, changes in water resources or water regimes reflect and permeate almost all other kinds of changes; even so, water is not evenly presented in the diverse fields. Nor need it feature equally at different moments in the same field. This is just to emphasize once again that our main objective has been to let our collaborators in the field decide what the central question is in any situation. Only by paying close attention to their own words and observations can we get close to what it means to *live* with actual environmental changes.

The book builds on a long methodological tradition of doing fieldwork along with people, where they live. The research in some cases has included year-long stays in a particular place of research; in other cases it has taken the form of a series of shorter pieces of fieldwork over a number of years. Yet each project has been specifically designed to encompass the overall research questions of our collaborative project, *Waterworlds*, designed to understand how natural and social processes are entangled. Answers have in some cases been elicited through surveys, but always alongside participant observation and continuous conversation.

Between us, we have made careful observations through participation in daily life and specific environmentally oriented activities in different fields. This has given us an extremely rich material for comparison and to address the general implications of living with major uncertainties about the future. The empirical material is heterogeneous, being made up of meticulously documented observations and concrete experiences with people in their environment. Out of the excess of conversations, photos, impressions, documents, and selected objects, stored in notebooks, computers, cameras, boxes, and not least in the embodied registers of memory, we have by turn presented, written and re-written preliminary queries and results. Collaboration within the research group has been intense; observations, readings, analyses, reflections, and so forth have been continuously shared. This has contributed to a process of cumulative understanding, which has been immensely valuable. As documented on the last pages in this book, the main bulk of the research is published in various specialized, academic journals and books, and will continue to appear there. The present book may be read as both an introduction and as an invitation to *Waterworlds'* backlist and the much larger, and immensely expanding research field of past, present, and future environmental change.

The future of the globe is deeply intertwined with the human capacity for reflection and remaking their world.

Yet there is another and even more important feature of collaboration inherent in the project, namely the collaboration with people in our various fields. They have shared their views, observations, and their theories about present predicaments and future challenges with us, the fieldworkers. Whatever else fieldwork implies in different fields, it is at base a matter of working *with* people, without whom there would not even be a field in the first place. We thank all the participants for sharing their landscapes, technologies, waters – and not least their time with us. Maybe it is a bold move to include so many important stories in just one book, yet we believe that it may advance a general sense of the lived concerns and creative thinking among people who are already responding to changing environments.

PORTRAITS

Each of the people in this book has their own distinct voice. Even so, we have chosen to portray some of them below as speaking for the many other people, who wonder what is happening to their immediate environment, and who – even in the absence of firm answers – must act upon particular expectations for the future.

ACONAN

PLACE
Recuay, Peru

TIME
November 2010

NOIMY SALVADOR lives in Aconan with her husband and their two little girls. In 1980, she was born in the altitudes of the neighbouring peasant community Catac, but she and her family have now moved into the old house of her grandparents close to the main town of the area, Recuay, where her children can go to school and her husband can find work.

She recalls how the snow fell when she was a girl herding sheep in the high altitude grasslands. Back then they always made snowmen. This year, Noimy explained, 'the rain has been delayed a lot' – meaning that they have not been able to sow in due time. When sowing is delayed, it usually means that the yield is less, and sometimes if rain then comes early, the following year it can damage the crops, especially the potatoes that may rot.

She explains that one cannot predict the rain. But animals also die. And as a mother she is worried about the health of her children: 'It affects both the sown fields and the animals, but it's not only that. It is the same with the health. So much cold. The children get sick. Or it is too warm, you give them a bath, and they get bronchitis.'

MURI BEACH

MII KAUVAI, chairman of the *Muri Environmental Care Group*, lives close to the beach on Rarotonga. She explains that the weather is getting unpredictable and that you see things that are not normal such as fruits that are having two or more seasons, for example, breadfruits and mangoes. Concerning watermelon, when there is suddenly a lot of rain, you lose your harvest. She is also worried about the beach, which is getting narrower. The trees have exposed roots which is telling her that 'We are losing our beach. I definitely want to do something about my beach. I want to put gabions down here, though, it costs 40,000 NZ$.'

According to the documentaries Mii has watched, the sea is actually intruding upon some islands in the Pacific: 'In the Cooks, on the island of Pukapuka, they used to grow taro, but in some parts of it, the seawater is mixing with the freshwater.' As far as she can see, 'We have seen enough evidence to say that climate change is something we need to take seriously. Maybe in ten years' time, people will have to start thinking of relocating. We have not seen too much on our island but examples from islands in the Pacific tell me that climate change is real.'

PLACE
Rarotonga, Cook Islands

TIME
July 2011

Laura Vang Rasmussen
and Anette Reenberg

TINTABORA

PLACE
Oudalan, Burkina
Faso

TIME
February 2010

According to **HAMADOU FARKA**, this February is very hot, hotter than they are used to. 'We do not have a thermometer in the village, but we know the temperature.' He explains that the changes have come gradually, but that it is certainly much warmer now than it was during the time of the big droughts (in the 1970s, for example). 'We have also noted that there is less water in our wells. The temperature change affects the crop yields. The cowpeas are not affected much, but the millet yields are much lower because of the higher temperature.'

The change in temperature is also causing serious health problems, Hamadou states, 'We have more mosquitoes – we cannot sleep in the open without nets as before, and the kids are suffering a lot from malaria. In addition, we believe that the increasing problems we have had with measles in the last years are caused by the shift in temperature. Furthermore, the rains are getting more violent. This is a big problem because our houses are made of clay bricks. They fall apart if the rain comes in concentrated showers with more than 100 mm per day, as we have seen recently.'

LIVING WITH ENVIRONMENTAL CHANGE

KANGERLUK

JAKOB JERIMIASSEN had just returned to the small village of Kangerluk as we passed each other on the path in the grass and started a conversation. He was pleased to be back, the weather was sunny and he had seen four seals on his way. He invited me indoors where his wife Ida was unpacking. We looked out the window framing the landscape as he explained about the social and environmental changes of the place. All his life he had been moving to many different places in Greenland for better hunting, fishing and job opportunities, but he always returned to Kangerluk where his wife was born. 'We used to catch a lot of halibut and there were plenty of porpoises. However, they were overfished by the European fishermen. We still have wolf fish and seal hunting is good.'

He pointed to the dusty and brownish mountains and assured me that they used to be covered with snow and ice even in the summer, 'It is really getting warmer!'

'Does that worry you?' I asked.

'It worries me that the river where we fish is getting dryer.'

PLACE
Greenland

TIME
September 2010

TEAORAEREKE

PLACE
Kiribati

TIME
January 2011

ANTEREA and **MWARIA** live with their children on one of the sparse plots of land left on the densely populated island of Tarawa. They have lived here since they finished their degrees and moved to the urban centre of Kiribati for work. They are one of the fortunate families who have been able to invest in a rainwater tank. When Anterea retired, he used his savings on a rainwater tank so that he would be better able to provide clean water to his family. Besides the rainwater tank, the family only has a well where they draw water for washing and cooking, but this water is not clean and cannot be used for consumption.

They try to keep the toilet and washing facilities as far away from the well as possible, in order to avoid contamination of the well water, but this proves very difficult on the small plot of land they own. Sometimes when extended family members run out of water, they will pay Anterea and Mwaria a visit with various containers, sometimes just a bottle, sometimes oil drums, and fill them up with rainwater.

CHIVAY

I met **ISIDRO HUARANCA** at 5.30 a.m. by a water reservoir. He was distributing water to farmers who came to claim their right to irrigation. Each farmer has the right to use a certain amount of water for each of their small fields on a specific day.

Isidro said that the weather had been cold that day. He told me how the climate has been changing during the last years. It is getting colder, but also warmer. During the day, it is warmer; there is a terrible, unbearable heat. During the night, it is freezing. The last years, there has been frost in the months when it did not usually freeze. These changes affect the production of plants, which are being destroyed by the heating sun and by the frost. Therefore, the plants do not grow as they used to.

The most delicate plant is the broadbean plant. If the flowers fall off,because of the frost, it does not flower again. The potato plant, however, is more resistant – if it freezes, it can sprout once more, though it is only 50 per cent, the growth is not the same any more.

PLACE
Peru

TIME
October 2011

BOH DIDA

PLACE
Toujounine,
Nouakchott,
Mauritania

TIME
April 2011

FATIMATOU, 8 years old, is the youngest of four children in a family living in the impoverished neighbourhood of Boh Dida on the eastern fringes of Nouakchott, the capital of Mauritania. Her mother, Leile, came to Nouakchott in 1986, following the great Sahelian drought, menacing the entire south-eastern region and decimating her family's herds dramatically. Having lived as nomadic pastoralists, the transition to sedentary life on the outskirts of the capital was challenging in many ways. There is hardly any water or sanitation infrastructure in the entire neighbourhood. Fatimatou explains how what bothers her most is the wind, which makes everything full of dust and which is cold at night and makes her cough all the time.

'Right now, it is not so bad, but soon it will change, I am sure. The wind (*el riah*) is always blowing here. The sand is everywhere, and I think it is also the reason why the TV signal is always so bad.' Nevertheless, Fatimatou likes living in the city because she can go to school – but she loves it when they, once in a while, take time to visit family members who still live in the *bâdiyya* (desert). For now, her dream is that her family will one day own a proper house and have running water.

PART ONE

WATER

WATER

INTRODUCTION

In this first part of the volume, we focus on water as a principal configurative force in society. The idea is to show some of the ways in which social life and community building are constituted by the access to water and to the resources that come along with a particular water body in the immediate environment. Whether water derives from rain, rivers, or wells, and however it is reached, the actual materiality of water – such as its liquidity, its variable quantity, its possible scarcity, its sudden absence, and its occasional solidity – all of it premeditate water's power at infiltrating social forms. This applies not only to freshwater, though access to clean drinking water is essential for survival and often subject to social regulation; also oceans and lagoons have the power to shape society by their being part of the larger resource space upon which social communities depend for their livelihood. Presently, many communities are experiencing notable changes in their immediate water resources that have become less predictable, both in terms of seasonality and quantity. This troubles people's perception of the immediate resource space and creates a sense of an uncertain future, as we shall see in some detail in the narratives below.

Concerns about water are always social concerns.

Generally, through the short descriptions from many different places, we show how water is not only the *sine qua non* of life in general, but also of community-making. Water configures societies in particular ways and generates its own standards of value. Rivers, canals, wellsprings, and oceans are complicit in the making of particular social worlds. Focussing on actual water issues reveals that its formative force is not mechanical, and not even causal in any direct way, because human ingenuity and social responsibility always enter into the equation. This is a key point in what follows; humans play an active part in taming, channelling, and distributing water according to their social and moral horizons. It is a question of a complex entanglement rather than a unidirectional causal link between water and society.

Before moving on to present concerns, it is interesting to recall Leonardo da Vinci's view of water as 'the driver of nature', and 'the vital humour of the terrestrial machine'. The illustrious Renaissance artist and scholar studied the elements closely and sought to understand their individual qualities by paying close, long-term attention to their manifestations. He began his study of water around 1506 and planned a major treatise on hydrology in general, as well as a geographical study of the entire water system of the Earth, to be followed by a discussion of military and civil hydraulic engineering, according to the editor of his notebooks. He never achieved it all, but he did make some very interesting observations of water in the process of realizing at least some parts of the grand project. He writes, for instance:

> Of the four elements water is the second in weight and the second in respect of mobility. It is never at rest until it unites with the sea, where, when undisturbed by the winds, it establishes itself and remains with its surface equidistant from the centre of the world.
>
> It readily raises itself by heat in thin vapour through the air. Cold causes it to freeze. Stagnation makes it foul. That is, heat sets it in motion, cold causes it to freeze, immobility corrupts it.
>
> It is the expansion and humour of all vital bodies. Without it nothing retains its form. By its inflow it unites and augments bodies.[1]

Leonardo da Vinci also addressed water's different forms, such as steam, mist, rain, snow, and hail, in addition to the sea, as well as its movement and propensity for seeking out the lowest lying places when flowing unhindered, and its power to wear down mountains and river banks over time. In a word, he described water as one comprehensive element, even if it appears in many forms and qualities. In a sense, this is what we are doing also in this first part of the book, where the driving force of water is seen in confluence with human imagination and interest. To illustrate the more general implications of this perspective, this Introduction is organized in a way that allows different qualities of water to be foregrounded, each in their turn.

ELEMENTALS OF WATER

Let us first discuss some elemental qualities of water, that surfacing in various forms all over the world, sometimes to quickly evaporate or disappear into the ground, sometimes to flow peacefully across vast landscapes, shaping people's experiences. In recent years, water has been seen as one of the great global challenges, and natural scientists have been called upon to find solutions to the expected future scarcity of freshwater resources. Many of these scientists take their point of departure in a particular vision of the hydrological cycle, that is a model of the connection between rain, freshwater, and oceans, a cycle that in recent years has been shown to be far less stable than previously imagined. Yet it remains a powerful model.

Introducing the hydrological cycle in the present context serves the purpose of distinguishing between water as a (largely scientific) abstraction, something which can be modelled and quantified, on the one hand, and water as an experience, something which must be socialized and qualified, on the other. Our focus is naturally on the second of these, yet the abstract notion of water often infiltrates even popular understanding and certainly is at work wherever water is being purposely engineered. The distinction took root in pre-modern times, as argued by Jamie Linton in his book, *What Is Water?* He describes the ideational transformation of water from being seen as a *vital substance* in pre-modern times to becoming a *modern abstraction* by way of hydrological enumeration.[2] At the same time, the idea of a hydrological cycle took root.

Of course, hydrology has had a long and uneven history with many sources, but it seems that in the first half of the twentieth century, the hydrological cycle became an established natural fact in science, through various treatises. It is still seen as one of nature's grand plans, much in the vein of Leonardo da Vinci's driver of nature. In the *Handbook of Hydrology* of 1993 it is described in the following way:

> The hydrologic circle is the most fundamental principle of hydrology. Water evaporates from the oceans and the land surface, is carried over the earth in atmospheric circulation as water vapour, precipitates again as rain or snow, is intercepted by trees and vegetation, provides a runoff on the land surface, infiltrates into soils, recharges groundwater, discharges into streams, and ultimately flows out into the oceans from which it will eventually evaporate once again. This immense water engine, fuelled by solar energy, driven by gravity, proceeds endlessly in the presence or absence of human activity.[3]

Since then, it has been clearly established that the system is far from stable, and that human activity, social demands, and political priorities always infiltrate and affect the water-machine – just like climate change possibly does these days. This makes it expedient to develop a more nuanced understanding of the place of humans and societies within the hydrological system, that were far too easily expelled from the modern abstraction, as we saw in the quote from the

As a source of life, coming in many forms, water configures social communities.

handbook above. People are never simply placed in the environment; they actively interfere with it, and increasingly so as the global population keeps growing and technologies multiply, deliberately affecting water's course and redirecting its power.

Conversely, water is never just an abstraction when seen from the point of view of humans, who experience its many forms and forces: ice, snow, seas, waves, rain, rivers, floods, swamps, wellsprings, ground water, dew, steam – each of which engenders particular meanings and sensations, and makes certain social forms possible or prohibitive. Once established, excess or shortage of any kind of water potentially threatens society, as it had become known and taken for granted; there is thus a balance to maintain, for a particular idea of society to flourish. In some places, people deliberately seek to influence the hydrological cycle as they perceive it, for their community to thrive. Thus, they demonstrate the human face of hydrology; we shall see how in one of the cases below, deriving from the Andes.

Although people in the richer parts of the global water catchment rarely have to go without fresh water, in less privileged regions it is still a recurrent question of life or death – for children, livestock, and potentially everybody. For all humans, water is a generative, and regenerative force. The existential meanings of water also include the sensory experiences of the shifting qualities of water, and their contribution to the deeper meaning of lives and places, all of them dependent upon access to water, whether firmly regulated or not, and linking people to the material environment and to each other. This is clearly an elemental quality of water, which transpires from the presentations from widely differing regions below.

This takes us to an implicit point about water, namely its agentive powers; water *does* something in society. Water irrigates, inundates, floods, dries up, and creates social tensions as well as transport systems. Water may create or obliterate value, for instance, when either inundating dry land or destroying the crops by flooding fragile fields. It also has a strong bearing on moral values, when it comes to sharing and distributing water resources within a community. Finally, water has deep imaginative implications; it carries people's thoughts towards other shores, further horizons, deeper meanings, and existential questions. In the presentations below, we get a sense of how this happens in actual practice.

FLOWS OF WATER

The agentive powers of water are closely related to the ways in which water moves and organizes people on its way. We may think of *rivers* flowing in their own pace and carving out riverbeds, testifying to the power of water in both the short and the long term, and transforming natural resources and social communities as they bend and twist. We may also think of artificially established *canals*, emulating natural flows, but having their own long-term social and political implications of maintenance and regulation.

An almost paradigmatic example is Veronica Strang's analysis of the transformations of nature and 'natural' resources along the Brisbane River in Australia, where people use the

LIVING WITH ENVIRONMENTAL CHANGE

Social communities deeply affect water's flow, mass, and usage.

water for a multiplicity of purposes, transforming it into different kinds of value, and where the river is therefore never the same:

> The Brisbane River starts high in the Jimna Ranges in a network of small streams that are often no more than a thread of green in the dusty hills. By the time it reaches the Port of Brisbane, it has been captured, used and turned into many things: beef and vegetables, fruit and wine – things that can be bundled into containers and shipped to the trading partners on which Australia relies.[4]

This analysis demonstrates how water, as the most basic ingredient in the transformation of natural resources into commodities, can become almost anything, but may also give rise to tensions between different groups of people. Thus, the closer the Brisbane River gets to the city, the more tension there is between industrial and recreational needs, for instance.

Rivers may sometimes overflow the banks and flood the surrounding landscapes, whether deserts or fields. In some cases this may be beneficial to the surroundings, in others it proves disastrous. Let us take one further look at the Brisbane River, where just below the region of primary production, reminiscent of colonial times, the river is captured by a couple of dams. They have a dual purpose: one to control the river and protect Brisbane from flooding, the other to store water for domestic and industrial supply. This is where "the river undergoes its first major physical and categorical transformation from being merely 'part of the natural ecosystem' into the vital commercial resource of 'water supply'". When such dams burst, as they did some years back, the flooding that they were explicitly designed to prevent, becomes even more disastrous. Below, we shall see cases from other regions, where bursting dams have created havoc in large agricultural regions, and where they have been abandoned because the required maintenance for preventing repeated bursts could not be met.

The remark about water supply above reminds us that in most places today, the chains of supply have to be hemmed in by solid constructions. Canals of one kind or another are built to supply freshwater to cities, to discharge wastewater, or to irrigate fields. Where canals have created new – and sometimes very old – flows of water and transport (while possibly contributed to the closing of others), there is also a distinct kind of social responsibility towards maintenance. This applies most forcefully when the canals are meant to supply cities with drinking water, or when they are built to relieve them of wastewater in the interest of hygiene. In the Western world, the last half of the nineteenth century was the time when great engineering projects were conceived that would literally change the atmosphere of the cities forever, by regulating the inflow of freshwater and not least the disposal of wastewater.

Along with the modernizing quest came a strong sense of clean water and sanitation being a public good, rather than simply a universal commodity, and this raised the expectations of society. This reminds us that the distinction between water and infrastructure is not always

Social water practices – such as damming, gardening, fishing, washing – connect people closely to the natural resource, whether plentiful or scarce.

easily maintained; for all practical purposes they fuse into one water-body that fosters a particular relation between a society and its citizens.[5] This is evident also at the community level, where irrigation canals must be maintained and access to the increasingly scarce resource regulated according to agreed rules.

In short, while the river or the canal may be one and the same when seen from a hydrological point of view, they bend and twist the human perception of resources and rights in distinct ways, and transform social and moral values all while they flow according to the laws of gravity and liquidity. Social life is both configured by and configures the flow of water.

WELLSPRINGS AND RESERVOIRS

By contrast to rivers and canals, making up their own infrastructure, and ferrying people, values, and imaginings up and down the flow, wells tend to centre social life, gathering people around the localized, still source of water. The value of water seems more obviously equal to everyone, but it is not necessarily the case. Even groundwater, which is a hidden water resource with immense importance to life all over the globe, not least in regions that are otherwise arid or semi-arid, is a subject of potential conflict, unless access is strictly regulated – and often even so. Access may be regulated by tradition and a sense of honour, as we shall see in a case from Mauretania, showing that while some kin-groups may have privileged access due to ancient rules, one cannot refuse water to thirsty people and animals whose own wells have disappeared under the weight of sand or simply dried up.

Wells may be extended in depth by engineered bore holes, and make new land reclamation projects feasible in areas with neither enough surface flow, nor enough wellsprings. This requires a huge investment in pumping technologies, which may only be possible for the few, creating new social tensions and resulting in illicit taps on the irrigation channels. If water is the limiting substance of production, pumps are thus a limiting technology in procurement. "The pump is not just a technology for delivering water, but a technology for building community."[6] The unequal access to this technology potentially creates fissures in a social community on the edge of water resources.

Water itself may fuel other technologies, as happens when it is used to make hydroelectric power, driving not only particular machines but also a whole new set of dreams for the future, as we shall see in a case from Greenland, where there is so far no shortage of water in the big picture, and where the huge amounts of meltwater may potentially alleviate the shortage of work by making large-scale industry possible. What is evident from the ways in which people manage water and regiment it with a view to proper distribution and possible futures, is the keen sense of timing necessitated by shifting water resources and the desire for a sustainable social life.

Too much or too little water is not only
a matter of volume but also of timing.

SEAWATER

Three-quarters of the Earth are covered by seawater; as we saw above, the oceans have been perceived as both the endpoint and the beginning of the hydrological cycle. In more mundane terms, the seas have played a major role in the history of humankind, connecting people or separating people from each other, to a degree that is almost unfathomable in the age of airborne travel. Deep and shallow seas have also provided endless communities with living resources.

Even when living on land, people rarely turn their backs to surrounding seas, if they are within reach. Rather, they explore and exploit it, cherish and dread it, cross it to find new lands, and navigate it to extract its hidden resources for consumption. Fishing is probably as old as humanity itself, and whaling and sailing on the seven seas have connected people across continents since the earliest times and provided communities with a living. The oceans have also been instrumental in shifting goods around during the commercial revolution and since.

Even the difficult, icy Arctic seas have been visited from faraway lands ever since the boats became solid enough, and local, coastal populations have lived from the immense riches of the deep, cold waters in a region that was largely perceived as uninhabitable in more southerly regions. Navigating and living on these ice-clad seas is a highly specialized skill, which testifies to human ingenuity and the ingrained capacity for finding a way to survive.

Another navigational feat is presented by the Pacific Islanders, whose ancestors migrated from South-east Asia and gradually populated the islands as they emerged – either from volcanic activity or from the horizon as the small vessels approached. The gradual population of the islands took place over ca. 2500 years from ca. 1300 BC to AD 1250 – when New Zealand was finally reached.[7] A couple of studies below deal with particular Pacific island communities, and they show how connections across the ocean are still vital to the sense of belonging, but also in some ways threatening. The islands may be isolated in the literal sense of the term, but by the movements of people and goods they have been integrated into a larger picture for a long time, and they still are, both with respect to possible deterioration in the wake of acidification, rising seas, and more violent cyclones and with respect to potential resettlement, if the islands once again become uninhabitable.

The fear of tsunamis has come to play its own part in the Pacific, which must be seen in the light of the Asian tsunami in December 2004, and the Japanese tragedy in 2011, where an earthquake and the resulting tsunami also destroyed a nuclear power plant. Seawater is in some situations a major destructive force, but also one which may eventually open new sources for both life and imagination. In the aftermath of the Asian tsunami, many people were resettled further inland, and in the example from India provided below, the tragedy has gradually receded into the background with the growth of new gardens and the delight in 'sweet' water, purer than in their old habitations close to the beach.

[1] da Vinci, Leonardo. *Notebooks*, selected by I. A. Richter; edited with an Introduction and notes by T. Wells (Oxford: Oxford University Press, 2008), p. 20.

[2] Linton, J. *What Is Water? The History of a Modern Abstraction* (Vancouver, BC: University of British Columbia Press, 2010).

[3] Maidment, D.R. (ed.) *Handbook of Hydrology* (New York: McGraw-Hill, 1993).

[4] Strang, V. Turning water into wine, beef and vegetables: material transformations along the Brisbane River, *Transforming Cultures, eJournal*, 1(2) (2006): 9–19.

[5] Carse, A. Nature as infrastructure: making and managing the Panama Canal watershed, *Social Studies of Science*, 42(4) (2012): 539–563. [p. 556].

[6] Barnes, J. Pumping possibility: agricultural expansion through desert reclamation in Egypt, *Social Studies of Science*, 42(4) (2012): 517–538. [p. 518].

[7] Nunn, P. *Climate, Environment and Society in the Pacific During the Last Millennium* (Amsterdam: Elsevier, 2007).

[8] Helmreich, S. Nature/culture/seawater, *American Anthropologist*, 113(1) (2001): 132–144 [p. 134].

What is important to note is that even while people live on land, their social life may be shaped by the sea. The coastline is not seen as the limit of the space for manoeuvring; rather it extends it to the horizon and beyond. This has deep implications for the sense of self and of the social space.

WATER IN FOCUS

What we argue in this part of the book is that water configures social forms, and, conversely, that people configure water, by defining and distributing the resources, and by taming and exploiting its liquid powers. The general message is that water is a powerful agent, not only for survival and production, but also in the making and maintaining of particular social values. Water both connects and disconnects, and it may open up or close down particular places or passages for people, agriculture, animals, and transport, fostering particular politics of solidarity or conflict.

In short, what distinguishes water in the present context is its pervasive power as a 'theory machine' in the qualitative study of community-making in a thoroughly globalized world.[8] This means that a focus on water enables new ways of seeing and theorizing about modes of connecting people and places, and of understanding the multiple ways in which social forms are enacted with a view to harnessing the life-giving power of water. In the following, we shall see what it means in practice to focus on fluid environments.

NARWHALS AND NAVIGATORS ON THE ARCTIC SEA

Summer scenery: a hunter silently waiting for narwhal in his kayak.

Arctic char drying in the sun on the edge of the Arctic Sea.

While the ice visually and practically dominates life in north-west Greenland most of the year, people living and moving about in the region have also depended very much on its open waters. The North Water, one of the so-called Arctic oases, i.e. patches of the otherwise frozen sea that is open for the better part of the year due to a particular algae production, has always been an important part of the resource basis of the people. Due to the rich micro-fauna, and a mass of fish and birds congregating by the North Water, larger marine animals such as the bearded seal, the walrus, the narwhal and the polar bear have been found within and around it, as have (human) hunters since times immemorial.

For a couple of months each summer, the sea would open up more generally, if not all the way to the Polar Sea, then at least in the broads and fjords where the settlements were found – for the same reason. This was the high season for hunting narwhal, moving north with the opening of the sea, and entering the fjord, on which present-day Qaanaaq is situated, through the Whale Sound, so appropriately named at least until recently. For the past few years, the seasons have become more or less unpredictable when it comes to the opening of the sea, and concomitantly to the arrival of the narwhal. The hunters have further noticed that the narwhals are increasingly 'confused' – about where to go and when; this is a serious matter because for the hunters, the narwhal is in some ways the most important game.

This is not the only reason for the narrowing of their opportunities, however. Another source of worry relates to international demands for protection and wildlife management. In the wake of global concerns with the changing climate, a general concern with bio-diversity and the protection of particular species has gained a new momentum. In the Arctic, the big marine mammals are being counted and controlled with a view to regulating the hunt. It is difficult to be against this, yet there are obvious clashes between local and international perceptions of critical mass and not least of the distribution of quotas. It is not that the hunters want to hunt freely and that they do not care; they care more than anybody, but they also know more than most. First and foremost, they have always lived in close dialogue with the animal world, and have always known only to kill to uphold their own lives.

They have also established and lived by their own measure of protection for ages, including rules that forbid the hunt of narwhal from motorboats and by rifles. Instead, they still hunt from the kayak with a harpoon on line; they go out in their dinghy with an outboard motor, but as soon as they spot a pack of whales they descend into their kayak and approach it silently, alert and with

The settlement of Qeqertat at the bottom of Inglefield Gulf.

High tide at Qaanaaq in Inglefield Gulf, NW Greenland. *Dinghies* with outboard motors are used for transport between settlements during summer.

the harpoon ready. The harpoon is fastened with a line, furnished with a sealskin floater that prevents the whale from disappearing into the deep. Only when the whale is secured, do they use their gun to finally kill it off, if necessary. A hunter said:

> We prohibit direct involvement of motor boats in the hunt. The reason for this is the fact that the narwhal is one of the most important resources in the Thule region. The hunter is requested to use his kayak, and the narwhal must be harpooned before it is shot.[9]

Whales are rarely wasted by this method, as they certainly are when simply shot from a motorboat, the hunters say. Narwhal is so far the main cash crop in the region, so to speak, and the hunters need it badly, given the prices and general costs of living in the North, where no subsidies make up for the price of transport – of fuel, food and everything else that is part of modern life. When whales are landed, relatives gather on the beach to have a share, and when winter darkness turns into collective stillness, they need the *mattak* (blubber, eaten raw) to fight off depression, they tell me. It is a well-known source of vital vitamins.

For a community based on the hunting of marine mammals, the concern about species protection is immanent. Yet the circumscription of nature's potentiality through international measures that do not pay heed to local variability threatens their sense of justice. For the people who have lived in the region for centuries, the polar bear, the walrus, the narwhal, and the seal are part of an environment in which the hunters equally belong; they play different parts in the ever unfolding environmental history, yet together they constitute a whole. This means that the removal of just one of these elements from the equation will shatter the constitution of a world made up equally of human and non-human agents.[10]

The opening up of the ice, eventually including (it is guessed) the direct strait to the Polar Sea and the North West Passage, has already created new traffic through the fragile ecosystem. Biologists have begun to warn the international community about the extent to which exploratory vessels and not least their extensive seismic activity in the deep waters may disturb the migration routes of the narwhals.[11] This affects the hunt, and goes some way towards a partial explanation of the 'confusion' experienced by the sound-sensitive narwhals. Yet another disturbance to the ecosystem derives from the increasing velocity and calving activity of the massive glaciers in the area, changing the balance between freshwater and saltwater and affecting the resource basis of the whales.

The hunters, for their part, have a deep understanding of their prey, and know how to position themselves without alerting the whale to their presence. Qujaakitsoq must again be given his say:

> We try to avoid making our own shadows when we hunt narwhal. The narwhal is a sensitive creature, and when it sees your shadow in the water, it will not come up. In order that we shall not make shadows, our hunting position is determined by the position of the sun. And we try to avoid making any noise. The narwhal is very sensitive and hears well. So we try to be quiet when paddling or walking on ice. We try to hunt in the way tradition teaches us. Our equipment is: the harpoon (*unaaq*), the bladder (*avataq*), and the throwing stick (*niutaq*).[12]

For both people and prey, life by the Arctic oasis is now circumscribed by environmental changes that converge with a number of other changes, relating to national politics, biological interventions, and a new international race towards the presumed riches of the Arctic seas.

The original navigators of the Arctic seas in their elegant kayaks will soon be dwarfed, maybe exiled, by larger international interests in the sea bottom, disregarding the sea and the fragility of the age-old ecosystem for large-scale economic returns for the country as a whole. Meanwhile, the changing temperatures of the sea have made halibut migrate north, and their size and numbers in the fjord have caught the interest of the hunters. Thus, while old resources are dwindling or at least less predictable, new avenues of income may be opening up. Social life will gradually change in the process.

Kayaks, ready for the next hunt with sealskin floater, harpoon, throwing stick, and paddle.

[9] Qujaakitsoq, U. (1990) Hunting regulations in Thule: a few salient features from the municipality of Qaanaaq, *North Atlantic Studies*, 2(1–2) (1990): 104.

[10] See Latour, B. (2005) *Reassembling the Social* (Oxford: Oxford University Press, 2005).

[11] Heide-Jørgensen, M.P., Hansen, R.G., Westdal K., Reeves, R.R. and Mosbech, A. Narwhals and seismic exploration: is seismic noise increasing the risk of ice entrapments? *Biological Conservation*, 158 (2013): 50–54.

[12] Qujaakitsoq, Hunting regulations, p. 104.

LIVING WITH ENVIRONMENTAL CHANGE

EPHEMERAL TSUNAMIS, EMOTIONAL WAVES, AND ENDURING ISLANDS

During my fieldwork in Kiribati, studying social responses to natural disasters related to water, I found myself suddenly very close to my object of study when one night in March 2011 the most powerful earthquake ever registered hit the coast of Japan, resulting in a tsunami warning across the whole Pacific region.

Around dinnertime that Friday afternoon my dad calls me on my ever so intermittent Skype connection. His voice sounds nervous as it is carried across the Pacific: "There has been an earthquake in Japan. They have issued a tsunami warning for large parts of the Pacific. Can you fly out of the island?" I glance at the map on my wall. I tell him that there are no flights and no lights on the runway. I cannot get off the island. And anyway, the distance to Japan is overwhelming. My father is aware of this. He is a seaman and has spent years sailing the Pacific Ocean. Soon after, my sister calls and gives me the latest news about the tsunami, as my slow internet prevents me from visiting news sites. We chat for a while about everyday things. I hang up to go and feed my three stray dogs – a part of my normal routine around sunset.

On my back porch I run into my neighbour, Cara. She reassuringly says: "Don't worry about the tsunami, I am sure it will be fine." As she finishes her sentence the secretary of the New Zealand High Commissioner pulls into our driveway. His family is in the car. Cara waves and shouts "Mauri", the I-Kiribati greeting. The secretary steps out of the car, and slowly walks towards us.

In a calm voice he says: "I don't know if you heard about the earthquake. We are driving to Bairiki, to the new tsunami-proof house. We have packed some food, some water, and a change of clothes. You are welcome to join us."

I turn around, walk into my house, and pack a bag. This turns out not to be so simple. As I fetch my laptop, I see missed calls and messages telling me to go somewhere safe. I call my sister – she is crying. I am walking in circles packing my bag: my passport, my documents, my laptop, and some water. I tell my sister that I struggle to understand if we are in any danger. "I am watching the news," she answers, "do you want to know, or would you rather not know?" I would like to know. "They are evacuating the entire coastal area of Hawaii," she sobs, "just hurry up and go to that house now."

The house in Bairiki has only just been completed and is not even furnished yet; still, it is by far the most modern house I have seen on Tarawa. We settle in with our bags. Two children are watching movies. Leaning over the railing of the balcony and talking on the satellite phone we get updates from the New Zealand High Commissioner: the wave

An island in a world of water. Tarawa is 2 metres above sea level.

LIVING WITH ENVIRONMENTAL CHANGE

has passed Taiwan, without much damage … the wave is supposed to hit the Philippines now, but there is no wave in sight … the wave hit Guam, and it was 80 cm.

The night drags on, it is getting late. I stare catatonically at the pitch-dark ocean. I have heard that there is no oral history of tsunamis in Kiribati. This comforts me. But we are on an atoll, only a 100 metres wide and just 2 metres above sea level. The High Commissioner continues to talk on his satellite phone. The wave is travelling slower than anticipated, and will not reach us until 3 or 4 o'clock. Some people are sleeping on the tiled floor, but I find it difficult to find rest. I am listening to the ocean. At 4.30, the High Commissioner receives another call. There is still a tsunami warning, but no one is sure where the wave is. We decide to go home, and I arrive in my village around 6 in the morning.

In the comfort of my own bed I start wondering about the night's events. I keep asking myself: whatever happened to that wave?

A concrete house where an expatriate, who works on Tarawa, lives.

Through the night its location was communicated to us via satellite phone. And then it just disappeared. It felt real when we were waiting for it. The following morning, Bruce, a motorbike-riding environmental consultant who had worked in the Pacific for decades, went to the beach to take his usual morning piss, as he so bluntly put it. He saw the ocean

Waiting for the tsunami. A group of expatriates are waiting for news about the wave.

A local thatched house on stilts made from local materials.

calmly withdrawing and then forming an unusually big, yet undramatic wave, before it settled into its normal ripples.

In the afternoon my landlady asks me teasingly: "So where did you go to hide last night?" She continues: "You know, in Kiribati, we have legends about the different waves: there are small ones, big ones, and tsunamis. In our legend, Nareau created the world. It was like a nut, there were two halves tight together. Nareau separated the two halves and they went to each side. One side went to the east, that is America, and one side went to the west, that is Asia, and in the centre is Kiribati." She smiles: "The continents protect us. They are like walls protecting us from waves. We have never had tsunamis, cyclones, or anything like that. I tell you this so that you don't have to be afraid."

Maybe there is a larger natural truth enfolded in the legends. According to the scientists, atolls are volcanoes scattered the Pacific Ocean. The last 3000–4000 years the volcanoes have been sinking into the ocean floor due to what is known as the subduction of the Pacific tectonic plate under adjoining

plates, creating volcanic and seismic activity known as 'The Ring of Fire'. The atolls emerging from the ocean are the products of coral growing on the sinking volcano. The coral creates fringing and barrier reefs, which partly or completely separate an inner shallow lagoon from the outer ocean, creating the characteristic circular or semi-circular atoll. Consequently, the explanation why atolls may escape tsunamis is that the volcano steeply ascends from the ocean floor, and therefore the masses of water travelling away from earthquakes, which eventually turns into a tsunami upon meeting the continental shelf, will pass the island as a calm swell.[13]

While the imagery of a tsunami rolling across the Pacific Ocean was, to me at least, associated with devastation and havoc, these islands, only just surfacing in the world's biggest ocean, are not a convenient image of vulnerability. While the atoll may appear as a vulnerable strip of land at the mercy of the waves of the enormous Pacific Ocean, it is exactly this formation, made up of growing coral that makes it resilient to the devastating wave of the tsunami.

13 Grigg, R.W. Darwin Point: A threshold for atoll formation. Coral Reefs, 1(1) (1982): 29–34.

LIVING WITH ENVIRONMENTAL CHANGE

SEAWATER TO THE MOUNTAIN TOP
THE HYDROLOGICAL CYCLE IN CHIVAY, PERU

At 4 o'clock in the morning on 27 August 2011, I was standing at a street corner in Chivay, a town with 6500 inhabitants located 3600 metres above sea level in Southern Peru. I was looking forward to seeing the offering rituals to the water springs, and a bit anxious by the prospect of ascending 1000 metres in a steep terrain by foot.

Chivay is the commercial and administrative centre of Colca Valley, surrounded by hills and snow-capped mountains. Approximately 80 per cent of the economy in the valley is based on small-scale agriculture, in spite of the semi-arid environment. For more than a thousand years, people in the Colca Valley have been building agricultural terraces on the mountain slopes to prevent soil erosion and irrigation canals to bring water to the fields. The water comes from mountain springs at an altitude of 4000–5000 metres above sea level, from where it flows down in streams and is collected in small reservoirs at night. During the day, the water is channelled down to the fields through a network of canals.

On this particular morning, I was meeting two men from one of the irrigation associations in Chivay. One was the *regidor*, the elected water allocator, and the other was the *paqu*, the ritual expert. I had been invited to accompany them up to the water springs in the mountains to make the appropriate offerings, which are made twice a year, while the rest of the farmers in this association were going to clean the irrigation canals and reservoirs in the area. We walked up the steep mountain and did not stop until we reached the first spring, called Turupuñuna, which means 'where the oxen sleep'. Here we met up with some other men who would accompany us in the walk and the rituals. They said that it was important for them to see the water sources and to know where their irrigation water comes from. While the *paqu* prepared the offering package with herbs, alpaca foetus, llama fat, maize, coca leaves and sweets, we made libations and drank some cups of wine and alcohol. The *paqu* poured wine and alcohol into two tiny cups, which he interred into a box by the spring, so that the spring could have a drink during the year: "Like we sometimes like to drink a toast, they can also be thirsty," the *paqu* explained.

The *paqu* was also carrying a bottle of seawater brought all the way from the Pacific Ocean. He poured some of the seawater into a small plastic container, and he covered it with a piece of cotton. After libations and invocations, he put these items – together with a starfish from the ocean – into the mountain spring. The *paqu* told me that he put the seawater in the spring "so that it will call for more water", and then he explained

The farmers in the semi-arid Colca Valley cultivate crops on agricultural terraces on the steep hillsides.

Colca Valley is criss-crossed by irrigation canals channelling the water to the fields.

that the cotton was "clouds, so that there will be rain". Finally, he told why he put the starfish there: "so that the water will continue to come out of the mountain". He continued: "This is water from the ocean. It will be absorbed by the hill and all of this spring, so that the water will continue to come out." One of the other men accompanying the *paqu*, explained it in this way: "They place the cotton so that it will absorb the clouds and that it will be rain, because the water comes from the clouds, through the air. Therefore we put the cotton there, so that it will rain." Another man told me that "[the seawater] brings the taste of the ocean."

It is as if the calling for rain is a ritual technique that invokes the hydrological cycle in order to call the water from the ocean and make clouds and rain in the mountains. We can see the miniature items as imitations of, but also as parts of, the ocean, the clouds, and other water bodies. The small amount of seawater, though separate, is still connected to – and a part of – the Pacific Ocean, and therefore the ocean's properties can be

enacted, like the ability to make clouds.[14] Through the ritual, the entire hydrological cycle is performed, and the ocean is enacted as the origin of all water.

Later, we walked further up the slope and stopped at two more springs where we repeated both the ritual offerings and the drinking. When we had finished in the afternoon, we followed the streams of water downwards from the high mountain. The people who had been cleaning the irrigation canals in the meantime had all gathered in a water reservoir, which had been emptied for water. As we approached the reservoir, people received us with cheers, music and drinks. They treated us as heroes for having been all the way up to the springs where the water is born. After people had finished the work of cleaning the reservoir, the celebrations started, with food, drinks and dancing inside the reservoir.

The *regidor* was in charge of the fiesta, during which they also elected a new *regidor* for the coming year. The *regidor*, who is elected for one year at a time, is responsible for the distribution of water among the farmers in his commission, and it is a duty every man should perform at least once in his lifetime. It is most work in the months with little rain, from September to December, when the rainy season should start. The last few years, however, people have started complaining that the weather seasons are moving. The rain patterns are not as stable and predictable as before, and the water level in many springs is decreasing. Farmers are thus even more dependent on irrigation, and the work of the *regidor* is as important as ever. It is also the responsibility of the *regidor* to make sure that the offerings to the water sources are performed. Twice a year, in January and in August, he and the *paqu* walk up to the mountain tops and give offerings and libations to the springs and the mountains so that they will continue to provide humans with water for irrigation. Extensive ritual work is involved in making the water move between the ocean and the mountain and back.

[14] Cf. Allen, C.J. When pebbles move mountains: iconicity and symbolism in Quechua ritual, in R. Howard-Malverde (ed.) *Creating Context in Andean Cultures* (New York: Oxford University Press, 1997).

Walking down from the mountain springs.

"Calling for water": the paqu places seawater and a starfish into the spring.

LIVING WITH ENVIRONMENTAL CHANGE

BURSTING BODIES OF WATER

A silent threat is growing below receding glaciers: lakes are formed as the tongues of the glaciers draw back up the mountain, and huge and growing bodies of water beneath them are contained only by weak moraine walls.

In 1941, disaster hit the city of Huaraz in Peru's Cordillera Blanca. Below the white peaks that adorn the eastern wall of the valley lie a number of lakes. One day in December, a gigantic piece of ice became dislodged from the glacier that feeds Lake Palcacocha and fell into the very same lake. The waves created by the vast chunk of ice exceeded the fragile dams that enclosed the lake, and within 10 minutes an enormous flood of debris, ice, water, trees, animals and humans reached Huaraz, killing an estimated 5000 people in the regional capital. That was most of the people living there at the time.[15]

Today, Lake Palcacocha has increased its volume compared to what it was on that devastating day more than 70 years ago. The disaster ignited a series of initiatives, putting Peru in the forefront of glacial lake management. But the accelerated glacial melt has made it quite a challenge, and since the 1970s – also seeing another great disaster in the Callejón de Huaylas, the 1970 earthquake – the rate of ablation has turned the valley into one of the iconic places of global

climate change. Beyond the aesthetics of the image, this means – as in any glaciated mountain range – that the high parts of the mountains become home to a lurking danger.

The glacial lake inventory that was initiated with the establishment of the Lake Surveillance Office (later the Office of Glaciology and Hydrological Resources) managed to keep count of the lakes of the Cordillera Blanca, growing in both size and number due to the melt-off from the glaciers. The weak moraine walls that are left behind as the glacial tongue moves upward mean that not only do older glacial lakes such as Palcacocha increase their size, but also that new and even more unstable lakes are formed. Experts of engineering are working hard at lowering the lakes by means of siphons and canals, thus seeking to reduce the threat from the high altitude bodies of water.

It is not only in Peru that people, politicians and experts fear the Glacial Lake Outburst Floods, that silent danger that grows day by day above the cities, pastures and

Lake Palcacocha with siphons continuously lowering the level of the lake and glaciers in the back continuously supplying water and eventual avalanches.

fields. But perhaps nowhere else have the authorities managed to institutionalize and systematize the efforts to control the dangerous lakes to the same degree. Yet even as the Office of Glaciology from their headquarters in Huaraz and through their field experts keep each and every of the now more than 800 lakes under close surveillance, seeking to control them under difficult circumstances, the movements of the elements – tectonic and meteorological – continue to wear down the icy formations and moraine dams in the high parts. That became evident in April 2010, when an ice block the size of a Boeing 747 fell from Mt. Hualcán into Lake 513 above the town of Carhuaz. A flood grew in size as it moved downhill along the Chucchun watershed towards Acopampa, but by

sheer luck, the outburst flood did not cause major harm to human lives. Accounting for livelihoods is a different matter. The event reminded the inhabitants of the valley of their vulnerability when it comes to the danger of the bursting bodies of water above their homes.[16]

Hazard zoning in Huaraz.

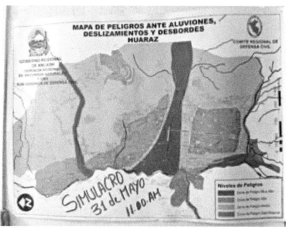

Huaraz at the bottom of
the valley.

WATER

Moraines formed by earlier glacial advances now containing the waters of Lake Palcacocha.

The glacial valley of Quebrada Cojup leading the water towards Huaraz.

In some areas, disaster management plans and funding for securing important infrastructure are in place. A map of emergency zones in the regional capital, Huaraz, shows where the dangers of a devastating avalanche of water, debris and ice are most likely to occur. But in the rural areas, no such devices are at hand. Fertile lands are often located in places of increased risk – should the lake above burst. People not only live with the threat of a glacial lake outburst flood, but more importantly, they must deal with the more mundane, everyday wearing down of river banks that erodes away fields and houses. That is a different matter, but it equally testifies to the situation in which people of the rural areas find themselves. Protection from the violently unruly waters goes beyond what can be dealt with locally.

Yet the authorities of Huaraz struggle to turn the coloured zones of the emergency map into zones of practice. The banks of the Quilcay River, where an outburst flood would be at its most violent and destructive, continue to be the home of people and their businesses. As much as the outburst floods are devastatingly real and facts of history that will most likely be repeated someday, they also remain rather elusive in practical terms. While everybody agrees that with glacial retreat, the threat of an outburst flood has increased, citizens and authorities prepare themselves in different ways for the event, converging at times, but diverging at others. Much to the despair of the glacier authorities, everyday life continues relentlessly and somewhat carelessly at the bottom of the valley from where the threat looks distant.

The bursting bodies of water that threaten to take away lives and livelihoods in mountainous areas across the world are a growing concern for politicians, policy-makers and people just trying to make do in their everyday lives. Huaraz, twice destroyed by natural hazards in the twentieth century, continues to grow as people from the countryside seek to improve their all too often meagre and impoverished situation. The invisible danger lurking above the city is sidelined by far more pertinent matters, as people accommodate to their immediate needs: there are children to feed, a house in the hometown to be improved, an upcoming *fiesta* to sponsor. Moving around the city, seeking opportunities, people push the possible danger from the bursting bodies of water to the back of their minds, in the interest of making a day-to-day living.

15 Carey, M. *In the Shadow of Melting Glaciers: Climate Change and Andean Society* (New York: Oxford University Press, 2010).

16 Carey, M., Huggel, C., Bury, J., Portocarrero, C., and Haeberli, W. An integrated socio-environmental framework for glacier hazard management and climate change adaptation: lessons from Lake 513, Cordillera Blanca, Peru, *Climatic Change*, 112(3–4) (2012): 733–767.

WHEN IT RAINS AND THE RIVER GROWS

By the end of January 2011, when the long-awaited rain season started, all Arequipans welcomed the rain with joy and happiness. I recall a day when I was walking through the city centre, on my way home from interviewing the director of an NGO engaged in environmental projects. All of a sudden the clouds burst and water started pouring heavily. I took shelter under an arch and watched the reactions of people to the pouring rain.

A man ran by on the street shouting: "*Tenía años de no llover así, !que chevere¡* [It has been years since it has rained like this! Cool!"]. Women and men, young and old would leave whatever they were doing and joyfully run to the nearest window to watch the rain falling from above. Within few minutes, people were selling umbrellas on street corners around me, while the streets, lacking drainage, started to resemble little rivers.

A drunken man walking in the rain stopped, looked at me and waved at me to come out into the rain. With his arms lifted towards the sky, he shouted, 'What is best, drought or rain?' He took off his soaked shoes and once again lifted up his arms, thanking God for the rain. Then he continued his walk. The heavy rains continued for days, then weeks, interrupted only for some hours each day by a clear sky. In these moments of sun, the three volcanoes embracing the city

would look out from the clouds and reveal themselves as majestic and beautiful beings, covered with snow, "wearing their ponchos" as *arequipeños* (the people from Arequipa) would proudly remark. Wherever I went, people commented on the rain positively: "Finally it is raining like it used to", and "This is Arequipa as we remember her." I was surprised by the joy and positivity that precipitation caused in *arequipeños* around me. The rain seemed to slow down the pace of urban life and generate a cheerful atmosphere.

It didn't take many days, however, before the singing of happiness turned into a choir of worries and blames, led by the media and orchestrated by people everywhere: "We live in a highly dangerous city, due to the natural disasters that can occur. In this time of rain, we have to be prepared" (Radio Rivereña). Rain is good and necessary,

The Chili River is bursting its banks, threatening the city after days with rain.

LIVING WITH ENVIRONMENTAL CHANGE

but too much rain puts pressure on all the hydraulic systems that run through the city, and generates risk, alerts, and emergencies. Every day, newspapers, local television and radio would tell about the damage caused by the heavy amounts of rain: collapsing sewer systems; homes built in inadequate locations being destroyed by water flowing down the mountain slopes in violent streams; river overflows destroying crops and irrigation infrastructure; cuts in the production of electricity and drinking water; rain causing damage in streets and historical monuments and buildings. With every urgency mentioned, some authorities were addressed and labelled as incompetent in responding to the problems. Other authorities used the same media to respond and reassure the populace that

they remained on alert and were perfectly prepared for the rains.

In Arequipa, the institution responsible for managing the sewage system is the municipal company for both drinking water and sanitation, SEDAPAR. When blamed for being responsible for the chaos of collapsing sewers during the rainy season, SEDAPAR stated that the problem was not caused by the state of sewers but by a lack of pluvial drainage, which was the responsibility of the municipal authorities. When no pluvial drainage system exists, all rainwater is led into the sewage system, causing major collapses. On days with heavy precipitation, rainwater and excrement alike flooded the streets of Arequipa. SEDAPAR administers a network of 2000 kilometres of pipes that run through

View on the Chili River after several days with rain. People watching the river from the bridge. Volcano Misti hidden by clouds.

Chili River, its valley, and Arequipa city seen from a neighbourhood in Alto Cayma.

In every home, water is necessary for everyday activities and well-being.

city, comment on the alerts and risks that corresponded to each level of discharge, and document the number of dogs, humans and cows caught in the tremendous flow. After one month of rain, the dams in the highlands had reached their maximum capacity of storage. In order to avoid the collapse of the dams, water was released into the Chili River in significant amounts, causing risks, damage and alerts downstream. According to the measurements of the National Peruvian Service of Meteorology and Hydrology, it had rained more in 2011 than in any previous years in the region of Arequipa. The amount of rainfall in January and February 2011 secured the agricultural production use and the general water use of the city for the entire years of 2011 and 2012. Some engineers stated that these variations in precipitation were caused by global climate change; others stated they were perfectly normal, since rain in Arequipa has always been cyclical, with some dry years followed by wet years.

On February 23rd, the level of river discharge of the Chili River reached 235 cubic metres per second. In spite of warnings against crossing the bridges, these were crowded with *arequipeños* stopping there, alone or in groups, to contemplate or take photos of the furious and potent river. Many people were remembering 15 years ago, when the entire neighbourhood around the river margin was flooded.

Urban life depends on a constant flow of water running through the Chili River and the different systems of water infrastructure. Great effort is daily put into controlling and securing the constant flow of water required for social and economic activities in Arequipa. Different institutions engage in measuring, testing, storing, calculating and distributing water according to availability. Most of the year this is an issue of securing enough water for the entire year, distributing use across the dry months. Heavy rainfall displaces normal efforts and generates concerns related to risks of flooding rather than to water scarcity.

17 municipal districts. On one day with heavy rain, up to 150 collapsing sewers were reported.

With the rain, the Chili River kept growing in volume and discharge; local media constantly updated the people on the volume of water flowing through the

LIVING WITH ENVIRONMENTAL CHANGE

THE ELUSIVE PLEASURE
OF RAIN IN THE SAHEL

Villagers walking towards an
approaching rainstorm. The
storm never made it to the
village.

The West African monsoon is characterized by its temporal and spatial unpredictability and variability. The monsoon fluctuates wildly across West Africa and over time "leaving some areas in some years well supplied, yet other regions and other years dry and parched".[17] The monsoon dynamic is a response to the contrast in temperatures and humidity between the African continent and the tropical Atlantic.

Sea surface temperatures in the Indian Ocean also influence the inter-annual-to-decadal variability of the monsoon. Beyond that, little is known about the West African monsoon. It is currently debated, for example, whether the Sahel watered by the monsoon is going to get wetter or dryer over the next decades. The GCMs, or Global Climate Models, used to predict future climate trends do not agree on this.[18] What characterizes the region is thus not some evenly spaced and predictable annual rainfall total average, but rather a high degree of spatial and temporal variability.

In Biidi 2, a village located in northern Burkina Faso and Sahel, rainfall variability is part and parcel of life. When and if the rain will fall is a central topic of conversation and concern in the village. One late afternoon in August 2007, for example, many of the villagers were congregated on the outskirts of the village after a long day weeding their fields. Standing on the dune upon which the village is located, they were looking south at a massive rain system clearly visible in the horizon. Trying to read the wind, the temperature, and the humidity in the air the villagers attempted to predict whether the rain would make it to Biidi 2.

Slowly the first drops came down and dust whirled up only to be caught again in the ever-increasing downpour. Water quickly collected in streams running through the village resulting in an array of activities. The adults and older kids busied themselves keeping the water out of the huts by placing sand bags prepared in advance in front of the door openings. The younger kids saved small chickens in danger of getting carried away by the water, constructed dams, sailed sticks and splashed around in the swelling streams while shrieking with joy. After the initial downpour, the rain settled down and fell gently almost the whole night. In the morning handfuls of saturated sand were picked up by the adults and tested for weight, colour, and composition. The verdict was good: the rain had saturated the soil. The rainfall event had turned out to be a good one.

Rain in the Sahel is almost always welcome but this event was particularly so. The last rainfall had been almost three weeks ago. Laughing and talking loudly, the villagers were not only happy the rain had been gentle and hence saturated the soil, but also that it had actually made it to Biidi 2. Only a week ago they had also stood on the outskirts of the village looking south. A similar rainfall system had been approaching. The massive rain cloud had been clearly visible, the temperature had dropped, and the wind

LIVING WITH ENVIRONMENTAL CHANGE

had picked up. But the rain never arrived. It stopped, went around 'or something', as a young man put it for lack of a better explanation. Biidi 2 and its fields and savannah got nothing. Frustration had been rife particularly since the rain had made it to Menegou, the neighbouring village. Menegou is only 7 kilometres away and they had a lot of rain: good gentle rain.

Watching, feeling, and hearing it rain somewhere else, somewhere really close like Menegou, yet not getting any is a disappointment hard to match in a dryland like the northern Sahel. The mood drops immediately once the villagers realize a particular rainfall event is not going to reach the village. Depending on the rain for their fields and cattle, this is understandable. Millet is the stable food crop in the village. Having no irrigation systems, the millet is totally rain-fed. Rain is particularly important in August as the millet flower in this month. Rain in August is equally important for the growth of wild plants, bushes and grasses on the

savannah. If it falls steadily and consistently in August, the savannah produces a lot of plants, which are used for grazing and later as hay to feed the cattle of the village.

The difference between a good and a bad rainy season is huge in terms of food production and income. During a good year, a household in the village can produce millet

Rainfall has become more extreme over the past decade. This has many consequences, one is erosion.

Cows drinking from a recently flooded river.

Typical household on the dry savannah.

[17] Hulme, M. Climatic perspectives on Sahelian desiccation: 1973–1998, *Global Environmental Change*, 11 (2001): 19–29.

[18] Christensen, J. H., *et al.* Regional climate projections, in S. Solomon, *et al.* (eds) *Climate Change 2007: The Physical Science Basis: Contribution of Working Group 1 to the Fourth Assessment Report of the Intergovernmental Panel on Climate Change* (Cambridge: Cambridge University Press, 2007), pp. 847–940.

[19] Nielsen, J.Ø. and Reenberg, A. Temporality and the problem of singling out rain as a driver of change in a small West African village, *Journal of Arid Environments*, 74 (2010): 464–474.

to last them between five and seven months, during a bad one, the harvest might last them only one or two months. For the rest of the year, they will then have to buy food. The villagers have many ways of obtaining an income but selling cattle is one of the more important ones.[19] Yet the cattle are very vulnerable during the early rainy season because they are weak from lack of food and clean water during the long dry season. Consequently no or little rain in July and August very often results in significant losses of cattle, again, meaning less money for food. In other words, in Biidi 2, the livelihood depends to a large extent on good rain

in August. But there are also other reasons behind the joy felt in the village when rain arrives. Getting wet, feeling the coolness of the rain on the skin, breathing an air free from dust, and sensing the temperature and the texture of the sand change between your toes, seeing the dirt get washed away and the colour of the landscape change to a pleasant soft green are simply just nice. That the sun for once is also hidden away behind clouds only enhances the feeling of having a respite from the harshness of the everyday life in northern Sahel so closely associated with dry extreme heat. Such pleasure is as elusive as the rain itself.

DAMS
MANAGEMENT
VERSUS LUCK

Because of the high water
levels, irrigation is now
possible during the dry season.

"In many cases, a life span of forty years or less is normal for a reservoir [created by a dam]. This seems a relatively short period in which to enjoy the supposed benefits, given the enormous financial costs, the high level of borrowing (and the resulting strains on the economy) and the disruption of millions of people's lives. The controversies in the winning of contracts for dams, and the irregularities in working out the ratio of benefits to costs, are well known ... and do little to disprove the view that dams are being built more for the benefit of the contractors and politicians than people."[20]

Fuseini is 20 years old, has a child, never went to school and lives in Galaka, which is in the north-easternmost region of Ghana. He makes a living from his boat, taking people across the river that is a major feature here. The river flows south from Burkina Faso, the border of which is so close to Galaka that the cell phone signals from the two countries get mixed up. Fuseini began doing boat work around the year 2000. His grandfather was a boatman, so Fuseini used to accompany him, and after he died, Fuseini took up the job. Fuseini has always had a hard time making enough money doing just one job, and has therefore diversified his livelihood strategies. This is the case for most people in this area. Fuseini has even stayed with an uncle in Côte d'Ivoire in order to look for wage employment. Even though Galaka seems isolated with poor roads, many of the people living here have similarly tried their luck abroad. Fuseini only stayed four months in Côte d'Ivoire, however, and apart from this brief sojourn abroad, he has

Flooding destroyed 20-year-old Fuseini's crops.

[20] Wisner, B., Blaikie, P., Cannon, T. and Davis, I. *At Risk: Natural Hazards, People's Vulnerability, and Disasters* (London: Routledge, 2004), p. 207.

LIVING WITH ENVIRONMENTAL CHANGE

Fuseini cannot transport people across the river if the water level is too high.

lived all his life in Galaka, where he now, in addition to his boat work, earns money from rearing animals, rain-fed farming and dry season gardening. Dry season gardening has become increasingly prevalent here – especially now that the river generally has a high enough water level to enable irrigation during the dry season.

Fuseini has heard that the water level in the river is determined by a dam at Bagre, upstream in Burkina Faso. Like most people living by the river in this part of Ghana, he feels rather ambivalent about the dam – his life opportunities are strongly determined by the dam. The dam is helpful because it means that there is enough water in the river to transport people by boat throughout the year and not only during the rainy season. Also, Fuseini can now do dry season gardening. The dam is problematic, however, because when there is heavy rainfall, the water level gets too high and the water authorities in Burkina Faso open the dam to avoid local flooding, which results in flooding downstream in Ghana instead. This is particularly tricky in relation to the rain-fed farming. Fuseini does not think it makes sense that they should open the dam, thus

When Burkina Faso opens the Bagre Dam because of high rainfall, areas downstream in Ghana can experience serious problems due to flooding.

were insufficient. He thinks the government should tell the Burkina Faso government that when they want to open the dam they should alert people in Ghana, they should also only open a bit at a time, so the water does not come in great quantities. The Burkina Faso government and the Ghana government have in fact tried to establish such procedures, but as will be seen, this is not an easy matter.

The Bagre Dam was completed in the early 1990s. It is located in Burkina Faso, but, as becomes evident from Fuseini's story, it affects Ghanaians downstream, positively as well as negatively. Dams are problematic in this way – on the one hand, they provide green solutions in the form of electricity and water for irrigation. On the other hand, dams lead to potential hazards, such as dam failures that are not limited to the Global South and can lead to serious flooding. Often dams merely shift a water problem elsewhere.

Dam failures are likely to become even more common with the unpredictable rainfall caused by climate change – rainfall and runoff reach levels for which the dams were not designed. This has been the case with the Bagre Dam. Models are predicting that due to climate change this kind of extreme and erratic rainfall will happen more often in West Africa. But many models also predict that drought will happen more often – the models disagree. This is a geographical area that scientists working with models find very frustrating – they cannot agree on what will happen; will there be more or less rain? The water level in the Bagre Dam is near to impossible to manage in order to optimize water usage options in Burkina Faso – and downstream in Ghana. Similarly, whether the local people living in this area will be most successful planting fields nearby the river, or further away, is a matter of luck. The question of whether the benefits of a dam outweigh its potential costs is thereby further amplified with the unpredictability that comes with climate change.

destroying the crops downstream to save crops upstream.

The first flood Fuseini remembers happened when he was about 10 years old. Between 2007 and 2009, he experienced flooding every year. Flooding destroys his crops, including maize, rice, early millet and sorghum. This has become a common problem for people in the area who have plots of land on lower grounds near the river. In dry years, these areas are good for farming, on the other hand, because they contain more moisture. It is hard to predict whether it will be a dry or wet season and therefore many keep sowing their fields close to the river only to find them flooded year after year. The flooding also affects Fuseini's business at the river as a boatman, because if there is too much water and too many waves, he cannot transport people, and his boat business is spoiled. In fact, when he went to Côte d'Ivoire it was because of the 2007 floods – his livelihood options in Galaka

WATER AS POWER AND DESTROYER

The largest lake in Greenland – Tasersiaq – is located far inland behind two glaciers, and it takes a real effort to get there. Even though some local people recall stories about caribou hunters camping there annually until as late as the 1970s, it is a place considered far away and rarely visited. Despite this, many Greenlanders relate to it as a place with historical and mythical connotations.

In particular, they have a sense of the place through the stories and watercolour paintings by the famous Aron fra Kangeq from 1858 until 1869.[21] They are part of Greenland's rich cultural heritage where land use and dramatic conflicts between Inuit protagonists play an important role. Even though the lake is no longer a physical destination for people, the old stories accentuate the powerful cultural position of the lake. The lake takes up a position as a sort of hibernating monument in the sense that it is neither used nor visited, but through naming, drawing and story-telling, the lake has been captured in social discourse and acts as a mnemonic for the historical actions of individuals and groups, both real and mythical.

During the oil energy crisis in the 1970s, Danish engineers looked into the lake's water potential, as furnished by water from both rain and melting glaciers. Their detailed studies indicated that the lake contained a vast potential for making a reservoir for a hydro-electricity plant. It could provide green energy for Greenland, attract industry from elsewhere and reduce the country's huge imports of fuel. Consequently, the country could forge a new position for itself. However, the plans were not pursued, and the engineers' reports are now hibernating in an archive in Copenhagen.

Therefore, it came as a positive surprise to the mayors of Nuuk, Maniitsoq and Sisimiut – the three towns located closest to the lake – that the Greenlandic government had been approached by an aluminium company with plans to use the lake as an energy resource for an aluminium smelter. The three towns competed to appear attractive as a smelter site as they all saw such a factory as a powerful mechanism to boost the local economy. The hidden lake and the melting glaciers suddenly emerged as a resource.

With the prospective construction of the

Maniitsoq anticipate cheaper
electricity and employment if
the hydro-electricity plant is
constructed.

New commercial sailing
routes are part of Greenland's
development plans.

LIVING WITH ENVIRONMENTAL CHANGE

The projected hydro-electricity plants are to transform hunting grounds.

The illustration (Knudsen and Andreasen, 2009: 9) indicates the complex land use pattern of prehistoric caribou hunters in the area to be flooded by a dam project.

Copyright: Greenland National Museum

hydro-electric dam, large areas around the lake are to be flooded (the waters will rise 20 metres) and like any other industrial project under development, the entrepreneur had to initiate archaeological investigations in order to survey and look into questions related to cultural heritage issues. The aluminium company Alcoa cooperated with the Greenland National Museum and Archives, then pursuing intensive archaeological surveys in the Tasersiaq area during 2007 and 2008.[22] The archaeologists returned with findings that – in the words of one archaeologist – were 'astounding'. However, the findings also raised concerns. According to the archaeologists, the huge numbers of cultural remains underlined the earlier importance of the caribou hunts in the interior and the big lakes as important cultural sites for Inuit. The carbon-14 dates from samples even indicated that the very first people of West Greenland exploited the resources of the interior. Therefore, the archaeologists recommended that special attention had to be given to these "complexes of unique and largely undisturbed contiguous cultural landscapes of the interior where traditional knowledge and legends of cultural significance for the Greenlandic population are associated".[23]

The site is probably the largest caribou hunting camp in Greenland that was also in use 4000 years ago. Even though the individual finds are interesting in themselves and point to palaeo-Eskimo activity so far inland, it is primarily the interplay and overall relationship of the complex of structures and the landscape itself that make up a substantial contribution to the understanding of the livelihoods of Inuit groups. As a consequence of these findings, the Greenland National Museum and Archives in November 2008 recommended that the cultural landscape should be preserved, and suggested that the Self-government of Greenland include Tasersiaq in the neighbouring area of Aussivissuit-Arnangarnup Qoorua (Sarfartoq), which is on the Tentative List as a UNESCO World Heritage Site.

The archaeologists' concern about the flooding of a cultural landscape of national and international importance suddenly became a potential 'show stopper' for the industrial dreams of the Self-government of Greenland and the inhabitants of Maniitsoq. The Greenlandic Parliament found itself in a predicament. The water had the power to run a large-scale factory but might in one powerful move erase important parts of the cultural heritage of Greenland. During discussions in the Parliament one MP made the following statement in order to put a pragmatic perspective on the matter:

Our honourable forefathers who pursued caribou hunting at Tasersiaq would in no circumstances want to stand in the way of the development of our country on the basis of their use of the area – on the contrary, it is expected that they would have wanted a use of Tasersiaq on the basis of the needs that are present today.[24]

In the end, the Parliament agreed to simply register, document and map the important archaeological finds and then allow the project to continue.

Three years after the discussions in the Parliament, the dam project is still only on the drawing board. Economic feasibility studies indicate that large cuts in the construction costs have to be made. The power of water can only be released by large-scale investments, and in 2012 a new framework Bill on international tendering in relation to large-scale projects was adopted by the Greenlandic Parliament. This Bill allows the entrepreneurs to cut the workers' salary costs and opens up the possibility of importing cheap labour. According to the Greenlandic Premier in his New Year's reception in Copenhagen:

> We now have the important regulatory framework in place, which will allow us to process applications to exploit our rich natural resources, which again will contribute to diversify and infuse resilience in our economy in the future.

Greenland is preparing itself to welcome the thousands of Chinese construction workers who are to build the dams and the factory and who thus are to release the true power of the lake's water. The lake has turned from being a monument of cultural heritage into a monument of Greenland's new position in a global economy of extractive industries, at least potentially.

[21] Aron fra Kangeq and Thisted, K. "Således skriver jeg, Aron", samlede fortællinger og illustrationer af Aron fra Kangeq (1822–1869), vol. I, II (Nuuk: Atuakkiorfik, 1999).

[22] Knudsen, P.K., and Andreasen, C. Culture Historical Significance of Areas Tasersiaq and Tarsartuup Tasersua in West Greenland and Suggestions for Salvage Archaeology and Documentation in Case of Damming Lakes (Nuuk: Nunatta Katersugaasivia Allagaateqarfialu, 2009).

[23] Ibid., p. 3.

[24] Aluminiumprojektet med udgangspunkt i de nu gennemførte undersøgelser, herunder den strategiske miljøvurdering (Nuuk: Inatsisartut, 2010).

LIVING WITH ENVIRONMENTAL CHANGE

NEW OPPORTUNITIES TURNING INTO DISASTER

As a researcher in the discipline of sustainable land use and natural resource management in the Sahel, I have travelled extensively for many years in the Sahelian region in the northern parts of Burkina Faso. I have always been impressed by people's ability to act in a flexible manner in order to handle the many challenges related to water availability in places with close to desert-like conditions. In these semi-arid environments, heavy rain showers may fall in one village, while the neighbouring village remains totally dry.

Likewise, the precipitation may vary considerably from one year to the other. The farmers have told me how their land use systems are geared to rainfall conditions that vary highly in time and space. They move their livestock around in order for them to find the pastures that are most productive at a specific moment, and they have adjusted their choice of crops and the location of their fields to best suit the actual water availability in a given year.[25]

When I discuss the classical land use strategies with the farmers, I am always impressed by their level of agro-environmental insight. The traditional knowledge systems actually contain a lot of useful knowledge, without the farmers having much access to scientific advances through agricultural extension services, often offering such information to the farmers.[26] While sharing their insights with me they also repeatedly stress the problems they face, using the traditional agricultural practices to sustain the food production for a constantly increasing local population.

When I visited a major integrated development project in the Oudalan Province

Intensive showers transform fields and pastures into open waters within few hours.

in northern Burkina Faso sometime in the 1990s, they explained their grand vision for an irrigation dam to me. I understood their reasoning. I had been following the development in the region, and I had noted the increasing awareness of alternative food products to supplement or replace their classical millet porridge. In the past few decades, rice had gradually been introduced in the small shops as a luxury commodity, and the prospect of growing their own rice was appealing to a number of the poor farmers, as well as to the agricultural extension service officers.

The idea of storing and utilizing the huge amounts of surface water, which runs

The Sahelian landscape is often covered with water at the height of the rainy season

LIVING WITH ENVIRONMENTAL CHANGE

The rain replenishes local water bodies, which for a period provide easy access to water for household consumption, e.g. washing.

The dam made for the rice irrigation scheme – one year after it was destroyed by a tropical rainstorm.

Only dunes remain dry with
scattered green vegetation fed
by the rain.

through the valley systems in the very short
peak of the rainy season, seems obvious. A
professional hydrologist proudly demonstrated to me how they planned to construct a huge dam across one of the large
valleys to the north of the provincial town
of Gorom-Gorom. It would then create a
temporary lake, sufficiently large to remain
a source of irrigation water well into the dry
season, he said. The following year I passed
the site again, and I could see how the dam
was constructed, together with a channel
system behind the dam. This was meant to
be the backbone of an extended area of rice
fields in a so far unused part of the valley
bottom. The local farmers were hopeful and
positive. We talked about their future rice
harvest, and they did not share my worry
about the long travel time they would have
to invest in getting to and from the rice fields
in the valley.

The time given to harvest the potential
benefit of the large investment became,
however, very short. On August 9th 2006, a
severe, tropical rainstorm hit Gorom-Gorom.
I only learned about this on the web-based
news, and later heard from my local friends
how the disaster had hit the province. In four
hours, the region received 136 mm of rain,
or around one-third of the 'normal' yearly
rainfall. On www.lefaso.net, I could read:

What is most striking is the destruction.
One of the city quarters is completely
wiped out except for a few houses. Two
others have half of the buildings left, and
the market place was severely damaged
with huge losses for the shopkeepers.
All in all, 965 houses were completely
damaged, and more than 5000 people
have lost everything.

(Author's translation from French)

Huge masses of surface water run-off
are a known phenomenon in the dry-land
regions. It rarely happens, but sometimes it
does. I remembered my layman question to
the hydrologist some years earlier: will the
dam be able to sustain an unusual heavy
rain if it comes? He replied with a firm 'yes'.
Unfortunately, he was wrong. The picture
on page 62 shows the dam when I passed it
three years after the disaster. All the installations surrounding the rice fields are wiped
out. The place has been transformed back
into a domain for pastoral use only. No-one
sees any obvious gain in trying to reconstruct
the dam. Although big rainstorms can be
expected only at large intervals, the bad
experience from 2006 has shown the extreme
vulnerability of the construction to events
that are 'normal' and could occur any time
again.

I can easily understand the local farmers'
initial enthusiasm. The immense cost of the
dam, which was covered by donor money,
was not an evident part of the farmers' assessment of benefits versus costs of the dam. The
money was a donation for the dam, not an
integrated part of a local peasant economy
evaluating costs and benefits against each
other. Hence, the success only became
transformed into a failure when the dam
broke and created a flooding catastrophe in
the nearby town. What was meant to create
a solid source of water in a drought-prone
region was not really able to absorb the
shocks and variability in the weather system
on a par with some of the traditional, but
less productive, strategies to manage water
scarcity in the agriculture. The dilemma is
recurrent and challenges strategic planning
in the entire region.

[25] Reenberg, A. and Fog, B.
The spatial pattern and dynamics of a Sahelian agro-ecosystem: land use systems analysis
combining household survey
with georelated information,
GeoJournal, 37(4) (1995):
489–499.

[26] Rasmussen, L.V. and Reenberg, A. Land use rationales
in desert fringe agriculture,
Applied Geography, 34 (2012):
595–605.

LIVING WITH ENVIRONMENTAL CHANGE

COASTAL GARDENS AND THEIR MAGIC

"Oh, the water is sweet here," my friend and field assistant Renuga often says when we walk about in the streets of Tharangambadi, a coastal village in the South-east Indian state of Tamil Nadu. Calling on people who live in the newly constructed part of the village where thousands of people have resettled after the Asian tsunami swept away their homes on the shore in December 2004, she almost routinely tastes the water from the pumps that have been established on the plot of many of the new houses.

As per orders from the Tamil Nadu state government, which undertook a huge rehabilitation programme in the wake of the tsunami, the new settlement is built further inland when compared with the original seaside settlement. The new homes are at a safe distance from the sea, a welcome side effect of which is the availability of sweeter water to the households, and their construction is based on disaster-resistant engineering. Modern houses on plots of land of equal size have been allotted to all affected families, who have gradually appropriated their new surroundings.

Quite literally so, since the houses in the new village are now for the most part surrounded by thriving gardens with neat rows of fruit trees, vegetables, palm trees and intensely coloured flowers. The sizeable plots around the houses, and not least a much better supply of sweet, that is, less saline, water and the move away from the sandy and somewhat arid coastal land to the new village have given the villagers a new opportunity of gardening, which most of the new house owners have taken to though it never really featured as an explicit prospect in the original plans for the re-housing project. The

Viewing the lush garden from the rooftop of my friend Renuga's newly built house.

lush and fast-growing gardens are the visible results of the villagers' initiative. The individual water pumps, though, are not officially approved. Formally, it is the responsibility of the authorities to provide water along the lines stipulated in the detailed plans for the re-housing project. Indeed, they do supply water, but in the eyes of many villagers the fact that right there, in the underground right next to their house, sweet water can be accessed by way of an inexpensive pump seems too good an opportunity to leave to the authorities to handle.

Certainly, the villagers are acting on fertile land; when we called on Aamani, a woman shopkeeper in her early forties, in her garden in the new village one day, she was equipped with a machete, chopping at a small papaya tree. The tree, she explained, had dried up because all of the other trees on her plot had stolen its sunlight. Too many plants were coming up, competing with each other to make it, and in order to ensure the best possible yield from her garden, she was now pruning her plot. Laughingly, she exclaimed that she had probably overdone the planting of trees a little, because she had been so thrilled by the new prospect of

LIVING WITH ENVIRONMENTAL CHANGE

having a garden around her house, growing her own fruits and vegetables, which she could sell in her shop that she had established in the front room of her house. We talk about her shop. Shifting to the resettlement village had greatly improved her business; for one thing, more people come by her house now, supplying her with more local customers. For another, before moving there, she had kept all her goods on a small trolley and had had no room for storage, let alone a plot of land to supplement her stock of sellable vegetables and fruits at no cost. This meant that she would sometimes run out of goods, missing out on business, because she would only buy and store exactly what she expected to sell. Now, as she and my assistant agree, she has to reverse the process of growth, so to speak, and cut away plants to keep the cultivation more in check.

Newcomers to the practice of gardening in Tharangambadi, Renuga and Aamani and I talk about how to go about it. Aamani expresses a sense that she almost has to do nothing to make the garden grow. It is as if the sweet water and the move itself to a new safe location make the garden magically appear. Compared to where she lived before, she has to do very little to produce fruits and vegetables, supplementing the income she makes from selling rice, dhal, sugar, cooking oil, tea, soap, and all such basic household items. She almost cannot believe her luck that after the tragic disaster, things have

Aamani's shop with homegrown fruits and vegetables on offer.

The shift from coastal land to more fertile grounds after the tsunami shows in the greening of the village.

Private and formal initiatives have ensured better access to less saline water in the relocation settlements of Tharangambadi.

turned her way. We discuss whether one can grow pineapples simply by throwing out the seeds in the garden and wonder how long this would take. I am not of much use in this regard; where I am from, we may have sweet water, but certainly no tropical sun to set off the pineapples. On her new plot, Renuga has become self-sufficient with tomatoes; throwing seeds into the garden will provide ripe tomatoes within a few weeks. Now we wonder if pineapples are equally accommodating. Aamani and Renuga laugh gently when I tell them about the care I have to take back in Denmark to even make

tomatoes ripen, moving them around all day long during the season to make them soak up every ray of sunshine.

As we make our way around the new Tharangambadi village, we see that sweet water has become a vital resident in the post-disaster resettlement village, somehow epitomizing new possibilities of securing means to survive and possibly prosper. In due time, Aamani and Renuga agree, they will have discerned the magic and know how many seeds to sow and how to make a garden that can sustain itself and its caretakers.

LIVING WITH ENVIRONMENTAL CHANGE

THE SPRAWLED WAY OF DETERGENTS

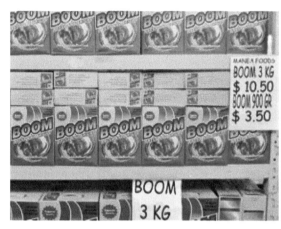

Soap powder on the shelves in
a local supermarket.

Muri beach, Rarotonga, with a
view to the islet Taakoka.

"Did you know that bananas grow very well in the waste water from the washing machine? The bananas grow strong from the nutrients in the detergent. I can show you. One of my neighbours has tried it out." Anne was not approving this agricultural technique, but she knew that it might hinder some of the nutrients in the soap from flowing through the insufficient sewage system into the tropical lagoon just 100 metres away.

In the hot season when the water is warm and calm without much overflow of freshwater from the Pacific Ocean, algae bloom is one of the visible consequences. Geo-scientific studies even suggest that high levels of nutrients may damage reefs and stocks of fish to the extent that beaches will eventually become deprived of all their sand, because sand is produced by the reef and the shell-fish, after which it is moulded and filtered by a host of sea animals.[27]

In some countries non-bio-degradable soap is banned, in other countries it is the cheapest available soap, boasting its qualities on boxes, cans, and bags with white whirls, clean bubbles and sparkling colours. It is, presumably, effectively cleaning your clothes at all temperatures, ensuring a bright result without stains and spots.

Some of the remarkable side-effects have come to the attention of an environmental care group in Rarotonga in the Cook Islands. First, people were warned by the National Environmental Service and local NGOs about the negative effects of over-use of fertilizers in the gardens in the hills.

Flushed into the lagoon, sometimes together with large amounts of soil sediments due to logging, this process causes high levels of nutrients in the shallow lagoon, to the detriment of the marine life. Second, it turned out that the extensive use of non-bio-degradable soap has the same negative effect.

Locally, residents founded an environmental NGO, and started to use soap nuts (a natural surfactant) and bio-degradable products in their households. They wrote letters to the importers of soap and to the government in order to put a stop to the import; they compared all the detergents on the market and taught school children at public Lagoon Days, and anyone else who cared to listen, about the negative effects on the waterways of the island. They applied for funds for an upgrading of the sewage system.

Becoming more and more engaged, members of the NGO registered that not everyone in the community changed their washing habits. The damaging detergents were still available in the shop, often in very

LIVING WITH ENVIRONMENTAL CHANGE

large quantities. Anne, a member of the steering group, was curious about this. To her, the change in washing (and cleaning) habits and techniques seemed perfectly logical, and she quickly developed a personal and embodied distaste for certain types of soap. Therefore, she laughingly confided, she felt utterly embarrassed, when she one day discovered that her own house cleaner was using the wrong soaps and cleaning agents.

Getting more and more involved in the NGO, and developing a deeper concern for the lagoon, Anne recognized that the cheap soap was a good buy for many people in the community with a strained budget. The

27 Nunn, P. and Mimura, N. Promoting Sustainability on Vulnerable Island Coasts: A Case Study of the Smaller Pacific Islands, in L. McFadden and R.J. Nicholas (eds) *Managing Coastal Vulnerability* (Oxford: Elsevier, 2007).

The tropical moist cloud-forest of Rarotonga. The average rainfall is between 2,000 and 3,000 mm per year.

A system of irrigated taro terraces in the high well-watered valleys.

higher prices for the bio-degradable soaps and the fact that many people did not really understand the exact biological mechanisms going on in the waterways were her explanation why some residents held on to the nutrient-rich soap.

Scrutinizing her own former use of soap that she now considered inadmissible, she became fascinated by the wider implications of soap use. Anne recalled her mother's use of soap and how the introduction of very foamy soaps was launched as more effective. The more foam, the better. But why? Does it at all help? Is it just a story told by the advertising industries? What do the bubbles indicate? And why do young women today, as she had been told, wash their often very long hair two, three or four times in a row to reach the right feeling of cleanness? In interviews she and other residents also linked the soap habits to the former colonial preference for the colour white in clothes, buildings and pathways. The colonial order was also a colour pattern. Another striking example with strong historical and colonial roots was pointed out to me in soap conversations, namely, that the church-goers are dressed all in white on Sundays celebrating the Holy Communion: suits, shoes, hats and dresses, spotless and shining clean.

Soap had become a bit of an obsession for her, Anne said. 'The soap lady' was one of her nick-names. She browsed the internet to learn more about nutrients, import bans, importers, water quality, and so forth, and quickly found a sprawled global network of people with related interests. "Go and see for yourself if you are interested," she said.

One of the threads in this network relates to questions of climate change. It is often noted on diverse internet pages, and claimed with more or less back-up from research in environmental assessments, that if beaches are washed away and naked bedrock is exposed, or if algae bloom becomes a more frequent phenomenon, lagoons and islands will be even more exposed to future changes in sea level. This was also the message presented in Muri by an environmental officer from the Cook Islands government who visited the lagoon. In a talk given to a small audience at an exhibition on environmental change in the lagoon, she said: "The best preparation for climate change is a healthy lagoon." Therefore, she welcomed the many initiatives by the local environmental group.

Soap is one ingredient among others floating through the island – in the groundwater, in streams, pits, wells and ponds – and eventually released into the lagoon. The movements of water from higher grounds through agricultural and residential areas is only partly visible to people living on the island, and the biological processes are intricate. Experimentation with ecological closets, water treatment and much more is ongoing, but the concern and expertise are not evenly distributed. According to the environmental group, things are moving much too slowly. Now that they have become aware of the strain they put on the waterways, they want to move on and protect the water resources.

LIVING WITH ENVIRONMENTAL CHANGE

DROUGHTS
COMPLEX SOCIAL
PHENOMENA

The light was blinding, the dust whirling, the heat suffocating. Toumame, the 12-year-old daughter of the herdsman Mohamed Ould Salem, in whose tent I lived during a stay among nomadic pastoralists in the south-eastern frontier provinces of the Islamic Republic of Mauritania in January and February 2012, looked at me with a mixture of curiosity, alienation and wonder. Moments earlier, I had asked her to explain what a drought is. A question which I found pertinent, given the fact that what was widely anticipated to become the most severe period of prolonged water scarcity since the so-called Great Sahelian droughts, which had menaced the region in the 1970s and 1980s, was currently gaining momentum.

The atmosphere in the camp, and indeed across the south-eastern frontier provinces at large, was saturated with anxiety as the nomadic pastoralists found themselves increasingly incapable of anticipating the polarized climate and hence navigating the ephemeral topography. I was hoping to gain an embedded understanding of how the increasing scarcity affected their livelihoods in the everyday routine, and the imminent drought seemed to encapsulate this question in a most acute way; hence my question to Toumame. She replied: "People die of hunger and animals die of hunger … All I

hope is that I will always stay with my family. Inch'Allah."

Despite the remarkably firm timbre of her voice, Toumame appeared profoundly anxious, and I was moved by how she equated the imminent drought with hunger, correlating water scarcity with an existential threat to the core constituents of her life-world: her parents and siblings. Following a long, ominous pause, in which she seemed to search for the right words, Toumame fixed her gaze upon me and proceeded to compose a rather poignant analytical definition:

Toumame, 12, photographed during a severe drought in the region of Hodh el Gharbi in south-eastern Mauritania, February 2012.

A nomadic herdsman outside his tent during a sandstorm in the region of Hodh el Gharbi in south-eastern Mauritania, February 2012.

Two women engulfed in a sandstorm. Oualata, Hodh ech Chargui, June 2006.

A drought (*jévef*) is when there is no water (*el ma*) and the pastures (*hatbä*) dry out. The animals find no food and eventually, they will die. That is a drought … This year is a year of drought (*am el-jévef*), and we are afraid our animals will die. We have to follow them where there are pastures … I don't know what will happen.

That evening, as I was attempting to make sense of the troubling situation which threatened to catapult this family into further vulnerability, Toumame's words made me think of a previous conversation I had had with a woman, named Khadija, in a nomadic camp in the *Mantega Rohuwiya*, a pastoral zone outside the remote city of Oualata, in a similar context of intensified scarcity during the peak of the dry season (*Seyf*) in 2006. At that particular time, the nomadic collectives had all fragmented into small units, which

were dispersed across the arid landscape. The men were herding on distant pastures, and the women, the elderly and the children remained in the tents not too far from permanent water holes. To my question of what was most important to her, Khadija responded:

> Our life is water. If we find water, we can relax, at least for a moment. If the rains don't come soon, it will be very difficult for us. Rain is important. If it doesn't come, we have to move closer to a well and wait until the rain comes.

From my observations living among the nomadic pastoralists, I understood that 'a drought' is not an objective phenomenon, which can be categorized as being merely natural. Rather, 'a drought' is a complex whole of elements that may derive from many domains, but which is experienced in

74   WATER

its totality for the nomadic pastoralists who are living in its midst.[28] A drought is no less social than it is natural, or, for that matter, political.[29]

To the nomadic pastoralists of Mauritania, water is considered *rahma*, a blessing from God. It is a purifying and life-giving – indeed sacred – liquid, which literally binds together the social fabric. Because it is so scarce, preservation and equitable distribution are a fundamental concern upon which life itself depends. Having undertaken recurrent fieldwork among nomadic pastoralists in the arid landscapes of Mauritania over a period of ten years between 2001 and 2012, I have come to realize how pivotal water is to their livelihood, indeed, as Khadija had said, their life is water. I have also experienced how a heightened sense of perplexity and anxiety permeates society as the weather polarizes and the appearances of pastures and water not only decrease but also become fundamentally reconfigured. The environment, quite literally, is becoming difficult to anticipate. Among the elderly nomadic pastoralists, genuine concerns over what they fear are irreversible ecological changes for the worse are preponderant and multiplying. In addition, the simultaneous emergence of nebulous assemblages such as the notorious AQMI (Al-Qaeda in the Islamic Maghreb) and the increasing political instability in the region at large, along with the unrest in neighbouring northern Mali in particular, are severely constraining their mobility. Paradoxically, in a context where mobility constitutes the primary means of survival, the nomadic pastoralists find themselves increasingly immobilized.

Droughts are complex phenomena in which a multiplicity of natural, political, economic and social elements converge to produce a form of escalating socio-political turbulence, threatening the social fabric of the nomadic pastoral livelihood in south-eastern Mauritania. Certainly, the situation in 2011–2012, when rains were entirely absent across most of the Saharan and Sahelian regions, and political instability escalated

in Northern Mali and beyond, the nomadic pastoralists among whom I worked were increasingly anxious and, in their own words, disoriented (*tounoussou*). Toumame and her family embodied this growing anxiety and disorientation, and as the pastures and water sources progressively dried out and the conflict in neighbouring Mali discouraged them from migrating with their herds towards more fertile pastures across the border, as they would normally do, Toumame became increasingly tense. What would happen to the family and would she stay with them or be forced to settle with relatives in the regional capital Aioun el-Atrouss?

Extreme water scarcity, particularly when combined with political unrest and economic disturbances, produces a context of crisis, in which core aspects of society, such as social relations and alliances, notions of morality, honour, solidarity and indeed integrity, surface as sources of uncertainty.[30] Hence, water and its absence afford a vantage point from which to ethnographically engage with the practical constituents of social life. In arid lands, water more often than not serves as a pervasive idiom for engaging with social and political issues of paramount importance to those who inhabit these hostile environments.

The well *Ain al-Argoub* outside the desert city of Oualata in the region of Hodh ech Chargui in south-eastern Mauritania, May 2001.

[28] Bonte, P. Pasteurs et nomades: l'exemple de la Mauritanie, in P. Bonte, J. Copans, S. Lallemand, C. Messiant, C. Raynaut, and J. Swift (eds) *Sécheresses et Famines du Sahel*, vol. 2: *Paysans et Nomades* (Paris: Maspero, 1975).

[29] Kallis, G. Droughts, *Annual Review of Environment and Resources*, 33 (2008): 85–118.

[30] de Bruijn, M. and van Dijk, H. *Arid Ways: Cultural Understandings of Insecurity in Fulbe Society, Central Mali* (Amsterdam: Thela Publishers, 2005).

LIVING WITH ENVIRONMENTAL CHANGE

PHOTO & TEXT   Laura Vang Rasmussen

WATER QUANTITY VS WATER QUALITY

Photo: Lykke Feld Andersen

Goal Seven of the Millennium Development Goals aims at halving the proportion of people without sustainable access to safe drinking water by 2015. In the beginning of 2012, it was, however, announced that the world had already met this goal well in advance of the 2015 deadline.[31] But what does sustainable access to safe drinking water actually mean? While safe drinking water refers to the quality of the water, sustainable access means that the water source is less than 1 kilometre away from its place of use, and that it is possible to obtain at least 20 litres of water per member of a household per day – according to the World Health Organization (WHO). Sustainable access to safe drinking water thus becomes a question of water quality as well as water quantity.

Although Goal Seven of the Millennium Development Goals has already been met at the global scale, Sub-Saharan Africa is one of the regions whose population has the least access to an improved water supply. Since the publication of *Drawers of Water* in 1972,[32] research on water supply in Sub-Saharan Africa has fairly consistently concluded that increasing the quantity of water used in the household may be more important than improving its quality in relation to health. But then it becomes vital to know how households in these areas, in fact, can achieve increased usage.

According to the World Health Organization's definition of sustainable water access, households in Sub-Saharan Africa may obtain increased usage if the distance to the water sources is reduced. However, an estimate of 20 litres per person to be sufficient for sustainable water access is most likely too low in, for example, the Sahel.

In the dry season, households have to use their domestic water supply also to support their livestock, and as the body temperature of an animal increases, so does its water requirements, implying that huge quantities of water are needed. During the rainy season, the domestic water sources are, by contrast, mainly used in the household for drinking, cooking, bathing, and domestic hygiene. Despite the differences in water requirements between the dry season and the rainy season, water is in general considered a scarce resource and the question of how to increase consumption is therefore extremely relevant.

In the village of Belgou located in the northern part of the Sahel, where I conducted fieldwork, people used water from four different sources: a river, small wells in the ground (French: *puits de terre*), an artificial pond (French: *bouli*) and a village pump. Almost all the water needed was

The main water source in Belgou, Northern Burkina Faso: a village pump.

carried by women and children, making several daily trips to the water sources to bring it home in containers. The amount of time spent on this task was substantial, as they had to walk to the water source, queue, draw the water, and walk home with it.

When the villagers of Belgou had to choose where to collect water, the choices seemed to be more determined by the distance to the possible water source than by the varying water quality of the four different sources. For example, people living close to the river primarily fetched water from this source despite the lower quality of river water compared to pump water. Nevertheless, they used the river water for drinking, cooking, bathing, and domestic hygiene. People who had to walk long distances to fetch water from the pump and the river, would likewise turn to their closest water source: small wells in the ground which would fill up with water during heavy rains. Just like the people who preferred to collect water from the river, considerations on water quality were indeed limited also when it came to the small

Photo: Ene Bugge

Photo: Anna Sofie Hjelm Pedersen

Small wells in the ground which during heavy rains fill up with water.

River water is used for drinking, cooking, bathing, and domestic hygiene.

An artificial pond on the outskirts of Belgou.

Photo: Trine Vannay

wells. Only when the river and the small wells dried up during the dry season, would the people living in the outskirts of Belgou have to collect water from the village pump despite the long distance.

The fact that the time spent carrying water was a more serious concern among villagers than the quality of the water became very obvious when a new pump was constructed in 2009. The pump was constructed by a development project and located 1.5 kilometres south-west of the village. The new pump was primarily intended for the people living on the outskirts of Belgou, for whom the distance to sources with water of good quality (the village pump) was long. In the rainy season, the new pump was intended to replace the previous strategy of fetching water of a poor quality by digging small wells in the ground very close to the homes. By contrast, in the dry season, the new pump would reduce the time spent collecting water as people used to be forced to walk the long distance to the village pump. Since the new pump was constructed within c. 200 metres from most of the houses, the planners of the development project had thought that this pump would be the preferred water source in the dry as well as in the rainy season. However, during the rainy season people continued to use the small wells located

practically just outside the homes rather than collecting water from the new pump. Only in the dry season, did the new pump seem to be of use.

Clearly, and significantly, people's choice of water resources seemed to be consistently determined by the distance to the water source, rather than by the varying water quality of different sources. Although living on the desert margins, people in Belgou did not perceive water as a sparse resource when talking about the different water sources. Quantity was not an urgent concern, locally. Consequently, with respect to the global question of how to achieve increased water usage in dry regions of the world in order to improve health, it became clear that people did not need more water sources; they needed closer water sources, as was often argued in Belgou. Thus, their concern was mainly a question of distance to the water sources rather than a question of either absolute quantity or of water quality.

Given the distance it had to be carried, the water that people had collected and stored in their homes was transformed into something similar irrespective of its source: Once in the home and ready for use, the nature of the collected water changed and it became a very sparse resource.

[31] UNICEF and World Health Organization. *Progress on Drinking Water and Sanitation: 2012 Update* (Geneva: UN, 2012).

[32] White, G.F., Bradley, D.J. and White, A.U. *Drawers of Water: Domestic Water Use in East Africa* (Chicago: University of Chicago Press, 1972).

MIRRORING

While the Arctic and the Pacific at first seem worlds apart, they do share a number of features, both physically and historically.

FIXED AND FLUID WATERS
MIRRORING THE ARCTIC AND THE PACIFIC

We know, for instance, that the two major climatic peaks recorded during the Medieval Warm Period (AD 700–1200) and the Little Ice Age (AD 1350–1800) have had major impacts on both regions and have later been typified as times of plenty and times of poverty, respectively. At the present time, a similar connection through warming is being established; if or when the ice continues to melt off the Arctic seas and the Greenlandic icecap (not to speak of the shrinking of Antarctica), this will affect the sea level in the Pacific and contribute to the vulnerability of the islands.

Conversely, with respect to the Little Ice Age, we know from the natural sciences that the transition to rapid cooling locked up (more) water in the Polar regions, while the sea level dropped significantly in the Pacific, by up to 1.5 metres.[33] Evidently, this induced some turbulence in the newly colonized island world. Reef surfaces were exposed which sustained many atoll communities, and new islands emerged, allowing more places for settlement and population dispersal, thereby both separating and connecting island communities.[34] At the other end of our oceanic continuum, in Greenland, the cooling made the Old Norsemen disappear some 400 years after they had migrated

to Greenland from Iceland in the tenth century.[35] Meanwhile, members of the last prehistoric Eskimo culture, the Thule culture, having migrated from the Americas and entered North Greenland about the same time as the Norsemen populated southern tracts, began moving south. The two groups did meet, but only one of them survived the Little Ice Age.

In more recent historical times, both the regions by the Arctic seas and in the Pacific have been subject to western dreams of exploration and colonization. In both cases, the image of isolation and remoteness has held sway ever since, quite independently of the lives actually lived by people in those places, for whom the island or the settlement on the Arctic coast was of course the centre of the world. In consequence, we find that in both cases community life is based on a dual outlook, both western and 'islandish'. The latter is partly due to the long-standing relationship to the ocean as a major feature of their immediate environment and an important natural resource basis.

Bringing the Arctic and the Pacific into one picture and showing the more complex relations that connect the two, as we have done above, already allows us to discover new things about both. Our point is that focussing on the ways in which the Arctic and the Pacific mirror each other will conjure up new images of a shared world. In the following we shall centre on the case of the circumscribed source of freshwater on the brink of the salty seas.

A high tide coinciding with a storm surge can be disastrous on a low-lying island.

Even in a spring snowstorm, the blue ice-cube of hard-pressed glacier ice stands out, echoing the blue house.

PACIFIC CHALLENGES: PERMEATED FRESHWATER RESERVOIRS

In Tarawa, the main island in the atoll nation of Kiribati, droughts can last years, even though the place is surrounded by masses of water. Kiribati consists of 32 small atolls, islands based on dead Pacific volcanoes. Together the 32 atolls have a combined land area of 811 km², but the surrounding ocean belonging to Kiribati is no less than 3.5 million km². The islands are scattered across the ocean in lines and clusters connected through voyaging routes from ancestral times until today. Before Kiribati became a British protectorate in 1892, the canoe was the only means to negotiate the ocean. The canoes were constructed without the use of nails. Instead the planks were tied together only using coconut string, which would not come undone if ruptured, but which

would scour even tighter, and still remain relatively flexible. Such canoes took voyagers to islands beyond the horizon, from where they were sometimes never seen again. During British colonial rule, inter-island travelling became prohibited, and locating a truly skilled navigator has been difficult ever since.

The rich history of navigation and settlement has recently been overshadowed by contemporary challenges, notably the fragility of the freshwater resources. The fresh groundwater resources on atolls form a lens under the surface of the ground, which balances on the surrounding salty ocean. This lens is usually 1 to 2 metres below the surface of the land, which makes it easy to access, but susceptible to pollution from humans. Contamination is imprinted in the groundwater, in a way comparable to how the sediments stored in the polar ice bear the mark of ancient volcanic eruptions.

WATER

At high tide much of the island floods.

At low tide, the shallow lagoon within the stone reef is not much of a port and the boats are stuck.

The natural qualities of the freshwater lens combined with the pervasive anthropogenic threats, such as global climate change and local overuse, make it one of the most vulnerable aquifer systems in the world.[36] Even so, this freshwater lens is the principal agent supporting life on the atoll. This shallow body of water allows plants, animals, and humans to survive in an otherwise fatally saline environment.

With the current challenges of unstable sea levels and changing precipitation patterns, the freshwater on the atoll is increasingly subject to over-exploitation, pollution, and saltwater intrusion. Freshwater scarcity is one of the major obstacles to continued life in the Pacific. The lens is breaking.

ARCTIC PREDICAMENTS: FLUID AND FROZEN FRESHWATER

Life in Greenland mirrors life in the Pacific in a number of ways. Even though the towns and settlements in Greenland seem to be linked through a massive landscape, partly consisting of ice – sea-ice, glaciers, and the ice cap – they are actually separated by the same token. Apart from airborne transportation, which is prohibitively expensive, there is virtually no passage between the settlements and towns except by the sea or the sea-ice, and the communities are nothing if not tiny islands in a vast and rather demanding ocean – sometimes frozen and passable only on dog sledge. The population is small (55,000 all together on the world's largest island, more than two million km², of whom 15,000 live in the capital of Nuuk), and each settlement, sometimes only inhabited by some 50 people or fewer, is of necessity a world unto itself, even while knowing about the others. Another mirror image is provided by the increasing fragility of the freshwater resources, in this part of the world locked up in the ice.

In the far North, the ice is melting and life is changing. Somewhat paradoxically,

LIVING WITH ENVIRONMENTAL CHANGE

it also affects the accessibility of drinking water. One would have thought, that with the run-off from the glaciers, and the thawing of the ice, it would have been much easier to access freshwater than before. If one looks at Greenland as a whole, it would certainly be impossible to claim that there is an absolute shortage of water. However, if we zoom in to one of the small towns or even smaller settlements along the coast, freshwater has become an increasing problem in quite a number of instances. Looking at Qaanaaq in the absolute North (home to some 600 people), the glacier from which the town has drawn its water during the summer has now melted down below its normal level, leaving only a trickle of water for the people. In the picture (p. 80), it is easy to see both how Qaanaaq has organized itself in relation to the rivulet, and how dry it is. One can also barely see the top of the former much mightier glacier. This also makes the water more prone to pollution from stray dogs, etc. There are other streams farther away, but not within walking distance – given that one must carry it back across a rough and stony summer landscape.

This leaves the inhabitants with just one other accessible water resource, that is the ice stored in the massive icebergs stuck in the sea-ice. These are only accessible in the period of reliable and solid sea-ice, since it takes either a pack-sledge or a heavy vehicle to transport it back to the town. Individual households may have their own 'ice-cube' outside of the house for their own coffee – 'this is the best'. The alternative, also for household water in general, is to have it delivered by a tank truck. This truck again gets it from a huge water tank in midtown (the biggest one in the picture on p. 80), which is constantly being filled and refilled with ice from the bergs, thousands of years old and tightly packed, when possible. Recently, another tank has been built, because the period in which one may assemble it for storage is shrinking, while the stream is also increasingly drying out.

Glacier cube for drinking water by family house in Qaanaaq.

MIRROR IMAGES

As noted above, the Arctic and the Pacific regions were geo-physically connected during the warm Middle Ages and the Little Ice Age. Today, they are connected through global climate change – rhetorically, climatically, and scientifically. Arguably, the meltdown of the Arctic affects the sea level in the Pacific, thus the fates of the two populations are linked through global warming. The interesting point in the present context, emerging from the unlikely comparison, is that in these regions so far apart, there is a remarkable similarity in the freshwater situations. While at first glance, glaciers and icebergs appear distinctly solid, while the freshwater lens on the atoll is by definition fluid, and embedded in the moveable substance of sand, they have a lot in common. Neither source is fixed, let alone solid, but nor are they simply fluid. They mix and move, according to season – and increasingly

The traditional I-Kiribati canoe is tied together with coconut string.

Approaching storm in an Arctic fjord.

33 Nunn, P., Hunter-Anderson, R., Carson, M.T., Thomas, F., Ulm, S., and Rowland, M.J. Times of plenty, times of less: last-millennium societal disruption in the Pacific basin, *Human Ecology*, 35 (2007): 385–401.

34 Nunn, P. *Climate, Environment, and Society in the Pacific during the Last Millennium* (Amsterdam: Elsevier, 2007).

35 Gulløv, H.C. (ed.) *Grønlands forhistorie* (Copenhagen: Gyldendal, 2004).

36 White, I. and Falkland, T. Management of freshwater lenses on small Pacific islands, *Hydrogeology Journal*, 18 (2010): 227–246.

so with the warming of the oceans – the Arctic and the Pacific alike.

In both cases, there is also a significant mixing of saltwater and freshwater. The transition between them is almost unmarked, and the freshwater resources in both cases depend on both the long- and the short-term rhythms of the salty sea. The images of an all-embracing global warming, is perceived as near to the mark in both cases. There is a point then, in mirroring the Arctic and the Pacific, because it allows us to see that they are equal parties in a network of global connections, affecting everyday life.

Oceanic navigation has allowed Pacific Islanders to negotiate the ocean.

LIVING WITH ENVIRONMENTAL CHANGE

PART TWO

TECHNOLOGY

TECHNOLOGY

INTRODUCTION

Why do we include technology as a central category in our explorations of waterworlds? The short answer is that water simply seems to attract and absorb technologies. Every waterworld abounds with ways of directing water from the ground or the sky into pipes, animals, bottles, plants, food, people, or any other kind of vessel or consumer. Water has to be handled in some way by every living community, and throughout history the diversity and the human ingenuity in devising means of handling water have been amazing – and continue to be so. In the Arctic, frozen blocks of freshwater are central to inhabitants in the dry winter season when the snow evaporates. In arid landscapes deep wells are dug, ingenious canals and dams constructed, and on atolls inhabitants live on a porous fresh water lens centimetres below the surface supplemented by quite another important water resource 5 metres up, sheltered by the thick husk of young coconuts. Everywhere water is handled with various technologies that in turn process and form water whether it is sprinkled, warmed, carried, drunk, poured, cleaned or deep-frozen. Humans and non-humans perform the waterworlds with many specialized skills and tools, and new technologies are constantly developed.

Water technologies are social devices and stretched between predictable and unpredictable modes of use.

Since water attracts technologies of so many orders, we have made some hard choices. As researchers doing fieldwork in some of the world's hotspots of climate change we could have approached the laboratories and offices of climate scientists and studied the ways they study and project the climatic changes of the Earth. Excellent work is being done by scientists using all sorts of instruments in order to refine our understanding of the complex processes in the atmospheric flux and meteorological patterns. And excellent work is done by historians who are carefully unfolding the societal implications of climate science through the ages. As a truth-producing activity, science is also a social activity and the practical aspects are co-produced. Anthropologists take part in understanding this production of theories and facts too, by asking questions such as: What kind of observations do scientists make?; and how do they match or differ from other kinds of observation?; how does the formalization of the data take place?; what kind of experimentation is involved?; how are projections made, tested and displayed?; and how are the practical consequences of the climate projections processed in the scientific communities and beyond?[1]

Obviously, we could also have turned to some of the high-technological hot spots of climate change such as engineering communities developing grand projects seeking to stall if not prevent climate change; they may do so by changing the weather by artificial rain-making or by changing the Earth's atmosphere altogether with large space sun screens.[2] After all, these high-tech universes attract much attention and stir controversies as examples of advanced human ingenuity or alternatively as yet another sad belief in a technological fix. Their importance should not be underestimated.

However, as fieldworkers in diverse environments we have a special interest in everyday technologies that people employ and rework in their homes and in the wider environment in which they live. Some of these everyday technologies are connected to large-scale infrastructural constructions such as industrial plants, water towers or major coastal protection devices. However, we have not focused on the technology itself to isolate and singularize it as a 'thing' or a 'machine'. Rather, the focus has been on the practical handling of the technology and its importance to the people with whom we lived and conversed. This is why rather different kinds of technology such as a sledge, a book, a date palm project, and an aluminium plant end up side by side in this Part. And this is why we present some quite extraordinary stories about these technologies. Sometimes we focus on how they are used before they are actually in place; at other times we show how they take on other uses than planned and expected, or how the most important outcome may even lie in their future replacements and successors.

Even though technology often connotes straightforward, rational, mechanistic usage, in social life it is more likely absorbed into the practical environment by adjustments, alterations, and alignment. Indeed, in this Part we show how technologies such as water pumps, lighthouses and maize cobs turn out to be surprisingly flexible, and how coherent practices arise in environments with even quite incoherent technologies.

A few words should be said about what we mean by 'technology'. In the first place, we have been searching for a category wide enough to include both advanced machinery, simple

     LIVING WITH ENVIRONMENTAL CHANGE

Fluid technologies dissolve into the environment, a quality mark in a world in which technologies do not travel easily.

tools, objects that are not constructed as technical devices but nevertheless used as such, and objects that clearly change purpose and functioning in actual use. Inner tubes for tractors, for example, are constructed for certain inflation pressures, but can also be used for carrying water. Second, we have been inspired by the so-called material turn in anthropology and other disciplines across the humanities and the social sciences in which physical objects are studied as inextricably embedded in the social fabric.[3] As such, objects may be more or less refined technologically, and more or less singularized as tools and commodities, but they are nevertheless always moulded, reworked, adapted, and absorbed by the environments in which they are put to use. Water technologies are both technical and social devices, co-produced, and stretched between predictable and unpredictable modes of use. This is why it is important to observe the technologies when in use and to follow their tracks when broken or dismantled, reassembled and recycled. The point is that even though 'technology' sounds clearly self-contained, demarcated, and advanced, in everyday practice it is closer to ordinary tools and simple objects. They are malleable, flexible, or sometimes simply fluid.

FLUID TECHNOLOGIES

> This is a paper about water pumps. More precisely, it is about a particular hand water pump: the Zimbabwe Bush Pump 'B' type. The paper is not critical, but neither is it neutral. For we happen to like, no, even better, to love the Zimbabwe Bush Pump in all of its many variants. But even if affection moves our writing, this is not an exercise in praise. Rather, we want to analyze the specific quality that attracts us to the Zimbabwe Bush Pump. This turns out to be its fluidity. So in what follows we lay out the various ways in which this piece of technology, so advanced in its simplicity, is fluid in its nature.

This is the opening paragraph of a paper by de Laet and Mol dedicated to a certain water pump with an eminent capacity to change and adapt to different environments and communities.[4] It may be characterized as a quite simple technology consisting of a few mechanical parts, yet it is also advanced with many well-thought refinements, checked and verified by the designer and countless communities. De Laet and Mol suggest that the distinct quality of this fine piece of technology is its 'fluidity'. The extraordinary capacity to pump water and keep it clean and healthy in different environments, the ease by which its users can repair and adjust it with local spare parts, and its integration into both the ground and the community of users makes it 'dissolve' into the environment. Its extraordinary fluidity is clearly a quality mark in a world where travelling technologies often have proved difficult to implement.

We have been moved too, in our explorations of water technologies and other devices central to diverse waterworlds. The careful construction of dog sledges in the Arctic, the

Even small-scale water technologies can change the mode of existence radically.

absolute central role the sledge plays for fishermen and hunters, the many details and parts that make up its strength and diverse uses, its squeaking and creaking, and the jolting comfort it offers the drivers makes it an outstanding piece of technology. Certainly, it too dissolves into the environment with no clear boundaries as it is assembled of driftwood, rope, spikes, fur and leather and topped with hunting gear, food, and so forth, all carefully arranged and secured in order to be able to move across great distances with dogs, hunters and a heavy catch. The sledge absorbs its environment, and dissolves into it. The same may be said, we think, about the tractor tubes, date palm projects and hammers when they work well. The fluidity of the observed technologies has been a recurrent theme in the *Waterworlds* project. Rather than isolating certain tools, machines or constructions by reducing the technology to its immediate purpose or design, we have been observing their use and patiently elicited their practical diversity. In some cases water scarcity has been the paramount problem, making up situations where even swift adjustments and small-scale water technologies have changed the mode of existence dramatically. The opposite way round, we have also explored cases where even the largest infrastructure projects did not reach far enough. In areas where taps and pipes run short, other technologies take over, and the system is extended by other sources and mobile carriers and containers such as trucks, plastic bottles, tubes, and donkey carts. Here, we have noticed how technologies are composed of a plethora of human and non-human components.

Obviously, questions have been raised about when and how we can observe and conceive of situations where the fluidity of the waterworld ends, and the waters, environments, and social structures become set, stiff, and rigid. When does a certain mode of existence become untenable? How can we foresee the breakdown of water infrastructures? What kind of water can be considered clean and suitable for drinking? The implicit search for tipping points in such questions is embedded in both climate science and in health care systems; the idea of clearly defined limits is also an important political measure. No doubt, limits are transgressed, occasionally and in some places. After a major flooding or during a pervasive drought, the breakdown of physical and social structures often entails calamities of catastrophic proportions. Every single animal, plant and human being needs water in certain qualities and quantities, not too little and not too much. Thus, we can readily assert that fluidity generally has limits. The more intriguing part is to identify where exactly this limit becomes manifest. Like our anthropological predecessors engaged in cultural comparisons across landscapes and continents, we tend to work with the hypothesis that neither entirely universalistic nor thoroughly particularistic conclusions are productive. It is rather in the space in between the universal and the particular that promising patterns for comparison emerge. One way to elicit these patterns is to write up cases, condense extended processes, and compile and compare a surplus of cultural variations in order to make some general claims – in between the universal and the particular. This is what we do in this book by presenting numerous specific cases that speak for themselves within the shared themes.

Technology not only shapes water and bodies,
it also permeates human imagination.

BODY TECHNIQUES

Neither climate changes nor technological changes are evenly distributed in the lived environment. People experience climatic changes in different ways, emotionally and socially. When drought strikes atolls, the water in the wells unavoidably gets more and more saline – a recognized fact by everybody, and measurable by tests and taste. However, the increasingly salty water does not necessarily worry the islanders to the degree that outsiders would expect. In this environment water is most likely already a bit salty, and as such an appreciated taste, just as very sweetened drinks, as we have noticed in Kiribati, are very popular. In fact, clean and clear water, pure H_2O, or "modern water" as Jamie Linton has it,[5] that health services and international aid organizations promote and provide is not necessarily regarded as 'nice' or 'right'. In many places it is certainly neither the normal, nor the ideal, water. In Kiribati, only visiting Europeans carry around plastic bottles with imported water, and since they seem to be doing it constantly, it is probably due to a permanent, genuinely sensed thirst and an incorporated knowledge of the importance of drinking at least 2 litres of clean water every day. Of course, people in Kiribati can get used to so-called clean freshwater and even learn to appreciate its taste and health-enhancing qualities, yet the example well illustrates that clean H_2O is not a universally neutral object and concern.

The differing taste regimes of water and the amount of water consumed across the world vary, indicate how water is incorporated in diverse practices with varying bodily techniques. The ways in which clothes and bodies are washed (and the amount of soap used), the sea navigated, and different sources of freshwater distributed and used differ. In that way, we may say that bodies 'do' water differently by processing and performing water with pliant technologies. Even the most automated and lifeless machines tend to develop skills, routines and coordinated supply lines around them. Water towers, irrigation canals, pumps and treatment plants need constant upkeep and thus assemble a web of activities around them.

When we put on a new pair of shoes, the position of our feet and our way of walking change. This is an observation made by the sociologist Marcel Mauss in his important essay on body techniques, and we can add that when we direct water along new pipes, dig new canals, add other chemicals, extract certain objects, drink new kinds of water, or consume water through fruits, vegetables and animals, our bodies change too.[6] At first, this may appear a trivial, yet also potentially life-saving or damaging change, but Mauss makes a more complex point, when he suggests that when we drink, for example, we are constantly in a series of assembled actions adapting to physical, mechanical, and chemical aims. This, Mauss stresses, is not only pursued by the singular individual, on the contrary, it is pursued "by all his education, by the whole society to which he belongs, in the place he occupies". In this way, the fluidity extends into the bodies.

Technology is in the widest sense coterminous with the social network.

[1] Hastrup, K. and Skrydstrup, M. (eds) *The Social Life of Climate Change Models* (New York: Routledge, 2013).

[2] Fleming, J. R. *Fixing the Sky: The Checkered History of Weather and Climate Control* (New York: Columbia University Press, 2010).

[3] Latour, B. *We Have Never Been Modern* (Cambridge, MA: Harvard University Press, 1993).

[4] de Laet, M. and Mol, A. The Zimbabwe Bush Pump: Mechanics of a Fluid Technology, *Social Studies of Science*, 30(2) (2000): 225–263.

[5] Linton, J. *What Is Water? The History of a Modern Abstraction* (Vancouver, BC: University of British Columbia Press, 2010).

[6] Mauss, M. Techniques of the body, *Economy and Society*, 2(1) ([1935] 1973): 70–88.

[7] Gell, A. Technology and Magic, *Anthropology Today*, 4(2) (1988): 6–9.

Technologies, we would say, not only shape water and bodies, they also affect human imagination. In Mauss' terms, it is so, because "[t]he body is man's first and foremost natural instrument", or "technical object". The human body is a multi-tool, with many skills and capabilities, used in *both* the construction of large square structures *and* in imaginative, magical actions. As we show throughout the book, the religious and magic technologies may show up right beside or completely intermingled with technical and practical tools, machines and high-tech installations. Seawater is carried to the mountain top in Peru in order to secure rainwater by people, who are otherwise experts in irrigation technologies. In the Pacific, traditional wayfaring techniques are acknowledged by professional navigators also using satellites and echo sounders. And, as others have remarked before us, sometimes we find a remarkable conflation of the magical and the technological. The anthropologist Alfred Gell identified several avenues between technology and magic in play, work and ritual, and notes how machines and technical objects that are ingeniously devised and cleverly manipulated can entrap users and observers and stand out as magical.[7] Conversely, magical actions often mimic technological manipulation of objects in order to produce substances such as water – or states of trust on a stormy ocean. The "technology of enchantment," he states, "is the most sophisticated that we possess."

In this part of the book we dwell on water-related technologies and follow some of the directions that their fluidity took when we were in the field. We have already hinted at our fascination with the practised technologies, often well-worn and with unmistakable traces of human and non-human use. We have chosen things, artefacts, tools, machines, plants and so forth that arrested attention and thus foregrounded certain kinds of knowledge and concern. Technology, in the widest sense, is seen as coterminous with the social network in the changing environment.

SEA LEVEL AND COASTAL PROTECTION

Over many centuries, the Pacific islands have been continually shaped and reshaped by the sea and the winds. Whereas the inhabitants through a thousand years have left few archaeological remnants, in the past few decades inhabitants, entrepreneurs and contractors have added to the changes dramatically by placing fixed structures and extensive protection devices along the coast.

Harbours, sea walls, jetties and causeways, devices and constructions such as tourist resorts and airports have been designed and built in order to secure the coast, yet it is also widely known that the devices in many cases have caused erosion and changed the shoreline significantly. Now, in times of global warming, the consequence is that present changes in sea level in many cases are difficult if not impossible to observe and foresee as an isolated driver of change.

Coastal protection devices are visible in many shapes and sizes all around the island of Rarotonga in the South Pacific. The main street and the local market with local food-stuff and tourist stalls have been enlarged and secured after a major cyclone hit the island in the 1980s. The prolongation of the

The coral sand beach in front of a popular tourist resort. It looks unspoiled and natural, but the coastal protection devises are definitely there, just outside the frame.

LIVING WITH ENVIRONMENTAL CHANGE

airstrip in the 1970s extended the island considerably into the sea. Harbours have been constructed, and many hotels and resorts have residential areas placed right next to or simply on the beach. In some cases, an attempt has been made to secure a beach by topping the upper beach with large boulders. In other cases, advanced concrete structures, wired boxes and groynes have been designed and installed by experts. The location of houses, platforms, swimming pools and the redirections of streams have also changed the processes of sedimentation considerably and thus created new shorelines.

The islands are malleable and the coastal environment so dynamic that the ongoing changes can be linked to many different interacting processes at once: seasonal and decadal weather patterns, extreme weather events and sea level rise in addition to the local constructions. Not surprisingly, the changing and unstable shorelines have led to endless conflicts among neighbours and various stakeholders. Some littoral regions have been tested for decades and the data contested accordingly. New protection devices are constructed and beaches fed with tons of sand.

Debates on observed changes are staged by local observers who are watchful and concerned by changes that may affect their own property, the marine life or any other part of an environment of concern that is intensely traversed by personal and collective memories. The intensified focus on global warming and its impact on small islands internationally has increased the number of scientific studies carried out on prehistoric and present changes, and computational models are used to estimate future wave transformation, storm surge and the rate of wave overtopping.[8] The studies do not necessarily point towards uniform conclusions.[9] However, findings suggest that the sea level changes at the seashores have profoundly affected Pacific islanders for centuries, and some point to sea level fluctuations as the most important single factor in making islands such as Rarotonga suitable for early human

occupation. Being the tip of a large volcano rising from 4,000 metres depth, rugged with mountains and high ridges, the coastal plain, now inhabited by all the towns and villages, is estimated to have moved since 4,500 years BP due to sea levels falling.[10]

Climate science projections state that the process is now inverted, and accelerated sea level rise due to global warming will contribute significantly to coastal erosion on the Pacific islands. Since 1993, at the Cook Islands' Rarotongan station, the net relative sea level rise has been 4.4 mm per year through to June 2011.[11] This is a twofold increase compared to the preceding decades. Presently, for local residents it is difficult if not impossible to observe directly, however. The monitoring stations are fixed structures capable of multiple types of measuring, securing data on the *absolute* sea level change, free from all the daily and seasonal changes. Oppositely, for the observers positioned on the shore, the variation of tides and currents exceeds the current rise in sea level.

Since the coastal areas in the Pacific are disturbed and unstable, every case of inundation should not be taken as an evidence of accelerated sea level change. However, if the sea continues to rise, the unprotected and ineffectively protected coasts will continue to recede. The projections for future sea level rise point in the same direction: rising! The removal of scrub and other plants on beaches, planting of trees, re-direction of streams, construction of ponds, dysfunctional sewage systems (and so forth) are also contributing to the inconvenient movements of the sand and water.

Climate change *is* involved in the loss of land in the coastal areas, but it merges with a profusion of coastal technologies and seasonal and long-term variability, making it extremely difficult to project the change at the particular coastline.

[8] Umeyama, M. Shore Protection Against Sea Level Rise and Tropical Cyclones in small Islands States, *Natural Hazards Review*, 13 (2012): 106–116.

[9] Ford, M. Shoreline Changes on an Urban Atoll in the Central Pacific Ocean: Majuro Atoll, Marshall Islands, *Journal of Coastal Research*, 28(1) (2012): 11–22.

[10] Allen, M.S. Holocene Sea-level Change on Aitutaki, Cook Islands: Landscape Change and Human Response, *Journal of Coastal Research*, 14 (1998): 10–22; Moriwaki, H. et al. Holocene changes in sea level and coastal environments on Rarotonga, Cook Islands, South Pacific Ocean, *The Holocene*, 16(6) (2006): 839–848.

[11] SEAFRAME. The South Pacific Sea Level and Climate Monitoring Project. *Sea Level Data Summary Report, July 2010–June 2011*. Available at: http://www.bom.gov.au/pacificsealevel/index.shtml.

A newly made construction redirecting a stream that goes from the interior of Rarotonga to the lagoon.

Sea wall and wave breaker outside the international airport.

Blocks from a ruined coast protection due to storms and cyclones.

LIVING WITH ENVIRONMENTAL CHANGE

URBANIZING WATER IN A CONTEXT OF SCARCITY

Nouakchott, the capital of the Islamic Republic of Mauritani, houses about one million people. In 1957, less than 5,000 people lived in the city, which was then under construction. Catalysed by a series of severe droughts in the 1970s and 1980s, vast numbers of destitute nomadic pastoralists who saw their animals succumb to famine, sought refuge there, and what was perhaps initially imagined as a temporary rupture of their nomadic livelihood became a permanent condition of life. Due to the rampant urbanization process and a general lack of government mediation, Nouakchott has grown into an infrastructural conundrum.

Nearly 80 per cent of the urban population, most of whom live in the precarious neighbourhoods on the burgeoning fringes of the city, do not have access to running water. General water shortages, lack of water pressure and high levels of water contamination are part of everyday life, and only recently have serious measures been taken to ameliorate the pervasive water problem. The so-called *Projet Aftout Essahli*, which brings in water from the Senegal River 200 kilometres south, represents the largest development project in the country since the 1980s and was inaugurated on the 50th anniversary of independence in November 2010.

Assembling a complex of social and natural actors and elements, the project is a particular form of socio-technological infrastructure, which literally urbanizes nature, in the form of water.[12] However spectacular and vast, this project solves only part of its objective of alleviating water scarcity: While the project significantly enhances the flow of water into the city, it does little to distribute it within the sprawling city. Distribution demands a complete renovation of the existing network of leaking subterranean pipes and an extensive expansion of the pipe system. This process not only demands billions of Euros in funding, but more significantly a

Mobile water vendors waiting to fill their barrels at a water hydrant in Toujounine on the fringes of Nouakchott, February 2010.

Two water engineers inspecting a control panel at the central water distribution station in the Ksar neighbourhood of Nouakchott, Mauritania, May 2011.

TECHNOLOGY

A woman begging for money near 'Carrefour Madrid' in Nouakchott, July 2006. The sign reads 'The Nouakchott of Tomorrow'.

Nouakchott de demain

لنبنى مستقبلنا مع مصار فنا

large-scale restructuring of the densely populated peripheral neighbourhoods. For the last
decade, such processes have been ongoing,
but they are slowed down by corruption,
political conflicts and the great difficulties
associated with the removal and rehousing
of tens of thousands of urbanites with no
formal title to the land upon which they
live.[13] Hence, while the *Projet Aftout Essahli*
has been widely used in political discourse
as a prime example of the resolution and
benevolence of the President of the Republic
and self-proclaimed 'President of the poor',
Mohamed Ould Abdel-Aziz, the paradox of
enhanced provisioning of water and inadequate distribution infrastructures remains
only partially resolved.

Urban water infrastructures are vast and
dynamic socio-technological processes that
depend upon constant repair and maintenance carried out collaboratively by a
complex of formal and informal actors in a
multiplicity of bureaucratic, technical and
economic institutions cross-cutting topographical and social scales. As such, these
infrastructures are fundamentally 'precarious
achievements', particularly susceptible to
malfunctions whenever a component or
node in the total assemblage fails to perform
appropriately.[14] The water distribution
terminal in the Ksar is a central node in this
fragile infrastructure and water engineers
like Nagieb, a smiling 42-year-old man and
indefatigable optimist, who is in charge of
the daily maintenance of the station, are
crucial to the continued flow of water to the
urban citizens. The following represents a
brief excerpt from a visit to the terminal in
2011, which illustrates the magnitude of the
task of ensuring water flows to the urban population, and exemplifies an optimism with
regards to the implementation of the project.

It is a great success. It is a great project.
The real relevance of the project resides
in the fact that we used to have very

TECHNOLOGY

real and acute problems with water. We could not satisfy the demand for water in the city, and since the inauguration of the Aftout project, we have not had this problem. Now, the problem is with the actual network, and that is the next thing we are looking into and working on right now. Our goal is to ensure water for each and every citizen in each and every house.

When do you think that goal will be achieved?

Well, with regards to the water distribution network, it is in progress and I think, by the way, that it is in a very advanced stage right now. I think that within 3 or 4 years from now, our objective will be realized, God willing. All people will have water. It is truly a great project … It is a very important mission. First of all, it is a humanitarian project. It is a national project … You know, water, we all know it is all about development, because with water, everything is possible. You can do everything with water. You cannot live without water. You cannot imagine life without water. There is no life without water.

At the foot of the hill on which the water terminal is established, the sprawling city of Nouakchott extends into the horizon. Situated in one of the most arid climatic zones of the world, the city has been defined by water scarcity since its inception, and the new and comprehensive infrastructural initiatives represent attempts at curtailing the effects of the increasing scarcity in the face of unmediated urban growth. This is a social, political and technological challenge, which, as Nagieb put it, is fundamental not only to the functioning of the city, but indeed to the nation-building project in the Islamic Republic of Mauritania at large. Unfortunately, realizing this immense project is a lot more complicated than what Nagieb thinks, and while a significant step has been taken in the establishment of the *Projet Aftout Essahli*, the extension of the distribution network is a much more demanding and time-consuming process, which might well remain unresolved for decades.

Meanwhile, most urban residents must be content with procuring water from one of the many water hydrants dotted around the city and console themselves with the fact that, at least, the chronic scarcity and soaring water prices have been partly resolved with the advent of the *Projet Aftout Essahli*. Now, they dream of one day having their own domestic water tap.

The construction site of the new main water reservoir for the city of Nouakchott, which holds 127,000 cubic metres of potable water, March 2010.

[12] Gandy, M. Rethinking urban metabolism: water, space and the modern city, *City*, 8(3) (2004): 363–379.

[13] Choplin, A. *Nouakchott: Au carrefour de la Mauritanie et du monde* (Paris: Karthala, 2009).

[14] Graham, S. and Marvin, S. *Splintering Urbanism: Networked Infrastructure, Technological Mobilities and the Urban Condition* (London: Routledge, 2001).

PHOTO & TEXT   Frank Sejersen

A JOB MACHINE POWERED BY WATER

The day the Greenlandic town of Maniitsoq was chosen as the site of the large-scale aluminium smelter, the town itself was buzzing with cheerful citizens. People were driving around town, honking the horns and waving flags out the car windows. To celebrate the occasion, the bakery even made a special cake dedicated to the American firm Alcoa which is going to build and run the factory. Indeed, the factory was perceived to be the (perhaps last) chance to save the town from turning into a place with a high rate of unemployment.

Due to Maniitsoq's excellent location, it is possible to provide electricity from the hydroelectric power facilities that are to be constructed nearby. The 1.5 kilometre-long factory is to produce aluminium from alumina, which is shipped to Greenland from locations far away. It is a huge piece of technology that is going to be introduced and it requires the damming of the biggest lake on the island and an additional one close by.

Seen from the aluminium industry's point of view, Maniitsoq stands out as a prospective and stable site for a smelter. From a Greenlandic point of view, a smelter offers job and tax revenue potentials for a town and the country as a whole. However, the mega-size of the project will have a potential impact on many aspects of the social and cultural dynamics as well as on the environment. The process by which technology (here a smelter) is anticipated being integrated into society can be termed a process of socialization. The socialization of technology is a process of socio-technological becoming

where members of society pursue critical reflection on social dynamics and societal vision triggered by the introduction of technology. From an aluminium producer's point of view, Greenland could potentially offer stability and a site with the right affordances for a profitable smelter. From a local and Greenlandic point of view, the factory could be inscribed in, support and expand the existing social and economic life. The factory thus acts as an interface between two different socio-economic systems. The interface position of the water-based technology may in fact also transform life in Greenland.

The smelter is expected to provide lots of jobs on the factory site and in sectors servicing it. Furthermore, an expected doubling of the town's population will create a town with much new potential. The factory is thus seen by Greenlanders as a job machine, primarily. For the Greenlandic nation as a whole, the expectation is that all these jobs will improve the financial situation of the self-governing part of Denmark. The aim

Small-scale fishing provides the main income in many small communities.

LIVING WITH ENVIRONMENTAL CHANGE

is to use the technology to produce jobs for Greenlanders; aluminium is just a by-product of the factory from this perspective. If this job machine criterion is not met, the piece of technology loses its value and does not function as expected. It may produce aluminium but not for the benefit of the country's economy based on tax revenues. To make it work for them, stakeholders have started a long process of assembling factory images that fit their aspirations. To prepare for the start-up, the Greenlandic government is urging people to educate themselves, to get ready to move to Maniitsoq and to set up new businesses. Locally, citizens have organized groups to plan how to reorganize the town and to brainstorm how to make Maniitsoq an attractive town to work and live

imagined future. Consequently, they are already pursuing practices that point towards an anticipated future, which only exists yet in reports, political speeches and public narratives. The way people anticipate the workings of the factory technology thus already is having an impact on contemporary life and the educational aspirations of people.

During the first phases of public discussion of the factory, the focus was scaled down to include primarily the impacts on the local environment and local businesses as well as the positive impacts on the national economy. Later, the scaling of the factory took different directions as the understandings of the technology and the job machine were elaborated. For some stakeholders, the factory was perceived as part of a larger global

Construction work has been on hold in some communities. Local entrepreneurs hope industrialization will boost activities.

in. Local entrepreneurs are rethinking their businesses to be able to enter the new job scene. All this is taking place as the preparation for a smelter, which is only in the stages of anticipation. The actual decision to construct the factory has yet not been taken, but people are being urged by the government to integrate it as an important part of their

industrial network. The factory transformed from a locally based technology primarily dependent on the water to produce cheap energy into a piece of technology dependent on raw material for the smelting process to be processed elsewhere in the world with high environmental risks. Furthermore, it became more and more apparent that the smelter as a

TECHNOLOGY

Maniitsoq is looking into how to become more attractive as a town in order to recruit and hold on to people.

Industrialization requires a mobile labour market. Consequently, many communities are to become depopulated.

unique piece of technology could only work if a stable workforce was available. Therefore, the government is eager to bring human resources to Maniitsoq. In a White Paper the government stipulates the consequences of this:

> It should also be taken into account that those moving to Maniitsoq from other parts of the country will, to a large extent, be socio-economically advantaged people. This means that some towns and settlements should expect to do without those people who they rely on in the local community and who may have been particularly enterprising or supportive in society.[15]

The factory's consequences thus are affecting community life in locations far from Maniitsoq and point to the transformative power of this particular technology on a national scale.

It remains to be seen how this job machine will work for Greenland, which remains a vast, relatively inaccessible and very thinly populated country. In any case, the challenge is not simply to adjust the factory project to benefit most from the water resources and to create jobs. The greater challenge is to determine how the technology and its global network will transform the demographic distribution of people and Greenland as a nation.

[15] Naalakkersuisut (*White Paper on the Aluminium Project Based on Recent Completed Studies, Including the Strategic Environmental Assessment (SEA)* (Nuuk: Greenland Self Rule, 2010), p. 21.

LIVING WITH ENVIRONMENTAL CHANGE

LIFE IN THE SHADOW OF A WATER TOWER

Water tower in Machabaya.
Sign with logo of the regional
government of Arequipa.

The water tower in the urban district of Machabaya, in the south-eastern part of the city of Arequipa, is a tall cylindrical construction, about 8 metres in diameter. With its body of grey massive concrete, it reaches about 18 metres into an often high-blue sky. The water tower is constructed to serve several functions: it penetrates 150 metres into the subsoil from where it pumps up groundwater, which is then stored in a white reservoir on top of the tower. It also serves as a point of distribution of water – through pipes and valves – to the urban population in its proximity.

Rosa receives her water from the water tower, which she also operates.

The water tower can be seen from far away, and on the white upper part it has written on it in sky-blue capital letters: REGIONAL GOVERNMENT OF AREQUIPA 2007–2010 (in Spanish, of course). Next to the text sits the logo of the regional government: a sun in movement, composed by various colours and bits. This visual aspect of the water tower marks its ownership; through the tower, the regional government is present in the urban settlement.

The water tower is connected to the ground by two thick metal tubes; through these, water is pumped up from the underground. Next to the tower there is a small square building, also of concrete; this is where the motor of the pump is located, as are the electric tables. It takes electricity to pump water from the underground up to the reservoir on top of the tower. And since it is not the newest automatic technology, it takes human interaction to supervise the pumping, storing and distribution that go on in and around the water tower – to control its capacities, and decide when to start and stop the pump that sucks up water from the underground to the reservoir, from where water is released to the households.

Rosa is one of three urban dwellers employed by the regional government to switch the pump on and off in the water tower. "Someone has to be here all the time," she explains; "we have to be attentive [*estar pendientes*] to when the water in the reservoir has been consumed, and more is to be pumped."

The water tower is fairly new, inaugurated in 2010. The copper mining company Cerro Verde financed the drillings, and the regional government of Arequipa financed the infrastructure as well as the operation and daily functioning of the water tower. "We don't pay for the water, it is subsidised

LIVING WITH ENVIRONMENTAL CHANGE

by the regional government," Rosa explains under her khaki-coloured cap. A chain link fence marks off the area of the water tower from its surroundings; not everybody has permission to enter. Around the water tower, a kind of suburban life is unfolding. Some people are watering the dusty road or little plants in front of their homes; a street vendor is selling newspapers, cigarettes, soft drinks and sweets from a stand; a few taxis are waiting for customers, and dogs are running around or resting in a shady spot.

The water tower assembles material and human efforts; it assembles public service, water governance, private and public investment and intervention, making urban life possible in a place with no surface water, and hence facilitating quotidian well-being. The concrete and metal constructions of the water tower work in interplay with pipes, valves, pumps, cables, motors, electricity, buttons, and human labour, responding to particular human needs. As such, the water tower functions as a firm assembled technology, working with regimes of public and private investment, and with the dynamics of regional politics and urban expansion.[16]

There are 14 towers like this one in the south-eastern part of Arequipa, where surface water is very scarce. For Rosa and her neighbours, these water towers represent life. Yet, the towers have consequences beyond the well-being of the urban population; for the farmers of the area they cause distress and a narrowing of their opportunities for making a living.

Mauricio is an agronomic engineer, and the technical chief of an organization of irrigation water users [*junta de usuarios de riego*] in the sub-basin where Machabaya and the 14 water towers are placed. In August 2011, Mauricio took me on a tour to the sub-basin where the *junta* operates water for irrigation. Under his wide-brimmed hat, which is typical of farmers in Arequipa, Mauricio showed me the dry lands of the sub-basin and finally took us to the urbanized area where we visited the water tower and met Rosa. What follows is Mauricio's

evaluation of the water towers and their consequences.

"This is the killer," Mauricio stated with an affective voice as we arrived at the water tower in Machabaya. The *junta* has close to 10,500 members who use water for the irrigation of their cultivated fields. Mauricio is emotionally affected and explains that the areas around this urban area used to be a fertile valley, where fruits and vegetables were cultivated: "Now the valley is dead, and the regional government killed it. Urbanization killed the valley, and most of the people living here are not even from Arequipa!"

The veins of groundwater feed the springs from which farmers and small-scale peasants take water to irrigate their fields. With the 14 water towers in Machabaya and its surroundings, constantly pumping up water for use by the population, the springs have dried up, and there is no longer enough water for irrigation. "We still pay and have our licence for water use, but as you see, not enough water reaches our fields. The people who live here have invaded the land illegally, they obtain their rights and the authorities even give them water," Mauricio states. "The law gives priority to population use, and so do the politicians, because urban populations represent votes. But I ask, what are the people going to eat when there is no more farming?" Mauricio clearly expresses his disgust of the water towers. The towers have physically transformed the landscape he has lived in since he was a child. Furthermore, they make farming, the traditional livelihood he knows, impossible. With the water towers and the migrant population urbanizing and invading his territories, and with the irrigated fields and valleys drying out, Mauricio sees the basis for life, for identity and status vanish.

This trip to the water tower and the terrain around it, where new urban populations and farmers are silently fighting over the same scarce water, shows how technologies, made to respond to human needs, are never simple and isolated technical solutions. As a technology, the water tower does more than simply transform groundwater to water

Volcano Misti and irrigated land in Arequipa city. Terraces are ancient irrigation technologies.

accessible for population use. The tower does not end where its clearly defined concrete stops, where the fence around it marks a limit, or in the homes where it provides water. It entangles conflicting modes of living, urban politics and daily practicalities, as well as memories of origin and expectations of future well-being. In this sense, the water tower becomes an entangled actor – a provider of well-being *and* a troublemaker simultaneously. While the sun shines from the logo of the regional government, down on the urban settlers, a dark shadow is cast over farmers who used to cultivate the land around it.

Valley where farmers used to grow crops and fruit. The water that once irrigated this land is now pumped to urban dwellers.

[16] de Laet and Mol. The Zimbabwe Bush Pump.

LIVING WITH ENVIRONMENTAL CHANGE

WASTE AND WATER
CONNECTED AND MIXED

Tarawa is a low lying island, but mountains of plastic bottles are forming.

A car wreck has found its resting place on the shoreline.

Waste and water management are two of the biggest challenges for the government of Kiribati, an island nation in the Pacific consisting almost entirely of small and low-lying atolls. Waste and water are entangled and changes in one frequently affect the other. Management often means inserting technologies in between people and waste or water. However, 'technology' does not necessarily mean an artefact created by Western science, which is then introduced to the local population. If we think of technology broadly, it also includes local ways of management and innovation.

Kiribati has one of the most vulnerable aquifer systems in the world, and the under-5 mortality rate is one of the highest in the Pacific region. Over-use, pollution, natural variations, and anthropocentric changes, such as climate change, make the delivery of water a difficult service to provide.[17] Each atoll island has its own aquifer system. The groundwater is often found no more than 1–2 metres below the surface of the sandy soils, making the groundwater easy to access, but also very vulnerable to human contamination and waste. Ensuring that islanders have access to clean and sufficient water is one of the greatest challenges facing the government of Kiribati. However, historically the open wells have been the only way to access fresh water.

The well comes in many variations. Some are merely holes in the ground, others have makeshift fences around them to prevent people accidently falling into them at night-time, others again are reinforced with concrete rings in an effort to prevent contamination from surface water running back into the well.

Often, the wells are located near the households, sometimes just within a few metres, which makes the well the centre of many daily activities and routines, but also exposes the well water to pollution from pit toilets, leaking septic tanks, and pig pens. The well itself also compromises the quality of the groundwater by exposing it to contamination from leaves and other organic and inorganic materials, sunlight, or seepage of mud and rainwater running into the well.

Usually, international experts and the government in Kiribati manage water supply systems, because designing and implementing them are believed to require expert knowledge and international funding. However, on the island of Tamana, locals invented a new inexpensive pump, which has been copied and used across the inhabited islands of Kiribati. Tamana is the smallest island in the south-western island group known as the Gilbert Islands in western Kiribati. It has an area of 4.9 square kilometres and a population of less than 1000.

Some of the basic characteristics of the Tamana pump are that it is portable, and that it is produced using locally available parts. The basic components of the Tamana pump are PVC pipes and simple fittings, often spare parts from broken-down solar pumps or

The Tamana water pump – a
local invention made partly
from waste.

electric pumps are used to make or maintain the pump. The design of the Tamana
pump relies on waste being reused in locally
meaningful ways. The costs involved in
making a Tamana pump range between
AUS$ 50–160, whereas a similarly efficient
hand-operated diaphragm pump is AUS$
1,800, and a solar-powered pump, running
on solar energy and not manual power, and
which relies on availability of spare parts and
sunlight, is AUS$ 20,000.

International agencies ascribe the success
of the Tamana pump to the fact that it is
entirely managed by the community, including financing, ownership, and maintenance.
The main problem facing water supply

projects in remote and low-income areas has
been the capital needed to maintain supply
systems and the availability of spare parts.
The earlier Southern Cross pumps installed
by UNCDF were simply taken out of production by the company. Consequently, some of
the Southern Cross pumps were abandoned,
others were appropriated into the Tamana
pump. Who exactly the inventor of the
Tamana pump is, and how it has become so
widely used, with no funding or international
agencies involved, remain unclear.

Innovative local solutions such as the
Tamana pump connect and mix water and
waste in new ways. But when this innovation
fails or when there are no ways of recycling
waste, it literally builds up in piles that is
difficult to imagine for people living in
countries with functioning waste management systems. On the main island of South
Tarawa, 40,311 people live on a land area
of 15.7 square kilometres. Only one village
on South Tarawa has a functioning sewage
system. The rest of the island relies on the
beach or pit toilets dug straight into the
groundwater. Similarly, only two landfills
exist on South Tarawa, which means that
litter often remains uncollected or is abandoned on the beach for the tide to carry it
out to sea. Abandoning litter on the beach is
an ancient practice on these islands, and it
was unproblematic, perhaps even beneficial,
when the waste was exclusively organic. But
today, piles of plastic, tins, and rusting car
wrecks dot the coastline.

Waste has historically been seen as a
resource in Kiribati, organic materials have
been used for land reclamations, where walls
of coral rocks were constructed on the coast
and then filled in with a combination of sand
and organic waste to create new land. And
composting has been an essential practice to
nourish the sandy depleted soils. In contemporary Kiribati, however, the waste has
changed, in many ways it is still considered a
resource, while it also creates new problems.
Today, waste consists of organic materials as
well as plastic, glass, and tins, but the waste
management practices largely remain the

Every day the tide carries away
waste from the shoreline.

Car batteries on Tarawa
waiting to be exported to
Australia.

[17] See the report *Country Programming Document UNESCO, Kiribati, 2008–2013* (UNESCO, 2009), p. 7. Cf. White, I. and Falkland, T. Management of freshwater lenses on small Pacific islands, *Hydrogeology Journal*, 18(1) (2010): 227–246.

same. Every early morning the never-ending task of managing the waste begins. Women and girls sweep their family land. Organic and solid waste are piled together, sometimes it is burned early in the morning giving the island its characteristic smoky smell or left in piles until the wind, the rain, or the tides undo the piles, ensuring that the women can once again repeat their morning task of keeping the areas adjoining the household presentable and free of waste. I witnessed

families who, in exchange for a small fee, asked the council waste truck to dump its waste into their newly constructed seawall where they were reclaiming land. The waste would serve to fill in the area inside the seawall creating a foundation of plastic, broken glass, rusty tins etc.

The mixing of waste and groundwater is a result of the groundwater resources, which are just below the surface of the ground combined with the high conductivity of the sandy soils of the atoll. This allows precipitation to run almost straight through the soils with no filtering or surface storage, mixing pollutants from abandoned car batteries, *E. coli* bacteria from human waste, and contaminants from animal husbandry with the groundwater. Thus, waste and water are not as distinct as one would most often think. They come in many variations as a result of projects of land reclamation, pumping of groundwater, and everyday clean-up activities.

LIVING WITH ENVIRONMENTAL CHANGE

INVERTED WATERING STRATEGIES IN SENEGAL

The arid and semi-arid grasslands in the region bordering the Sahara Desert have been used for animal grazing for centuries. The very high variability in climate, specifically the spatial and temporal variability in precipitation both within and between years, is well documented and known to be a major challenge for local livelihood conditions. Vegetation dynamics in the pastures are more or less determined by daily rainfall, because plant growth is determined by distribution, number, quantity and intensity of individual rains. For this reason, the human strategies guiding the pastoral societies have been characterized by *mobility* as a means to cope with a highly fluctuating production base.

The Ferlo region is such a place, located in the Sahelian zone of northern Senegal. The heaviest precipitation occurs in July, August, and September and the mean annual rainfall for the period 1986–1996 was approximately 200 mm in the north and 400 mm in the south.[18]

Historically, the rangelands of Ferlo served as a grazing area for pastoralists who had to move around – i.e. pursue large-scale migration – due to the lack of permanent water supplies and fluctuating grazing resources. Hence, an efficient use of natural resources is achieved by pastoral mobility, i.e. moving the herds, adjusted to the spatial and temporal variability of fodder resources. Pastoral

mobility between different agro-ecological zones meant that a larger number of animals could be kept, as compared to a situation where the livestock was permanently kept in one zone. By using dryer areas during the wet season and more humid areas during the dry season, livestock was ensured sufficient and high quality grazing in the larger part of the year. As temporary water holes dried out during the dry season, pastoralists moved north to the Senegalese river valley or south and west to the Peanut Basin.

In the 1950s, the French colonial administration made the first boreholes equipped with motor pumps in Ferlo. This meant that the area could be used on a permanent basis,

Used tractor tubes have become an important commodity on the local market in Northern Senegal.

Tractor tubes on donkey carts
serve as efficient means of
water distribution.

Moving herds in Northern
Senegal.

and some pastoralists also started rain-fed
agriculture, especially in the southern part
with the highest rainfall. Since the great
drought in the 1970s, many pastoralists
have abandoned their cultivation, however,
and only a small percentage of the area is
cultivated today. Even though many pastoralists have become semi-sedentary, mobility is
still an important part of livestock rearing in
various ways.

Water is crucial for pastoralists, in terms
of providing water for the animals' daily
needs. New forms of mobile behaviour have,
however, developed in the northern part
of Senegal, supported by the imagination
and innovative spirit of a specific group of
herders.

In short, the historical development is
as follows. After the boreholes were drilled
in the 1950s, many Fulani herders gave
up their traditional migration and settled
around the boreholes. With the event of the
serious droughts in the 1970s and 1980s, the
pasture production was insufficient to feed
the animals. The herders were severely hit,
not least because they waited to move until
very late, when the animals were already

weakened. When the drought hit again
in 1983/84, a large number of the herders
decided to stay in the Ferlo region, where
a new system of water transport has created
a novel platform for prosperity. In the same
period, pastoralism has been changing from
an emphasis on cattle rearing to greater
dependence on sheep. Sheep have higher
drought resistance and a shorter reproduction cycle, hence allowing the herders to
recover their losses more quickly. Furthermore, small stocks were in higher demand
following the conflict between Mauritania
and Senegal in 1989.

The most important factor in this transformation of the pastoral systems was the
invention of a new system for carrying water

[18] Adriansen, H.K. and Nielson, T.T. The geography of pastoral mobility: a spatio-temporal analysis of GPS data from
Sahelian Senegal, *Geography
Journal*, 64 (2005): 177–188.

[19] Juul, K. Post drought migration and technological innovations among Fulani herders
in Senegal: the triumph
of the tube! *IIED Drylands
Programme Issue Paper*, 64
(1996).

TECHNOLOGY

over long distances: the use of huge trac-tor-type inner tubes and a donkey cart.[19] A major challenge during the dry season was to ensure optimal fodder conditions while limiting energy losses related to watering. If the cattle have to graze more than 15–20 kilometres away from the watering point, they will spend too much energy on walking and lose weight. For smaller animals like sheep and goats, the maximum distance is as low as 5–6 kilometres because they require more frequent watering.

Instead of moving the dry season camps near to the watering point as usual, the technological leapfrogging offered by the tubes enabled the herders to stay in the most productive pastures and bring the water to the animals. In this way, the introduction of tubes to carry water over long distances constituted a technological revolution. Moreover, the 'triumph of the tube' was made possible because donkey carts were

widespread in the region, introduced as part of the general attempt to mechanize the agricultural sector and gradually adopted by the herders in the course of the 1980s.

The success of the pastoral production and the higher survival and reproduction rates of the herds were closely related to this new dimension of mobility; the new means of water transport hugely expanded the accessible pasture areas. In other words: while the situation in northern Senegal has been made more difficult due to events of agricultural encroachment and severe drought periods, a simple but smart, techno-logical innovation, related to water transpor-tation, enabled more animals to survive by making better use of the grazing. As a result, many herders became richer than they were before the drought forced them to migrate to the south.

Instead of moving the animal herds to the large wells, the water is transported to the grazing land.

LIVING WITH ENVIRONMENTAL CHANGE

COBS AS TECHNOLOGICAL SOLUTIONS

Charles works at the Ghanaian Ministry of Food and Agriculture (MOFA), which is responsible for delivering agricultural extension services, such as bringing new research and technology to farmers. New seed varieties are an example of this. The seeds may look 'natural' – but they have been developed in collaboration between MOFA, farmers and researchers.

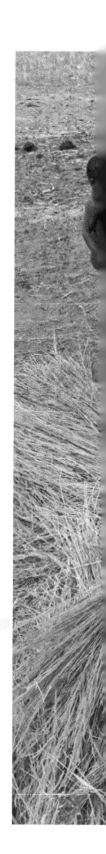

Charles explains: "We go to the field to find out what problems farmers are facing, and farmers will raise problems. When we go back, we now sit down to see how we best can help the farmer and this is where we bring in research to find solutions." One major problem that MOFA, the farmers and the researchers have worked on together to find a solution was drought. Today, however, unusual and extensive flooding is causing new major problems.

The assemblyman Joseph has experienced many changes in his surrounding environment that cause new problems in need of new solutions. He links these differences to the changing climate as well as human actions. He lives in a compound dwelling in the area where Charles carries out his agricultural extension services. It is located in the north-easternmost region of Ghana, with Burkina Faso just on the other side of a nearby river. Joseph explains the changes he has seen:

When I was a child, all the trees and grass made walking places difficult, you would be chased by wild animals, but now everything has been cleared off, and people don't even know what a monkey is. We used to cut grass for our rooms, but everything is now bare, these transformations are now changing the weather. Everything has gone bad, we don't know whether it is due to the weather or human beings.

In this region, 30–40 years ago, farming used to be done primarily during the rainy season and on the lands surrounding individual compounds. The missing trees, grass and monkeys, however, are symbols of the perceived consequences of over-cultivation, erosion, deforestation and bush burning. The soil is now exposed to heavy rains, and the fertile soil will be washed downstream in the event of flooding. Problematic rains are becoming more frequent and there is general

The assemblyman Joshua
feels that the environment has
changed significantly.

LIVING WITH ENVIRONMENTAL CHANGE

Old and new varieties of
seeds.

A storehouse for seeds.

The area behind the structures
used to be forest, according
to Joshua.

agreement, both locally and globally, that
there is a link to climate change. The culti-
vatable areas are thereby reduced and local
agricultural extension agents like Charles
lament how the population has started using
the land along the river, where the soil is
moister and has more nutrients. As explained

by Charles, this is problematic for several
reasons. Cultivating on the riverbed causes
siltation of the river – in the event of flooding, plots near the river are also the most
exposed. Extreme flooding in 2007 made this
threat apparent to all, but some are unable to
find alternatives, and therefore continue to

TECHNOLOGY

cultivate this land in the hopes that they will be able to harvest before potential flooding.

In the early 1990s the Bagre Dam was built upstream in Burkina Faso. While the dam produces electricity and enables irrigation year-round during normal rainfall, it frequently has to be opened during unusually heavy rains causing devastating flooding. In addition to the 2007 flooding, there were, according to the local population, also floods in 2008 and 2009. This affects the local people in many ways. Their compound houses made out of mud collapse when entrenched in water for extensive periods of time, and sometimes they collapse on livestock – or, even worse, on people. Furthermore, as most of the people here are farmers, the flooding of exposed agricultural fields is a problem practically everyone experiences. Besides depending on their produce for food and fodder, the local people need to sell some of the produce to raise money to pay school fees and to buy clothes and soap. They also need money when somebody in the family is getting married, needs treatment at the hospital or is commemorated at a funeral ceremony. After a period of flooding some people are thus left without a home, without food, without cash – in short, without a livelihood. By sharing the homes that are still standing, and the little food that is available within extended family networks, people survive, but droughts and floods lead to prevalent famine on a yearly basis.

Charles explains that one solution to the problem of flooding is to cultivate new varieties of seeds, such as early maturing crops that can be harvested before the flooding usually occurs. Like all other compound houses, the assemblyman Joseph's compound has a storehouse for seeds. He has many different seeds in the storehouse, some that are traditional and some that are the new varieties that Charles is talking about. Take, for example, millet. The assemblyman has millet cobs of both early and late millet. Millet is used to make TZ (or tuo zafi), the most important local staple, which comes in the form of a thick porridge. When late

millet is planted along the river, it takes from five to five and a half months before it can be harvested. When the farmers plant during the first rains, which usually come in June, then, as has happened several times, all the crops will be destroyed if there is flooding in the beginning of September. The farmers are therefore encouraged by agricultural extension agents like Charles to sow early millet, which can be harvested after only three months. The farmers used to prefer late millet, because the yields were higher, but because of the floods and the availability, often through donations, of optimized seeds developed through research, it has become more preferable to cultivate early millet.

Local farmers are similarly shifting to a new kind of maize. Maize is primarily used for food, such as TZ. Maize is also used to make 'kenkey', a kind of TZ, which is rolled into balls and eaten with stew or soup, which often contains fish and a lot of *peppe* (spicy pepper). Referring to two different coloured maize cobs Charles clarifies that the whiter maize is an improved variety of the yellow maize. MOFA and the farmers are working together to develop new seed varieties that mature early, have higher yields and nutritional value – thus obtaining better market prices. "Flooding and research continuously optimize seeds," Charles proudly summarizes. While Charles' enthusiasm is understandable, problems remain and new problems keep developing. Sometimes the seeds will not germinate because the soil is either too moist or too dry. Sometimes the farmers cannot afford to buy new seeds to replace those lost in the flooding. The flooding is destructive, but also leads to new research and development. Problems and opportunities thus keep taking new forms and shapes, in this case the problems and opportunities led to technological solutions in the shape of cobs of millet and corn.

THE IMAGINED WATER PUMP

Mamadou planting bushes for a development project in the dune on which Biidi 2 is located.

The West African Sahel went through major episodes of drought in the 1970s and 1980s. While Sahelian populations were accustomed to droughts, these droughts were significant not only due to their severity, but also because they prompted extensive international aid and development assistance.

A large part of this aid manifested itself in both large- and small-scale technological solutions. Donors initially focused on large-scale changes in food production and distribution systems, but from the late 1980s onwards, development efforts began to focus on local participation and a better targeting of aid. The delivery of small-scale technologies to people in the Sahel became common and was often organized in projects run mainly by European NGOs. Despite a shift in the 2000s towards programme or sectoral support among many of the major donors in the region, external funding for small NGO projects persists. The NGOs provide, among other things, technologies such as water pumps, tools, wheelbarrows, and improved seeds for the fields and gardens.

In Biidi 2 – a village located in northern Burkina Faso – large-scale projects as well as smaller NGOs arrived in the aftermath of the major droughts experienced in the early 1970s and 1980s. During the 1970s and 1980s the aid delivered consisted mainly of famine relief, but from the early 1990s these projects and particularly NGOs became a more integrated aspect of everyday life in the village. Since then, at least 25–30 NGO projects have been carried out in the village. Famine relief, micro-credit loans, education and transfers of technologies are the most important aspects of this aid. Almost all permanent buildings such as the school and the granary, tools, improved seeds, and other simple technologies like pens and books used in the village have, for example, their origin in a project. The large number of projects that arrive in the village means that the villagers rarely distinguish them by name or donor. The projects arrive each year at the end of the agricultural season in December. The length of time a development project stays depends on its scale and aim; some stay only weeks while others stay for years, undertaking major work such as planting trees and bushes to stabilize the dune upon which the village is located. The technologies they leave behind often stay much longer.

Understandably the villagers of Biidi 2 prefer to participate in projects that make sense locally. The women in the village, for example, are very keen on micro-credit schemes and work well with projects delivering such aid. But local enthusiasm for a project can be quite independent from its perceived relevance among the villagers.

Asoman, a middle-aged man, explains why in this sense all projects are 'good': "Because by being here they [project workers] see how good we are at making projects come through and therefore other projects also want to work with us. This is why we work with projects we consider *tiidude* [to be difficult]." An example of this is a Northern NGO that wanted to plant date palms in the sand dune on which the village is located. The NGO had soil samples taken and sent off for analysis to a university laboratory in its home country. It was established that soil in the upper part of the dune was suited for small plantations of date palms. Even though the villagers strongly disagreed, they quickly realized that they could not "argue with the soil tests" as it was put by Layya, a young man. Instead of arguing, the villagers then wholeheartedly engaged with the project and

helped plant and take care of the palm trees. Not surprisingly, at least to the villagers, the date palms died a couple of years later, possibly due to poor and loose soil, but this did not make the project a fiasco for the villagers. Secret cuttings of the original trees by garden owners in the village had meanwhile resulted in a large amount of young date palms in the gardens located at the foot of the dune. More importantly, however, the villagers argued that because of their cooperation with the first project, two other NGOs from that country had since arrived. One of these was talking about establishing a new water pump in the village.

This pump is very much longed for. Currently, water for washing, cooking and drinking has to be collected from a pump established by an Italian project some ten years ago at the foot of the dune. Of all the

Fetching water from the water pump. This is the only water pump in the village.

TECHNOLOGY

The river below the village. Loose sand is making the river shallower each year.

Sign saying that Biidi 2 is the site of development work.

'development technologies', as they are called in the village, this pump is by far the most important. While the walk to the pump is not that far, walking uphill in loose sand with water buckets balancing on their heads and in their hands is, however, hard work. Getting a pump in the village would hence free up much time and make life less cumbersome, particularly for the women.

A pump also provides a clean and reliable source of water. According to the women, the children are less sick since the establishment of the pump. Moreover, the villagers are increasingly concerned about the ever-diminishing availability of surface water. The combination of heat and drought results in loose sand. Despite the efforts made by projects to stop the movement of sand by, for example, planting trees and bushes, the sand is picked up by the strong winds in January and February. Moving across the landscape the sand settles in indentations in the ground such as holes and riverbeds. This makes them shallow. Consequently, less water collects in them during the rainy season (June–September) and higher evaporation takes place. This means less surface water is available for drinking during the many dry and hot months until the rain starts falling again. A water pump would alleviate the problem of diminishing drinking water. In this respect, "working for the date palm project was a good investment", as it was put by a group of women. Now all that is missing is the fruit of this investment, for the water pump is still not there.

UNPREDICTABLE SIDE EFFECTS OF NEW TECHNOLOGIES

A young girl grinding millet in the traditional way in Belgou, Northern Burkina Faso.

Located in an arid landscape notorious for the lack of water from October to May, the village of Belgou in Northern Burkina Faso continues to rely on millet and sorghum as the main stable crops. Due to the low amount of rain and the limited soil fertility, millet and sorghum are in fact the only crops it is possible to grow in this marginal area, but even in the best years, the harvest only covers three to four months of the food requirements.

Many development projects have focused on technology improvements aiming at higher crop yields. Planting bushes to fix sand or constructing dikes in the fields against surface water and soil runoff have, for example, been some of the main technologies introduced in Belgou. Such technologies have primarily been targeted towards men as they are responsible for most agricultural activities like preparing the fields for cultivation, sowing crops, weeding and harvesting.

The strong focus on technologies aiming to improve crop yields in a milieu with insufficient rain is underpinned by the fact that Belgou is primarily inhabited by the ethnic group, RimayBé, for whom agriculture is a major part of their identity. As one man explained: "We were born in the fields. The field is your home – you have to have a home." When a hammer mill driven by a diesel-engine was given to Belgou in 2010 by a local NGO, it did therefore not receive much attention from the men as this new technology unexpectedly focused on women's work rather than crop yield improvements. The NGO aimed to decrease women's labour burden as the NGO was concerned about the fact that women simply did not have any time for rest and leisure after completing all their tasks. Especially, the preparation of Millet-Tõ, the principal cereal recipe consumed in Belgou as well as in other parts of Northern Burkina Faso, was considered an extremely labour-intensive process.

With the new hammer mill, women would be able to save a lot of time in the process of preparing Millet-Tõ. The traditional technology used for the preparation was described in the following way: After the millet had been harvested by the men, the women and young girls started to grind the millet grains. A wooden mortar and a pestle were used to grind the grains into flour. The mortar was about 60–70 cm high, with a diameter of about 30 cm. The pestle was heavy as it weighed about 3 kg, and was about 1.2 m long and 6 cm in diameter with bulbous ends.

LIVING WITH ENVIRONMENTAL CHANGE

Approximately 2–3 kg of grain would be placed in the mortar, and about 250 ml of water added. The water was accordingly mixed with the grain, and the pestle would then be held in the hand of the women or young girls and worked up and down striking the grain. This process would be carried out vigorously by one, two or three women, each

Millet ready to be grinded, Belgou.

Harvested millet is transported from the fields to the village where women begin the grinding process, Belgou.

working at about 60 strokes per minute. It would take one woman 4 hours to pound 2–3 kg grains into flour, and 4 hours would be about the maximum time to carry out this type of physically demanding work. Pounding for 4 hours would, however, only cover about one-third of the food requirements of an average household, as one person on average consumed a little less than 1 kg per day, and the average household size was about 7.5 persons. The processing of the about 7 kg grain required for one household would thus entail about 12 hours of work per day, for three persons or more.

The worries expressed by the NGO concerning the fact that women simply did not have any time for rest and leisure after completing all their tasks seemed thereby justified. As the young girls or women who took part in the Millet-Tõ preparation also had to allocate time to other tasks such as

the actual cooking of the Millet-Tõ, cleaning and collection of fuel and water, and taking care of the children, the 4 hours spent each day on millet grinding appeared somewhat like a huge burden. Due to the time-consuming millet grinding and the other mentioned labour tasks, these women complained that they had limited or no time left for leisure, rest or engagement in other activities.

When the new hammer mill was given to Belgou in 2010, it greatly reduced the

20 Nielsen, J.Ø, D'Haen, S. and Reenberg, A. Adaptation to climate change as a development project: a case study from Northern Burkina Faso, *Climate and Development*, 4(1) (2012): 16–25.

21 Bierschenk, T., Elwert, G. and Kohnert, D. The long-term effects of development aid: Empirical studies in rural West Africa, *GIGA German Institute of Global and Area Studies/ Institute of African Affairs*, MPRA Paper No. 4217 (1991).

The labour-intensive way of grinding millet, Belgou.

time spent on millet grinding from about 4 hours to 1 hour per day per person. But surprisingly, it did not cause more leisure and rest time for the women. Rather the hammer mill enabled them to reallocate the time saved from millet grinding to engage in other non-agricultural activities, like the men did every year after having finished the agricultural work. The technological change from manual millet grinding to a hammer mill thus provided the women with an opportunity to gain an income, which primarily used to be reserved for the men. By having their own income, women also began feeling that they could gain more power in the household.

In that sense the new hammer mill brought with it a number of unpredictable side effects, and it had thus more widespread consequences than the local NGO ever imagined. This is in line with recent findings from the Sahel that have shown how project encounters are always part of a chain or flow of events located within broader frameworks.[20] The outcome of development projects is therefore often inconclusive and unpredictable as was, for example, also seen with the numerous irrigation projects in other places in the Sahel.[21] These were intended to promote vegetable cultivation among women, and for a time, the projects were very successful as yields increased. This was precisely what had been intended by the development project, but it also led to unexpected developments: the new wealth of the women fuelled the envy of other groups, for instance, their husbands. This in turn led to the development of a new property structure, with the men now becoming the owners of the fields with vegetables. They thereby took over the profitable production of vegetables themselves.

Such social changes, which are detectable only in the long term, are thus typical examples of the unintended consequences of a technology improvement induced by development projects. Hence, it becomes hard to categorize technology changes as either entirely successful or entirely disastrous.

LIVING WITH ENVIRONMENTAL CHANGE

SCALABLE AND FLUID SPRINKLERS

In 2011, the World Bank-funded irrigation modernization programme, PSI, directed by the Peruvian Ministry of Agriculture, started up in Colca Valley.[22] Through educational and financial support, the PSI engineers encourage peasant farmers to change from traditional irrigation methods based on gravity and furrows to modern sprinkler irrigation systems.

The engineers emphasize the water efficiency versus the evaporation and filtration in the earthen canals: "With traditional irrigation you use 30–35 per cent of the water, and you lose 60–65 per cent along the way; in technical irrigation the efficiency is 70–75 per cent." After having experienced success on the coastal plains, the PSI programme was extended to the highlands. According to their webpages, the objective is to: "Contribute to the increment of agricultural production and productivity in the highlands, promoting the sustainable change from a traditional agriculture to one with a higher profitability, through the technologies of the irrigation systems and the associations." On the same webpage, PSI announces that: "Through 12 years of trajectory, the experience of PSI has been successful and has served as replica, so that the public and private institutions can repeat the strategy of modernization of irrigation with an integrated focus on development in diverse areas of the country."

PSI presents its technology as replicable, and aspires to implement "scalable projects", which are those that can expand without changing its nature. Making projects scalable takes a lot of work, which means excluding ecological and cultural diversity from scalable designs.[23] However, these technical systems are not easily adaptable to the steep mountain terrain with tiny fields and terraces. Moreover, the systems are expensive and the local groups need to finance 10 per cent of the installation. Most peasant farmers cannot afford this, and continue to irrigate by flooding their fields and directing the water with the skilled use of a shovel. Hence, the implementation depends on several conditions: topography, economic capacity and motivation to learn new skills. Some farmers were eager to engage with new technologies, hoping to improve their livelihoods.

Alfredo is a farmer in Chivay who constructed his own system based on experiences gathered from various places. By adapting the technology to an irregular topography and a

The skill of directing water in furrows is still highly valued in Colca.

LIVING WITH ENVIRONMENTAL CHANGE

PSI and a sprinkler supply company demonstrated the technology at the irrigation organizations' annual meeting, 2011.

A modern sprinkler system saves water and enhances productivity in PSI's pilot project in Colca.

Home-made sprinkler systems can work well in steep terrains.

precarious economy, he created a pragmatic solution: a homemade sprinkler irrigation system to water his bean plants. Alfredo attended a course in modern irrigation some years ago, and he took some advice from the engineers and combined it with knowledge from his training as a topographer and from his work experience in a mine. "They say that you need to have unevenness in the terrain, but that is a lie, it is not like that, I have adapted it, because I have worked in mines," he told me. Since the required 25 metres of hydraulic altitude would not leave any space to plant in his 2-hectare field, Alfredo experimented with 2.5 metres of altitude, making a system of tubes of different sizes in diameter, regulating switches and sprinklers. "It worked, it gave results," he told me.

Alfredo has practical knowledge produced by his engagement with a particular environment, and he adapts a technology (which is designed for other conditions) to a vertical terrain with small fields in a situation where he has no means to invest much money. The question of whether the sprinkler systems work cannot, it seems, be answered with a clear-cut "yes" or "no". Instead, there are many grades and shades of "working"; there are adaptations and variants. The type of sprinkler system that Alfredo assembled can be said to have fluidity because it is adaptable, flexible and responsive. Consequently, and a bit surprisingly, this fluid property is what makes it stronger than inflexible technologies.[24]

In September 2011, I joined a group of visitors from an irrigation association in

another highland region who came to learn about other experiences in irrigation. First, we visited Alfredo together with one of the PSI engineers, and we were all very impressed by his system. However, the engineer pointed to the fact that the hydraulic pressure was not as strong as it should be, and that the system was not optimal. Alfredo reflected on this when I interviewed him later:

> It does work. But when they came to visit and see my irrigation system, the engineer said that it would not work with less than 25 metres. But I had only 2.5 metres. You saw that it did work, but you cannot refute the engineer, right? What would I say to him? He wins by talking, right, but it is another thing to do it in practice.

Afterwards, the visitors went to the neighbouring village Yanque to look at a sprinkler system that is considered to be PSI's most successful pilot project in Colca. Here we met Camilo, the leader of the project's 18 farmers, who cultivate a total of 10 hectares of land. The system is installed in optimal conditions: the water is collected in a reservoir 50 metres up in the hillside, and goes through a tube to an engine-driven water pump. From the machine house, the water is pumped out in the tubes and sprinklers in the flat fields by the riverbank. Camilo emphasized the benefits of the system: it saves time and water and produces good beans.

> It is a great facility. You can irrigate 1 hectare with 8 litres per second. The savings are great. When I irrigated by gravity, I had to use 70 litres per second for 12 hours to irrigate 2 *topos* [less than 1 hectare]. And the production is much better with this system. The irrigation creates micro-climate when you irrigate in early morning and it prevents the frost from destroying the plants.

The PSI engineer was also proud to be able to show a modern system that worked well:

A PSI engineer posing with women in traditional Colca dresses.

This is the technical way of doing technological irrigation. No one will take away that willpower, that creativity that we saw this morning [referring to Alfredo], because that is how great projects emerge. But with a little technical management …, this is the way. It's necessary to have certain technical considerations. If it [pressurized irrigation] worked without these systems, do you think that [PSI] would have made the direct investment? Obviously, this is fundamental.

The sprinkler systems can certainly improve productivity with less water. However, while they can be repeatedly used in the flat coastal landscape, they meet new challenges in the mountains. While the high-tech system requires an engine-driven pump, the cheaper sprinklers and hoses that Alfredo uses seem to be easier to use, at least in his small and steep field. The reason is its fluidity: it is flexible and easily adaptable to a difficult environment. This shows that relations between technologies and humans are contingent, transformative and diverse, and that one can never be sure of the outcome.

[22] Programa Subsectorial de Irrigaciones, available at: www.psi.gob.pe.

[23] Tsing, A. On nonscalability: the living world is not amenable to precision-nested scales, *Common Knowledge*, 18(3) (2012): 505–524.

[24] de Laet, M. and Mol, A. The Zimbabwe bush pump: mechanics of a fluid technology. *Social Studies of Science*, 30(2) (2000): 225–263.

DRY TECHNOLOGIES AND COMMUNITY BUREAUCRACIES

Meeting of the Irrigation Users' Committee with the secretary noting everything in the Book of Acts.

Irrigation channels criss-cross the Andes, bringing water to the dry soils of the peasants' fields. To obtain water, people must deal not only with the amount of water and the physical terrain, but also with concerns of others and matters of the social terrain.

When water flows across the terrain in the Andes, it traverses a number of obstacles that each require technology-dependent solutions: bridges across gorges, sluices that direct water, inlets that capture the water from the riverbed, reservoirs that store water, and different arrangements that distribute water to its fields of destination. But none of this would happen, had people not taken the effort to organize themselves. Irrigation in Peru is organized in a nested hierarchy of organizations: it is the Irrigation Users' Committee who are those in direct contact with the flow. These are the groups who depend on the water for their livelihoods. Every once in a while, the users will be summoned by their president to a general assembly, in which small and large matters are discussed.

At the meetings of the Irrigation Users' Committee in the high Andes, the politics of water are as important as the water itself when it comes to watering the fields. Authority and legitimacy of water politics are therefore technologies of water management that are just as important as the very irrigation channels through which the water runs or the disperser that sprinkles the crops with the much-needed water in times of dry skies. Technologies of water must therefore include the administrative regalia that surround the governance of water. Without these, water would not flow anyway.

At the meetings of the Irrigation Users' Committee, two particular artefacts can be thought of as technologies of water governance and management as they serve as instruments that make the water flow. The Book of Acts and the rubber stamp have both become pivotal to the management of political life in the Andes.[25] Flows of water must be maintained; and as important as the shovel and pickaxe are the Book of Acts and the rubber stamp. The Book of Acts makes sure that everything that is agreed upon at the meeting is remembered. Decisions, queries, unruly subjects and future working parties are noted down meticulously, and at each meeting, previous decisions and unfinished pieces of business are vigorously discussed. And the rubber stamp signs the agreement, making it official by bestowing legitimacy upon it.

The governance of water is highly literate: those who cannot write must, nonetheless, sign the Book of Acts with the mark of their

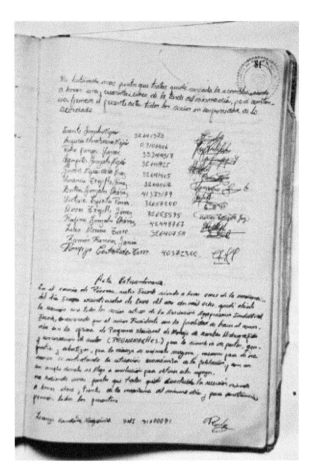

An older Book of Acts signed
by the participants of the
meeting, granting legitimacy
to the decisions made.

index finger. The meetings that the Book of
Acts is meant to report are, indeed, very different from the clarity and unity of voices of
the Book of Acts in itself. At meetings, fierce
debates and even attacks are not unusual. On
occasions, certain people will try to oppose
the book, challenge the local authorities and
go outside the usual perimeter in order to
force through their particular needs. This
happened when one man had presented a
host of names to the authorities in order to
establish an Irrigation Users' Committee;
that is how an irrigation channel becomes
real and legible in the eyes of state officials.
Like a birth certificate of a child, people
would tell me. In itself of little controversy,
had it not been for the covert manner in
which the presidency, the community – and
thus, the Book of Acts – were left in the dark
about this. Not including the community

in the process was a way of delegitimizing
its authority and its right to govern its own
water. But as soon as this knowledge came
to the president's attention, matters were
brought back into the regular spheres of
water politics. Consequently, the management of the irrigation channel could be
recorded and formalized through the book
and the community.

Even in smaller matters of sharing water,
antagonisms may arise as individuals may try
to ensure their sustenance. Differences are
great, because the water flows across plots of
lands. Equity is hard to obtain in a terrain
that is rugged both in topography and in
social relations. But once written, disagree-
ments are flattened; the topography of the
terrain is as rugged as ever, but rhetorically,
the Book of Acts evens out social differences
and obstacles. By putting the decisions onto
paper, the cacophony of voices is presented
in unison. For the presidency who must act
accordingly, the Book of Acts turns the many
into one, and through that magic the flow of
water becomes a possibility.

The literate politics of water governance
therefore rely on the ability to make the
many into one, on crystallizing the will of
the general populace into a single statement.
The Book of Acts is a book! It is the written
word, the format of governance that only
reached the Andes when the *conquistadores*
arrived almost 500 years ago. Since then,
letters have been an ambiguous matter in
the Andes; it has been the language of those
in power, but also an efficient way to attain
legitimacy in local power struggles. Those
who know how to read and write are those
who know how to deal with authorities
outside the villages, and in that sense the
increase in schooling is also democratization.
As technologies go, skill and knowledge are
necessary. Even though the many become
one through writing, the governance of
water is nothing without the hierarchy. The
hierarchy is expressed through a different
technology, which captures the written word
and the literacy of water governance in a
different way.

TECHNOLOGY

Communal work often follows the decisions taken in the meeting, in this case constructing a bridge across the irrigation channel.

As a technology, the rubber stamp is that which authorizes the decisions. Without the stamp of the presidency (and the stamp on the first page from the public registers which initially turn any notebook into a Book of Acts), the words written onto the lined pages would be nothing but words. But with the stamp at the end of the text, accompanied by signatures and fingerprints, the words attain meaning. The rubber stamp is thus a complementary technology of water governance, which enables the flows of water. Without the stamp of the Irrigation Users' Committee presidency, no meeting could be convened, no working parties arranged, no aid solicited from the local governments.

Without these dry technologies of water governance, it is unlikely that water would flow to where people need it. The flows of water are contingent on the abilities of the presidency of the Irrigation Users' Committee not only to organize labour parties,

A few men negotiating politics on the side.

but also to communicate their needs to the relevant authorities. In that way, the dry technologies of water management create legibility, serving as a way both of hierarchizing and ordering the many voices of concern and desire, and a way of making sure that state institutions and others with a budget may help to increase the amount of water reaching the fields.[26]

25 Salomon, F. and Niño-Murcia, M. *The Lettered Mountain: A Peruvian Village's Way with Writing* (Durham, NC: Duke University Press, 2011).

26 Scott, J. *Seeing Like a State: How Certain Schemes to Improve the Human Condition Have Failed* (New Haven, CT: Yale University Press, 1998).

LIVING WITH ENVIRONMENTAL CHANGE

A LIFE JACKET STORY

Certainly, the people of the coastal village of Tharangambadi in South India know that the sea is not always benevolent. While providing a source of income and food for the majority of the population, the neighbouring Bay of Bengal is also the site of tropical cyclones, whipping up the water during the annual monsoon time, which locally goes by the name of 'rough season'.

Heavy rains transform dusty roads into little rivers, stopping village life for a while. Tragically, in December of 2004, the Asian tsunami furthermore swept away hundreds of lives primarily from among the fishing population of the village. The settlements closest to the sea were shattered and left unrecognizable. In the wake of the disaster, numerous humanitarian organizations, public agents and private actors came to Tharangambadi to offer both immediate relief and long-term development to the affected people.

A host of new things have appeared in the village, each of them packed and delivered with their stated purpose. Some objects were to replace lost ones; others were novelties in the village landscape, explicitly aimed at developing village life. In terms of shape and size, the delivered aid items range from a massive and durable cyclone shelter now towering near the newly built re-housing settlement, to small pieces of soap gradually disappearing with use. Upon delivery, the objects have been appropriated, adjusted, welcomed, ignored, sold on or left untouched – interchangeably and depending on specific situations. Whether seen as quick detergents or long-term solutions, the many post-disaster interventions have come to work in multiple and often unpredictable ways,

proving the point that there are many ways in which something can work or fail.

As technologies for making the coastal zone liveable (again), the many delivered objects have come to imply whatever people have made of them over time and in their own pace. Clever design and information packages do not necessarily make an object work as intended. In Tharangambadi, success and failure of the humanitarian and post-disaster interventions were not a binary opposition.

Brand new life jackets, among other things, have been donated by the official state fisheries department. Financed by a tsunami relief programme, it was decided that the fishing communities in the tsunami-affected areas need to improve safety onboard; the authorities, it seemed, handed out life jackets to materialize their concern for people's safety. Unused to such tangible measures of precaution, so far the fishing people of Tharangambadi have piled the life jackets in the storage rooms of the village temple. The reflectors on the life jackets beam at the flash from the camera in the light of the late afternoon. Stored carefully in the temple, but out of practical use, the life jackets are ambiguous as a protective technology and somehow temporally suspended.

Life jackets in mint condition stored in the village temple.

LIVING WITH ENVIRONMENTAL CHANGE

At the time of writing, the life jackets have yet to make their way to the boats. Not because the fishing people simply say they see no point in wearing the jackets when at sea, nor because they do not know of fishermen drowning in rough weather or because of misconduct or bad luck. Maybe the fishermen are just not really ready to acknowledge that kind of danger and that kind of precaution. As if wearing a life jacket to sea would somehow emphasize the danger of the trade. Danger, it seems, must be relegated to a domain outside of routine, rather than pertain to the fishing practice in general. One way to locate a danger that life jackets might respond to is within a register of incipient and future climate change, which is perceived locally to have made and increasingly make the sea less knowable. As of now, the life jackets are weighed up against an already established bodily technique of fishing, with which they collide. Until further notice, the fishermen seem to trust their well-tested practices adapted to the sea they know of, rather than the newly provided technology that is tailored to a sea of the future.

For the time being, then, the life jackets are seemingly allowed to point either back in time towards the tsunami or forward to unknown conditions. If they point back, this is so because the life jackets were occasioned by a disaster relief effort, which suddenly brought many more or less useful things to village. Thinking back, the villagers hint at a kind of humanitarian whirl gripping donors and recipients alike, none of whom had ever experienced a precedent situation. Along with a host of other surprises and changes, the wake of the disaster was often referred to locally as "tsunami time" – a pervasive sense and practice of mutual configuring of the disaster and village life.[27] If the life jackets also point forward, they do so because the villagers connect them to an anticipated future of accelerating climate change, the beginning of which the fishermen have already noted from a combination of local observations and media reports from around the world. The tides have changed, they say, and the sea is not what it used to be; more frequent and forceful cyclones have started to come onshore from the Bay of Bengal. Accordingly, the fishermen explain, routine precautions such as the life jacket may eventually – and sooner than they might like to think – come in handy. If the sea comes to be at odds with the people whose livelihood domain it is, novelties might be just what are needed, even if they initially sit collecting dust in a storage room. In light of this, the

Rough waves and dark skies off the coast of Tharangambadi.

[27] See Hastrup, F. *Weathering the World: Recovery in the Wake of the Tsunami in a Tamil Fishing Village* (Oxford: Berghahn Books, 2011).

Mending fishing equipment on the beach of Tharangambadi. So far, life jackets are not part of the standard gear.

Boys playing with life jackets in the water.

stock of lifesavers in the temple is much appreciated, though some fishermen appear slightly embarrassed to admit it. One can never know what tomorrow brings, and as a precautionary technology, the life jacket may be just slightly ahead of its time.

Meanwhile, some of the dust is easily washed off. Even though delivered for serious reasons, whether in response to the tsunami or to anticipated climate change, and furthermore explicitly to be used by adults, as the print on the front asserts, the life jackets have become a toy for some of the boys in the village, enjoying the lightness of a day off and their own controllable version of rough waves. When they come of age, other changes might have depleted the waters so that fishing will no longer sustain them. What other technologies to stay afloat will they then have?

LIVING WITH ENVIRONMENTAL CHANGE

UNPACKING THE DOG SLEDGE

When in 1932, Knud Rasmussen looked back upon his achievements as an ethnographer of the Eskimo peoples, he said poetically: "From the bottom of my heart I bless the fate that had me born at a time when polar research by means of dog sledges had not yet become out-dated."[28]

His chosen mode of transport was not only a means to get from one place to another, but also to inscribe himself into the Arctic topography in a similar way to the people who lived there more permanently. From this perspective, it was impossible to keep an external perspective upon the life of the Arctic hunters.

For better and for worse Knud Rasmussen became as much part of the landscape as the Eskimos were, and by travelling like them and most often with them, he took on the perspective of their life world. In his writings, Knud Rasmussen claims that in his work, the Eskimo is the hero; we understand what he means and his praise is well taken. But there is a sense in which it is actually the dog sledge that becomes the main protagonist in his narrative. Moving along with the Eskimos opened a new way of perceiving their social life as deeply intertwined with their technologies; this made the first ethnographies possible, as well as more recent anthropological work in the Thule region, where people are still predominantly living as hunters.

Even though these days one may in principle get to the farthest regions by means of airplanes or helicopters, there is no way for the hunters to access their hunting grounds other than by sledge for the better part of the year. During a couple of months in the summer, when the fast-ice has broken up, kayaks and dinghies serve as means of getting to areas where narwhal, sea-birds or musk ox live, but for most of the year, the dog sledge is sovereign. During long hunting expeditions, the sledge is both a means of transport and a home to the hunters.

As technology, the sledge is simple and sophisticated at the same time. Since time immemorial it has been made out of driftwood, when available. The North-western part of Greenland was never on the main routes for driftwood, hailing from either Northern Siberia or Northern Canada and being pumped there by the Polar Express – the ice current dominating the Polar Sea and shipping driftwood southwards along the east Greenlandic coast, round Cape Farewell, and then (with luck) up again along the west

A dog sledge dressed with hides, etc. The hunter has left his travel costume, bearskin trousers and sealskin *kamiks* on the sledge.

Canvas tents erected upon sledges, serving as sleeping platforms.

coast. While in the Arctic region generally, finding productive sites for encampments included an attention to driftwood resources, in the Thule region, this was very difficult, and most often impossible due to packed drift-ice, when the sea was not actually covered by solid sea-ice. This resulted in temporary isolation and periods of technological decline and impoverishment; in its own way it also provided a creative impetus, however. Lacking wood, people would build sledges from whale bone, walrus tooth, hide and sinews. A specimen was brought home to England, and given to the British Museum in 1819, by Captain Ross, who gave the first vivid portrait of this isolated group of Eskimos.[29] Whether made of wood or bone, the Thule sledges were narrower and lighter

A hunter and his gear.

than the sledges further south. Even today, when timber can be imported, the distinctive construction remains. Wood is still a scarce resource, because it is an expensive import that can only reach the region in the short summer season that just allows for one or two supply ships to reach the shores.

The apparent simplicity of the sledge relates to the construction out of the material at hand, and the conjoining of the appropriate pieces by straps made from the skin of bearded seal – like the dogs' braces and the long dog-whip; if need be, this can be replaced by another material, such as nylon rope. It seems that anyone can make a sledge, at least with some practice. Yet it is a highly sophisticated technology, expressed in its accurate proportions, the flexibility of the entire construct, owing to the use of pliable straps for holding the planks together, and not least the gear which is as much part of the sledge as anything. The sledge is never naked when en route. On the contrary, it is fitted out with numerous items without which it would not serve the purpose of the hunt, and this is where the sophistication of the technology is paramount, and betrays its double purpose as a means of transport and as a home.

It is covered with reindeer hides, upon which the hunter sits when not running along with the dogs or moving slowly in front of the sledge, measuring up the ice and its solidity with a stick and a trained eye. Underneath the hides, often other items are stored, such as large pieces of canvas for makeshift tents, and (in modern times) large pieces of plastic that may serve a similar purpose, but which also serve to cover the meat that will be laid out on the sledge after a successful hunt, and which will again be covered by canvas and hides, on top of which the hunter sits, the hunting rifle and the ice stick within reach. There is always a wooden box behind the driver, in which a burner, a can of kerosene, and a cooking pot are stowed, along with a thermos, possibly a kettle, a cup, and some utensils. There may also be an extra pair of mittens, maybe a cap. Hanging on

the handle posts, there is invariably a sliding shooting sail (to the left), behind which the hunter will eventually move invisibly towards his prey on the ice, extra braces for the dogs, surplus strapping for everything, and a canvas bag suspended between the posts, containing matches, tobacco, sunglasses, cartridges and other such smaller things that must be kept dry and ready to hand. Everything is in an exact position, and any interference with the order is inadmissible. Life may change in a split second, if the technological minutiae are not in their place. The hand stretching out for the rifle or for the mittens must not fail its purpose.

When night comes, or when sleeping becomes necessary under the midnight sun, a tent is raised over the sledge, serving as sleeping platform for the hunter, and allowing him floor-space besides, so that he may keep his *kamiks* (boots made from skin) and weapons within reach. Sometimes, two sledges are joined together, and some four people may share the platform, lying across both of them.

Technology is not separate from social life in these surroundings – nor, indeed, elsewhere. The dog sledge is of use only if the human agent – in our case, the hunter – is free to engage in a coupled flow of perception and action, demanding a high degree of concentration and flexibility of movement.[30] This skill must be matched by the dog sledge, where everything must be in place, yet also eminently flexible and easily replaceable. This allows the sledge driver and the sledge to merge into one whole actor, able to constantly make corrections of movement due to imperfections of the ice and detections of moveable targets, such as the seal or a polar bear. In anthropology today, notions like techno-cultures or techno-natures point in the same direction, but such hybrid terms actually continue to break apart what is really one. What is more, they tend to subvert the kind and degree of human ingenuity that connects them, and which is so conspicuous in the High North, where social practice is technological by default.

28 Rasmussen, K. *Den store slæderejse* (Copenhagen: Gyldendal, 1932), p. ii.

29 Ross, J. *Voyage of Discovery, Made Under the Orders of Admiralty, in His Majesty's Ships Isabelle and Alexander, for the Purpose of Exploring Baffin's Bay, and Inquiring into the Probability of a North-West Passage* (London: John Murray, 1819).

30 Ingold, T. Walking the plank, in T. Ingold, *Being Alive: Essays on Movement, Knowledge and Description* (London: Routledge, 2011), pp. 51–62.

LIVING WITH ENVIRONMENTAL CHANGE

MIRRORING

In social science the question of what kind of societies and solutions technologies co-produce is an ever-present theme.

WATER TECHNOLOGIES
MIRRORING GREAT EXPECTATIONS IN GREENLAND AND GHANA

During our field research in Greenland and Ghana respectively, the significant role of two technologies, involving factories and trees, were repeatedly highlighted locally as providing for possible solutions and positive societal changes. These technologies are both relevant in light of recent climate changes and "operate on water", so to speak.

The Greenland ice sheet dominates the island and takes up more than 80 per cent of its total area. It has always been a moving entity producing icebergs but today the melt-off is increasing rapidly due to global warming. The Greenlandic government is therefore looking into ways to harvest the enormous quantities of run-off water produced by the ice sheet for hydroelectric production on a large scale. The aim is to offer industries cheap and green energy in order to boost the ailing Greenlandic economy and to create an economic basis for greater self-determination. Thus, there are great expectations for the introduction of this water technology, and the industries to be sustained by it, as social and political changes are anticipated. Of particular interest is the construction of the large aluminium smelter in Maniitsoq.

Children marching as part of a VSO UK event with signs promoting tree planting.

School is over.

In Ghana, many NGOs emphasize the importance of tree planting as a way to solve the problems of climate change. At an event for school children in northern Ghana arranged by the British Volunteers Overseas (VSO UK), the children thus carried signs that simply read 'CLIMATE CHANGE: PLANT MORE TREES' and 'CLIMATE CHANGE: EVERY TREE MATTERS'. This emphasis on trees is rooted in research that blamed local populations in West Africa for mismanaging their natural resources. Despite the science behind such studies being heavily critiqued for being based on a simple causal relation between drought and tree cutting that is difficult to verify, a widespread narrative maintains that by educating the local population to stop destroying their trees and teaching them how to plant and care for seedlings, reforestation could lead to increased rainfall, and drought avoided.[31] In this sense, while trees are part of 'nature', they can also be perceived as "a technology utilized by humans to create certain environmental changes"[32] – in this case, to produce rain.

On paper, these two solutions to environmental problems in the shape of water technologies seem simple. The reduction of

LIVING WITH ENVIRONMENTAL CHANGE

livelihood options in Greenland is solved by planning a factory that utilizes the melting water and thereby produces jobs. The problems of drought and climate change in Ghana are solved by planting trees. In fact these solutions are so simple that they can be easily schematized (see the relevant diagrams on p. 150). Furthermore, the expectations for the benefits of these water technologies are high. By moving beyond paper and models and into the field, however, it is possible to gain a better understanding of how the local populations have been interacting with these imagined or perhaps largely imaginary technological solutions.

TREES AS A TECHNOLOGICAL SOLUTION?

During fieldwork in northern Ghana on climate change and development in the context of the severe floods of 2007, many conversations touched upon trees and their relationship to environmental changes. A common view was: "By planting trees you can get more water." Locally, trees were perceived as a water-generating technology – a solution to the problems of drought. An international development practitioner also put it like this: "Trees make the earth more fertile, they can improve the local climate and they are a very important resource that reduces vulnerability." The engaged development practitioner described how local people in Ghana would tell her that trees give more rain. However, she was aware that there was uncertainty about the idea that the presence of trees can lead to very local rains. One counter-argument, for example, posits that trees can act as pumps, and thus drain the soil of water and exhale it into the atmosphere. Trees are, however, able to reach water resources that other plants cannot, and they can help hold on to the earth during flooding. "In northern Ghana there are large tree planting projects – mango is a big hit!," the development practitioner continued and went on to explain that development organizations drive the mango seedlings to the villages and

give them to some "resourceful" men they know in the villages who then plant them. People are happy about the trees, and they want to plant them. While trees may be useful, however, they do involve hard work, and the organizations experienced a discrepancy between the energy spent on planting compared to growing them – a discrepancy which resulted in a success rate of less than 20 per cent.

In northern Ghana, it is easy to find several of the "resourceful" men who have been given seedlings by an NGO. One such man is Seidu in the village of Busanga, which is close to the border between Ghana and Burkina Faso, and which is right by the Volta River. Seidu is 33 years old and never went to school. He makes a living from rain-fed farming, dry season onion cultivation, rearing of animals and selling onions. During a discussion about the 2007 floods the conversation turned to trees:

> I participated in the planting of the trees, I was even given some mango seedlings which I planted. But the seedlings were given to me after the rains almost stopped, so some of them died. Also the problem with planting trees is that in the dry season, many [people] have gone into rearing [animal husbandry] and the animals go to drink from the river, and then they eat the trees, so we can only protect the trees if we have some wire netting around them.

Houses in Qaanaaq, built on wooden poles and permafrost. This technology is gradually melting down, and houses begin to slant.

Infrastructural expansion in Maniitsoq is expensive and complex.

Tree seedlings are among the prizes at the national Farmers' Day celebration.

When asked whether he had been able to see any positive effects yet from the trees that had been planted, he replied:

> The advantage is that the roots are able to hold the soil particles together, so the erosion won't happen. And the mango, when it begins fruiting our children will eat the fruits. The trees are very helpful to the riverside, I have observed that erosion does not affect the land there much again, once the trees grow up.

Far away from the river, but close to where the VSO UK climate change event for school children was held, one can meet Prosper who has not planted trees and who has never been to the river. Prosper had to take off two

weeks from school when the flooding was at its worst because the roads were so bad that he could not get to school. Also, the schools were filled with people whose homes had collapsed. When asked whether his teachers had talked about what could be done to prevent damage from the flooding in terms of agriculture, he replied: "They said that we should plant trees, avoid cutting down our trees, all those things." Reflecting on whether the teachers had explained the reasons for the flooding, Prosper responded: "They really did, they complained about how a lot of people have engaged themselves in doing galamsey [small-scale gold mining], cutting down trees for firewood for money, all those things were part of the reasons." Prosper laughed nervously when asked: "But did the teachers say why tree cutting was bad?" He couldn't remember exactly what the teachers told him. One wonders how the teachers managed to explain that tree cutting can lead to both too little rain, as the original narrative would have it, and too much rain.

LIVING WITH ENVIRONMENTAL CHANGE

MEGA-TECHNOLOGIES AND GREAT EXPECTATIONS

During fieldwork in Maniitsoq a meeting with a small group of active local citizens lobbying for the construction of the hydro-electric complex and the smelter was set up. Asked about how the factory would affect the town, a local teacher responded:

> We are of the opinion that Greenland is aiming at becoming more independent. It is impossible right now. We are unable to become 100 per cent independent before we get some resources to cover our expenses: police, legal system, the prison service and not least the block grant that we get from Denmark every year. But that is only the beginning. If we establish a smelter we may be able to cover 10 per cent of our expenses ... It is a stable turnover that we can count on. Stability. The smelter can be one of the pillars. It will become a huge workplace that will generate a stable income. But the start-up is important – and how it is organized ...

When asked whether he thought Greenland is ready for this new industry, the teacher responded:

> Everything has to have a beginning. It does not happen from one year to the next. Maybe, it will take a generation. Our generation demanded a lot from the environment and the fish ... The fishermen welcome Alcoa [the aluminium producer]. Then the fishermen can sell their fish to more people.

The future smelter in Maniitsoq is going to produce aluminium, but for Greenland the factory must produce jobs for Greenlanders in order to meet expectations. Thus to make the technology work in that direction the Greenlandic government has proclaimed that people have to be re-educated and re-settled, towns and businesses should be re-organized, laws and rules should be re-negotiated, and time and space should be reinterpreted.

Rain and melting ice will generate the water needed to power the hydro-electricity complex linked to the aluminium smelter.
Source: Drawing: Carsten Thuesen. Copyright: Geological Survey of Denmark and Greenland (GEUS).

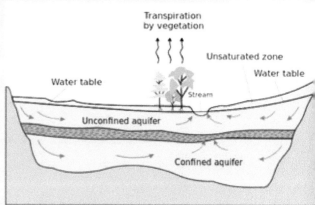

The hydrological cycle schematizes how trees play a role in precipitation.

TECHNOLOGY: A GOLDEN SOLUTION TO PROBLEMS?

Even though we compare quite different water technologies (trees and factories) located in two distinct places, a striking similarity emerges. They are regarded as golden solutions to big problems. The importance given in Ghana to the planting of trees in order to avoid climate change, because trees are believed to generate rain, remains powerful even in a situation where the supposed climate change comes in the shape of too much rain. By promoting the technology of tree planting as a simple and easily implementable solution to the problems of climate change, other potential dimensions of climate change, such as flooding, are largely ignored and other solutions to reduce consequences are not explored.

As the development of the factory project in Maniitsoq progresses, the critique of the project in Greenland is becoming more qualified and specific. The requirements, in

31 Leach, M. and Mearns, R. Environmental change and policy: challenging received wisdom in Africa, in M. Leach and R. Mearns (eds) *The Lie of the Land: Challenging Received Wisdom on the African Environment* (Oxford: James Currey, 1996), pp. 1–33.

32 Gardner, R. Trees as technology: planting shelterbelts on the Great Plains, *History and Technology: An International Journal*, 25(4) (2009): 325–341 [p. 325].

33 Feenberg, A. *Critical Theory of Technology* (Oxford: Oxford University Press, 1991), p. 8.

34 Winner, L. Do artifacts have politics? In D.G. Johnson and J.M. Wetmore (eds), *Technology and Society: Building Our Sociotechnical Future* (Cambridge, MA: The MIT Press, 2009), pp. 209–226 [p. 211].

35 Hughes, T.P. Technological momentum, in D.G. Johnson and J.M. Wetmore (eds), *Technology and Society: Building Our Sociotechnical Future* (Cambridge, MA: The MIT Press, 2009), pp. 141–150.

terms of social and cultural re-engineering on the national scale necessary to make the technology work, are becoming clearer. The technology gives Greenland a new position in the world that demands new forms of political navigation. In order to make the technology work, the Greenlandic government is also encouraging people to move closer to the proposed factory and thus is pushing for rapid urbanization.

In both Greenland and Ghana, the use of these particular technologies may address some societal problems but they also narrow our focus in certain directions and reshape the local societies in new and unpredictable ways. The question is thus: Is technology the means that humans use to pursue social and cultural projects and ambitions or are humans modelled by technology? The idea that technology can be applied in the service of human projects is an instrumentalist understanding that stands in opposition to a substantive theory that questions the neutrality of technology.[33] Feenberg points to Ellul and Heidegger who argue for a substantive theoretical understanding of technology as constituting a new type of expansive cultural system that restructures the entire social world as an object of control. Implicated in this – according to Feenberg – is the idea that "[t]echnology is not simply a means but

has become an environment and a way of life."

The general point is that by choosing to use a particular technology, humans make many unwitting cultural choices and are affected by the technology itself. The construction of an aluminium smelter or tree planting may, from this perspective, require the establishment, structuring and maintenance of a particular set of social conditions as the operating environment of that technology. Winner terms this relationship "the political qualities of artefacts".[34] He argues for a dialectic perspective on the political quality of technology: the use of artefacts may have intentional or unintentional consequences for society, authority and power but may also, due to the design, use, maintenance and running of crucial technological systems, tend to eclipse other sorts of moral and political reasoning. Hughes proposes the concept of "technical momentum" in an attempt to bridge technological determinism and social constructivism and he suggests that the investment of money, effort and resources to develop, maintain and use technological systems – be they trees or factories – can make it difficult, if not impossible, to change those systems.[35] From this perspective, the technological system thus both shapes and is shaped by society.

During the winter (2011), citizen groups met on a weekly basis to sketch out new town scenarios.

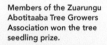

Members of the Zuarungu Abotitaaba Tree Growers Association won the tree seedling prize.

LIVING WITH ENVIRONMENTAL CHANGE

PART THREE

LANDSCAPE

LANDSCAPE

LIVING WITH ENVIRONMENTAL CHANGE

INTRODUCTION

Before embarking on the grand tour of the distinct landscapes visited below, it is useful to stand still for a moment and reflect upon the notion itself. We may start by listening to Simon Schama, whose work on *Landscape and Memory* enlightens us on the inner meanings of the notion of landscape. The key message is that it is our own perception that makes the difference between raw matter and landscape.

A landscape is not simply a natural place; it is *lived*.

The word itself tells us as much. It entered the English language, along with herring and bleached linen, as a Dutch import at the end of the sixteenth century. And *landschap*, like its Germanic root, *Landschaft*, signified a unit of human occupation, indeed a jurisdiction, as much as anything that might be a pleasing object of depiction. So it was surely not accidental that in the Netherlandisch flood-fields, itself the site of formidable human engineering, a community developed the idea of a *landschap*, which in the colloquial English of the time became a *landskip*. Its Italian equivalents, the pastoral idyll of brooks and wheat-gold hills, were known as *parerga*, and were the auxiliary settings for the familiar motifs of classical myth and sacred scripture. But in the Netherlands the human design of the landscape – implied by the fishermen, cattle drivers, and ordinary walkers and riders who dotted the paintings of Esaias van de Velde, for example – *was* the story, startlingly sufficient unto itself.[1]

In the Scandinavian languages, 'landscapes' were also units of communal jurisdiction each with their own law and system of justice until comprehensive kingdoms became fully acknowledged in the Middle Ages. Again, we understand that the landscape is not simply a natural space; it is a socially defined place. This is a point of departure for the present part of the book, recognizing also that the landscape was to get additional meaning in the Romantic period of painting, being something mainly *seen* and praised for either its beauty or its terror. In other words, landscapes are significant in the context of this book, because they are *lived*. Conversely, human and social life itself formats landscapes in particular ways by incorporating them in particular visions of social life.

ATTENDING TO LANDSCAPES

Social communities, societies, and modern states are of necessity located somewhere, as were the ancient landscapes. They are not simply put on top of natural landscapes, however, they are formatted by them, and contribute to their shaping. As will become clearer in the course of reading the following chapters, the ways in which people attend to a particular landscape open up for diverse ways of perceiving it. What meets the eye when looking on mountain slopes, riverbeds, desert pastures, urban waterways, fishing waters or glacier bursts, is already half-interpreted within a particular mode of living.

This also means that people do not necessarily agree with what they see. It is relative to personal pasts and present interests, at least in part, but also to different degrees of social attention. Nomads in the desert hinterlands of Mauretania will see potential grazing land, where others would only see an empty space. Likewise, where tourists visiting Greenland will experience a

People live *within* landscapes and cannot perceive them apart from social interests.

deep sense of wonder at the rapidly calving glaciers and marvel at their beauty, the geo-physicist and the seal-hunter may either see a global climate drama or an encroaching disaster to a particular settlement. Forests may be symbolically loaded with economic plenty or with (mythical) terror; the same goes for rivers, mountaintops, and much more. In other words, the landscape is inevitably humanized the moment people attend to it.

Part of this humanization is reflected in certain affective ties with the environment, or a particular *topophilia* with the term suggested by Yi-Fu Tuan. He says about such ties:

> These differ greatly in intensity, subtlety, and mode of expression. The response to the environment may be primarily aesthetic: it may then vary from the fleeting pleasure one gets from a view to the equally fleeting but far more intense sense of beauty that is suddenly revealed. The response may be tactile, a delight in the feel of air, water, earth. More permanent and less easy to express, are feelings that one has toward a place because it is home, the locus of memories, and the means of gaining a livelihood.[2]

In fieldwork, the method by which we – the contributors to this book – have approached the lived landscapes of different groups of people, we have sought to come to grips with the feelings that people have towards their home landscapes. They are indeed difficult to express, and the more so because these years, the upheaval of the landscapes where we have deliberately placed ourselves is so conspicuous. The means of gaining a livelihood are called into question, and memories become destabilized. It could be argued that the boundary between the domesticated landscape, such as the Dutch from where the term was exported to Britain, and the wilderness beyond it is becoming increasingly permeated. Wilderness, of course, is as much a state of mind as is the tamed landscape of sociality and production, but the point is that in significant ways, wilderness now seeps perceptibly into the social order along with the destabilized seasons, giant waves, unpredictable rains, and disappearing ice.

For the contributors to this book, it has been essential not only to move into different landscapes but also to discern how people attend to them. This is achieved by moving along with people within their own landscapes. In the course of moving along, the fieldworker seeks to detect the significance of the current upheaval with respect to the implicit imaginations and sensations of the landscape, whenever it is stumbled upon in the practices of cultivation, way-finding, and getting from one place to another.

THE SPATIALITY OF HABITS

A recurrent theme in the snapshots of social landscapes given below is that habitual patterns of socio-spatial action are up in the air. People, whose livelihood is moveable by definition, such as Arctic hunters or Saharan nomads, are now challenged by unprecedented openings or closures in their well-trodden landscapes, but this is not all there is to the issue of spatiality here. In all landscapes, people live by numerous spatial habits that have gradually been installed in their bodies and affected their perception of the environment. Humans have been called 'ceremonial animals' precisely because of their deep-seated spatial habits.[3]

While above, the human dimension of landscapes was highlighted, here we must make the inverse claim about the deep impact of landscapes upon human self-perception. Clearly, hunters' long-term experience of a particular seasonality in the landscape and among its animal inhabitants, or farmers' reliance upon regular changes between wet and dry seasons, deeply affect the ways in which they think about the world, and how they act within it, of course. In a microscopic move, Pierre Bourdieu has shown how the entire world-view of the Kabyles could be detected in minute spatial details of the house.[4] He re-invented an older notion of 'habitus' to cover the ways in which spatial (and other) practices become installed in the body as natural, and thus forgotten as the outcome of particular histories and social interests.

What becomes clear from the meanderings through different landscapes presented below is precisely the degree to which social habits are also spatial habits. The range of this claim can be seen from the degree of unsettlement that people experience in the wake of environmental changes, even when the actual consequences seem to be minor, and sometimes have not yet really happened. We can see how planning a particular industrial development in Greenland implicitly calls for a re-modelling of a vast region – way before the industrial project materializes. An entirely new industrial landscape may emerge out of the hunting hinterland, as may indeed a landscape of cultural heritage, suddenly calling for protection. And we shall see how urban development on vertical slopes in Peru cannot simply be achieved by the hard work of transforming the dry mountain landscape into a liveable space, but equally requires a complete refashioning of the legal routines, because access to water has to be regulated in new ways. This is related both to a new sense of water scarcity and to a destabilized urban landscape, calling for new forms of vertical regulation.

This last observation reminds us that the spatiality of social habits affects a much broader field than the actual bodily movements of people through particular environments. It also embraces vast domains of regulation, policy, and planning, where – once again – the social forms must be kept in check along with the fluid environment. Places and people are co-constituted.

Social habits are also spatial habits; it creates a sense of unsettlement, when the environment changes.

THE ELUSIVENESS OF PLACE

To introduce another notion of momentous, if implicit, impact upon our perspective on landscape, we can again look at the Arctic hunter. There is no way he can determine his catch beforehand, but when setting out he naturally presumes that under the given circumstances of season, weather, and wind, the trip will be worth his effort. The element of uncertainty that adheres to any hunt is thus tempered by an activity of forecasting the potential promise of the environment. The imagination of the future always balances between such uncertainty and promise in a community where the horizon of knowing expands and contracts in both expected and unexpected ways, and of course the more so, the less certain the season. From his experience among Nunavut reindeer hunters (in Arctic Canada), Hugh Brody has expressed this with reference to the habitual movements in the landscape:

> Hunting itself, however, must defy the habit as well as follow it: no two seasons are identical, animal migrations are never wholly predictable. Hunters, following well-worn trails, must seize new opportunities, adjust the pace and direction of their movements to follow, intercept or find the animals upon which life depends. At each point along the seasonal round, individuals must assess and process a vast amount of information. The habit and pattern of mobility set the scene; action within the scene keeps changing.[5]

What we sense here is how the non-human prey upsets the habitual movements along known trails in the landscape. This is the first indication of the elusiveness of place, and, in this case, its distinction entirely dependent upon particular stories and hunting luck. However, the implications are general and apply to all places of importance to humans. They become singled out as 'important places' for many different reasons; individual persons attach different meanings to a place, as well as different times, and different potentials – whence the instability or elusiveness of places.

With Doreen Massey, we want to underline that this has nothing to do with a deconstruction of place, nor is it a disclaimer of its possible distinctiveness. It is rather to renew the significance of place, by its also being an event – a product of a momentary marking of its significance. Massey says:

> What is special about place is not some romance of a pre-given collective identity or of the eternity of the hills. Rather, what is special about place is precisely that throwntogetherness, the unavoidable challenge of negotiating a here-and-now (itself drawing on a history and a geography of thens and theres); and a negotiation which must take place within and between both human and non-human.[6]

Within particular landscapes, people engage in multiple strategies to safeguard the world.

In the process of history and scientific development, new places may gain prominence and old places lose their importance. In such processes, unknown landscapes emerge in ancient, and well-trodden regions. With the current environmental changes, whether already experienced or just feared, the elusiveness of place may turn into a serious sense of displacement, disrupting people's sense of who they are in the process, as we shall demonstrate in the cases presented below.

The thrown-togetherness of place has a direct bearing on the humanized landscape. Glaciologists and peasants may agree that the glaciers are shrinking rapidly in the Andean highlands, but the glaciers do not necessarily belong to one and the same landscape. In one sense, the landscape is geophysical and heavily laden with scientific knowledge, deep geological times, and global temperature curves; in another it is practical and heavily laden with memories, years of famine or plenty, and a recalling of times when the white mountain tops could still be called upon to protect the people on the slopes. Presently, there may be a degree of convergence between such distinctive landscapes, because the sustained international debate of climate change leaves no one unaffected and incorporates most people in the know.

LANDSCAPE LITERACY

The aim of our collective endeavours has been to create a body of knowledge about people's perceptions of and placements within particular landscapes in times of upheaval such as the present era of global climate change. 'Upheaval' itself suggests that strong forces are at play, and in the studies below there is a definite sense of *unsettlement* in the wake of increasingly strong indications of environmental change. All while people continue to sow their seeds and set out their fish-traps, there is a deepening concern about the stability of the landscape. The elusiveness of place may turn into veritable disappearance in some of the hotspots of climate change that we have studied.

The experience of unsettlement is not simply a worry about physical changes as such, but incorporates also the potential breaking of the affective ties with the environment, and the upsetting of spatial habits. While, arguably, all places are elusive, once the ice melts under one's feet, or the river dam bursts and wipes away the year's crop, the elusiveness is much too real for comfort. Whatever the local actualities of environmental change, what we have wanted to understand in each of our fields, is how they affect everyday lives and strategies for the future. Within our collaborative project, the attempt at understanding has been premised on our actual emplacement in the different landscapes. Again, this is more than simply travelling 'out there'; it is a particular commitment to achieve at least a degree of *landscape literacy*, or an ability to read the vernacular landscape – beyond scientific categories. While one can immediately observe the lie of the land, it takes more time and effort to experience it as a socially formatted landscape and sense its many meanings to people living there. This is where the method of fieldwork is invaluable. As Tim Ingold has it:

LIVING WITH ENVIRONMENTAL CHANGE

Landscapes gain shape and significance through human activities, movements, and imaginations.

What truly distinguishes anthropology, I believe, is that it is not a study *of* at all, but a study *with*. Anthropologists work and study *with* people. Immersed with them in an environment of joint activity, they learn to see things (or hear them, or touch them) in the ways their teachers and companions do. An education in anthropology, therefore, does more than furnish us with knowledge about the world – about people and societies. It rather educates our *perception* of the world, and opens our eyes and minds to other possibilities of being.[7]

In the following short reports from various fields, it has been an axiom that they should reflect a located perception of the environment rather than a view from above, or from a distant scientific perspective. We would never claim to have understood the landscape in exactly the same way as our collaborators in the field; no two people ever think in exactly the same way, not even when at home. What we have aimed at is simply to sense the world from the perspective of our companions.

The fieldworkers have engaged in conversations not only with people but also with landscapes.[8] This is more than just a metaphor for the engagement with landscapes, it also implies that we – as scholars – have attempted to understand the particular responses from the landscape to human action and query. Landscapes are never unaffected by human presence, but marked by farming, mining, draining, hunting, gathering, and constant evaluation with a view to future opportunities. Thus, the idea of conversing with the landscape is implicated in the idea of landscape literacy; both emphasize the agency and inscribed significance of landscape itself. There is no way in which we can relegate landscape to an external 'nature', waiting to be embraced by human interpretation and social exploitation. As suggested above, they co-format each other.

[1] Schama, S. *Landscape and Memory* (New York: Alfred A. Knopf, 1995), p. 10.

[2] Tuan, Y.-F. *Topophilia: A Study of Environmental Perception, Attitudes, and Values* (New York: Columbia University Press, 1990), p. 93.

[3] James, W. *The Ceremonial Animal* (Oxford: Blackwell, 2003).

[4] Bourdieu, P. *The Logic of Practice* (Cambridge: Polity Press, 1990).

[5] Brody, H. *Living Arctic* (London: Faber and Faber, 1987), p. 89.

[6] Massey, D. *For Space* (London: Sage, 2005), p. 140.

[7] Ingold, T. Anthropology is *not* ethnography. Radcliffe-Brown Lecture in Social Anthropology 2007, *Proceedings of the British Academy*, 154 (2008): 69–92 [p. 82].

[8] Benediktsson, K. and Lund, K.A. (eds) *Conversations with Landscape* (Farnham: Ashgate, 2010).

The agency of landscape has been discussed in anthropology for a long time, not least under the rubric of animism, building upon the axiom that somehow nature speaks back to humans. There is also a good deal of attention paid to non-human agents of other kinds, whether sand or sea, weather or wind. The general point here is that while the questions addressed in the chapters below focus on the landscape, at the same time they implicitly range across the entire scale of human interest and imagination and defy any easy classification. Most importantly, all of the questions and suggestions derive from our thinking *with* the world – or some part of it – rather than *about* it, and from dwelling and moving within it, rather than simply observing from above or afar.

HUALCA HUALCA
MOUNTAIN LORD AND LIFE SOURCE

From 15 to 17 October 2011, the villagers of Pinchollo in Colca Valley went up to the Hualca Hualca Mountain, their main water source. The local Irrigation Commission organized the event, and apart from the farmers, several local authorities took part: the mayor, the justice of the peace, and the leader of the peasant community.

As an anthropologist interested in water, I was invited to join them. After a Catholic mass in the local church, a procession was led by the priest and the farmers' patron saint San Isidro Labrador, who gave the travellers his blessings. Around a hundred people set out on foot or horseback, with mules carrying the food, cooking gear, blankets and shovels, and we arrived at the camping site after a day's travel. Next morning we walked up to the foot of the glacier and gathered where the melt water starts flowing down to the village. We stayed for several hours, making offerings to Hualca Hualca so that he would continue to provide the village with water and life. This mountain rises 6025 metres above sea level, and is one of the most powerful *Apus* in the Colca region, since he provides several villages with water. *Apu*, which means "lord" in Quechua, denotes the mountain as a guardian for the territories he overlooks and as a powerful being that people can communicate with through offerings.[9] The leader of the peasant community of Pinchollo stated that:

This is a ritual which we make for our Apu Hualca Hualca. We, the authorities, watch over our people in Pinchollo. The organizers in the Irrigation Commission,

together with the mayor, and the leaders of the peasant community, we make an offering, a ritual, so that he [Hualca Hualca] will receive with a lot of good will and affection, and so that we will not lack water in the next year. The water is fundamental for us, for our plants, for the humans. We live from the water, and that is why we make this offering, with a lot of affection and devotion. And I know that tomorrow, the water will increase with 3 or 4 litres per second. We have this hope and every year we do this.

The offerings, consisting of alpaca foetus, llama fat, maize, coca leaves, sweets, fruit, flowers, wine and maize brew, were burnt on a fire or interred in the earth. When the leader of the Irrigation Commission presented the offerings to the mountain, he asked Hualca Hualca not to forget them, to give them more water and to protect the people of the village. After the offerings were made, a bunch of ice fell down from the mountain side, and this was taken as a sign that Hualca Hualca was thrilled and telling us: "Look, here is the water!" After the offerings, we shared drinks with each other and with the mountain, and there was music and dancing. A band with a harp, a mandolin,

The place where the melt water starts flowing from the ice that is left on Hualca Hualca.

163

LIVING WITH ENVIRONMENTAL CHANGE

and a guitar played this song dedicated to Hualca Hualca:

Apu Hualca Hualca
Cerro poderoso
Desde aquellas nieves
Bajan nuestras aguas
Para el regadío
De nuestra campiña

En el sitio de Achumani
Hay una ventana
Donde antiguamente
Pagaban al Apu
Con una doncella
Al Apu Hualca Hualca

Lord Hualca Hualca
Powerful mountain
From those snows
Our waters flow down
For the irrigation
Of our lands.

In the place of Achumani
There is a window
Where they in the old times
Paid to the Lord
With a maiden
For the Lord Hualca Hualca.

The next day we walked to Achumani, where the water springs out of an opening that looks like a window. The story goes that in ancient times, human offerings were made to Hualca Hualca: in times of crisis, a young girl would be chosen to go into the mountain through the "the window", and she would go voluntarily because Apu Hualca Hualca called her. Hualca Hualca is venerated for being the source of life for Pinchollo, and this is meant in a quite literal sense since the melt water is the main water source for the village. One of the elderly men, Nazareno, told me that:

Without Apu Hualca Hualca, without the snow-capped mountain, there is no water. If there is no water, there is no

A farmer posing with the Peruvian flag by a virgin figure made of ice.

life. Without Hualca Hualca, our village would not exist. That is why we make libations.

On their way down from the mountain, women and men used their shovels to clean the earthen canals so that the water could flow more easily down to the village and the cultivated fields. About 60 per cent of the fields in Pinchollo are irrigated with water from Hualca Hualca, while the rest of the land is irrigated with water from the state-owned Majes Canal. In recent years, people are increasingly blaming global warming for the glacier shrinkage on Hualca Hualca and the decrease of water in the springs, which are fed by rainwater and glacial melt water. The Andean tropical mountain glaciers are known to be visible indicators of climate change, due to their sensitivity to increased temperatures, and during the last 35 years there has been a 22 per cent reduction of the total glacier area in Peru, and a reduction up to 80 per cent of glacier surface from small glaciers.[10] When the frost season ends, the melt water flows with an increased volume

[9] Allen, C.J. *The Hold Life Has: Coca and Cultural Identity in an Andean Community* (Washington, DC: Smithsonian Institution Press, 1988). Gelles, P.H. *Water and Power in Highland Peru: The Cultural Politics of Irrigation and Development* (New Brunswick, NJ: Rutgers University Press, 2000); Gose, P. *Deathly Waters and Hungry Mountains: Agrarian Ritual and Class Formation in an Andean Town* (Toronto: University of Toronto Press, 1994).

[10] Bates, B.C., Kundzewicz, Z.W., Wu, S. and Palutikof, J.P. (eds) *Climate Change and Water*, Technical Paper of the Intergovernmental Panel on Climate Change (Geneva: IPCC Secretariat, 2008); Vuille, M., Francou, B., Wagnon, P., Juen, I., Kaser, G., Mark, B.G., and Bradley, R.S. Climate change and tropical Andean glaciers: past, present and future, *Earth-Science Reviews*, 89 (2008): 79–96.

LANDSCAPE

A breathtaking view to the mountains on the other side of Colca Canyon.

and intensity that destroy the canals and erode the soil, and people are not able to use it for irrigation; it gets lost in the river. Nazareno said:

> In August and September there is a strong flow that starts in the glacier, it is the melt water. The white snow can no longer be seen after September. There is less ice than before. … If the glacier disappears, there is no life any more; there is no village any more. The mountain supports us. Who will contain the thaw? Earlier the snow of Hualca Hualca reached the bottom, as far as the foot of the mountain, as far as the geyser. Now there is little snow.

Others emphasized how mountain springs and cushion bogs by the foot of Hualca Hualca have dried up in the past few years.

The offering contains alpaca foetus, llama fat, coca leaves, maize, sweets, cigarettes, fruit and flowers.

These experiences of a changing environment and a dwindling life source lead to new uncertainties about the future and whether the coming generations will be able to live in Pinchollo. For how long will Apu Hualca Hualca be able to safeguard the landscape of the mountain dwellers?

KNOWING LANDSCAPES OF WATER IN KIRIBATI

In Kiribati the landscape is made of water, and navigation skills have since time immemorial connected the islands.

The landscape around the islands of Kiribati is inviting and seductive with pristine blue lagoons, coconut trees hanging lazily over the beaches, and a far horizon where sky and ocean merge into one.

However, it is also a treacherous landscape, which can be dangerous to move through. Unsuspected waves and reefs, strong currents, and outbreaks of bad weather make moving in this landscape of water a hazardous activity. In the eight months during which I did my fieldwork on the main island of Tarawa, several people were lost at sea. Traditional navigation is a highly specialized skill that connects the vast ocean and the tiny islands into one landscape.

Teueroa is a navigator who can make long inter-island journeys on the Pacific Ocean, and she can read the weather. She was born on the island Maiana, but now she lives on the main island, Tarawa. When she was born, her father took her umbilical cord and sailed into the ocean, "to the place where the current ends". When Teueroa told me this story she paused and explained that where the current ends is where the ocean is very deep. He put the umbilical cord into his mouth and jumped onto the outrigger and then proceeded to jump into the water. After swimming for a while, he spat out the umbilical cord, and allowed it to sink into the deep ocean. Then he swam backwards in the direction of the canoe and sailed home. Puzzled, I asked Teueroa why he swam backwards to the canoe. Her answer was that it

was so that he could keep an eye out for the creatures of the ocean.

This is a variation of a well-known ritual in Kiribati in which the umbilical cord connects the new-born within the extended family and grounds the new-born to family land. When the umbilical cord falls off a baby boy, one of his grandfathers wears the cord on his right wrist for three days. After three days it is carefully wrapped and put away in a safe place. In the case of a baby girl, the cord is worn by one of her grandmothers. This is done so that the child will follow in the footsteps of its elders.[11]

Teueroa's father did something rather different. Instead of tying the umbilical cord to an older female relative's wrist as a way of connecting and grounding her within the extended family, he took it to the sea and allowed it to sink into the deep ocean, thus connecting and grounding her in this fluid space. When I heard that he swam away backwards to the canoe, my initial idea was that it was a sign of respect, as when you walk backwards out of the public meeting-house (*te maneaba*) as a sign of respect to the congregation gathered inside. However, he actually did so to keep an eye out for the creatures of the ocean, implicitly comprising both trust and betrayal, the

In Kiribati from an early age, children play in, work in, and explore the ocean.

intimate and the treacherous. The landscape is, thus, not a neutral background to human activities; at times it is family, at times enemy.

Navigational skills have allowed a handful of people from these islands to journey in this ocean world and to predict sailing and weather conditions. Navigators have interpreted the formation and colour of clouds to identify islands over the horizon. Birds and species of fish would give an indication of distance to land. Star paths were followed when travelling greater distances. And most impressively, ocean swells, reflected from faraway islands and reefs, would echo through the canoe and the navigator, and would be recognized like the face of an old friend.

Traditional navigators use models of the movements of the stars to predict weather.

These skills have continually been tested and adapted to changing natural and social conditions, enabling interaction with the environment throughout history on these islands. Teueroa's skills rest on generations of knowledge passed down through family lines. Her father, who passed on the skills from his ancestors, about the stars, the weather, and the currents used for sailing, passed them on to Teueroa. He taught Teueroa from an early age how to *be* in the landscape. For a navigator, it is not sufficient to have knowledge of the ocean, you have to *know* it. How it feels, tastes, and behaves. When it is welcoming, dangerous, or deceitful. Teueroa told me this story:

> The first time I learned to travel I was 14. I was on the local canoe with my father from the island Maiana. My father asked me to pick up something, as I leaned down my father pushed me into the sea. So I fell into the sea and you know how I tried to survive. I was crying and calling my mother, but my father sailed away. I can't really remember how long I was in the sea for, but when I looked at the canoe, it sailed away and disappeared. I was crying in the middle of the ocean, calling my mother. The ocean there is very dark and deep. But that was a test for me to overcome the fear of the sea, because if you are going to be a navigator, if you are going to be a traveller, you cannot be scared of the sea. My father came back, he put me on the front of the canoe and then he said: "Tell me, where is the land?" I pointed, and when it was wrong, I got smacked. Then I tried to remember again what I had learnt. So I identified the land according to the cloud.

Why did Teueroa's father throw his daughter in the ocean? What kind of cruel exercise was this? We can only speculate as Teueroa's story does not reveal the full answer. Teueroa learns much of her knowledge through repetition, memorization, and models. But being thrown in the ocean is a very different lesson indeed. Her father's lesson could be that the landscape can be treacherous, unreliable, and uncertain. While in the ocean,

A traditional navigator observing the horizon.

the waves washed over Teueroa's body, and the current dragged her along. Teueroa is learning about the landscape not by quantifying it or observing its parts, but by qualifying it, being in it, feeling it on her frail, young body. Teueroa's father demonstrates that even navigators may lose their way, their orientation, and their ability to move in this world of ocean and islands.

Even if the world seems uncertain when Teueroa floats in the ocean, her experience is equally important as knowing the landscape by memorizing star paths or recognizing swell patterns. When her father rescues her from the water, he demands she set the course and take them home. A difficult task when the world seems uncertain. When Teueroa is wrong, he slaps her face, as if to say: "Use your other skills and knowledge about the landscape to take us home." Knowing the landscape, then, is equally about applying ancient skills of navigation and recognizing that you are always at risk of losing your way.

11 Talu, A. *Kiribati: Aspects of History* (Suva: *Fiji Times and Herald* Ltd, 1979).

LIVING WITH ENVIRONMENTAL CHANGE

BORDERS AT SEA

In most cases when I asked the fishermen upon their return to the village of Tharangambadi, where I did my fieldwork, where they had gone during the day, they would reply by stating the number of hours they had been away.

Pointing loosely towards the Bay of Bengal in one direction or the other, they would often say "We went seven hours that way." Other common responses would be statements like "We left at three o'clock in the morning – it was pitch dark", or "The trip took four hours, up and down." To me, the visiting fieldworker, this was a fine and apt way of responding to my question about where they had been, as I probably would not have been very familiar with any of the land- or seamarks that the fishermen might otherwise have named to indicate their location during their working hours. Even though the fishermen could obviously specify in more detail where they had gone if I asked them to, I usually left it at that. Time as the marker of space when the fishermen were out at sea seemed to match my sense that the waters bordering the village constitute an unfathomable expanse; curiously, in this case hours seemed a more tangible measurement than location.

At times, though, clear boundaries and differentiated space do surface at sea and in the daily lives of the villagers and remind them that, despite all the boundlessness, it is also a territory. During my fieldwork in Tharangambadi in 2011, I noticed that all the local fishing boats recently had the number 1093 painted on them. This, the villagers explained, is the toll-free telephone number by which the Coastal Security Group, a division of the Tamil Nadu Police, can be alerted in cases of emergency and if any suspicious behaviour is observed on the waters. My friend and field assistant Renuga elaborated that the number had been painted on all the boats both to remind the fishermen of the hotline if need arose, and to scare off anyone with terrorist and other suspicious plans. It should be clear, she told me, to all parties to any potential incident that the sea is not a safe haven for acting against rules and customs. Social relations and regulations are not suspended at sea. In recent times,

The Tharangambadi fishing
fleet, advised to roam only in
Indian waters.

Prints of the number by which
the coastal police can be
alerted of suspicious behaviour
at sea.

The authorities have yet
to make people change
to offshore fishing on big
mechanized vessels.

LIVING WITH ENVIRONMENTAL CHANGE

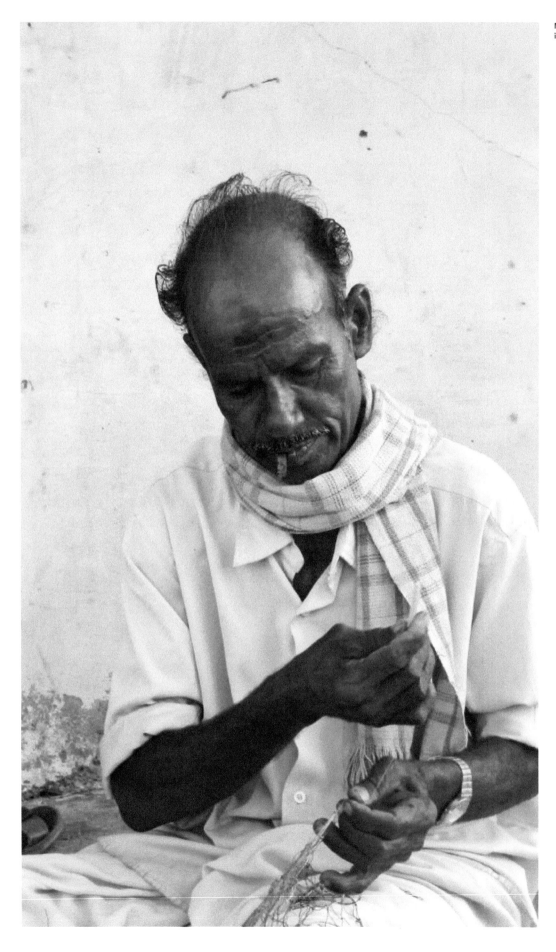

LANDSCAPE

accordingly, the fishermen of Tharangambadi have begun taking cell phones on their
fishing trips, making it technically possible
to alert authorities as well as getting in touch
with one another; one more reason for
adding the number to the boats and raising
awareness about coastal security.

From an official policy note issued by the
Tamil authorities I learned that the Coastal
Security Group was formed with the objective of preventing people from smuggling
fuel, medicines and other substances and of
detecting and blocking the entry of so-called
anti-social and terrorist elements into Tamil
Nadu by the sea route. Not infrequently, I
heard talk of fishermen from Tharangambadi
and other fishing hamlets along the Tamil
coast being arrested and even attacked by the
Sri Lankan navy accusing them of fishing in
Sri Lankan waters and illegally crossing the
International Maritime Boundary Line that
separates India from Sri Lanka.

Newspapers report on the issue and on the
consequences of such alleged cross-border
fishing and suggest that the Sri Lankan navy
is unduly brutal, because they suspect that
the Tamil fishermen are somehow allied
with the Tamil Tigers on Sri Lanka. The fishermen in turn claim that they only, if at all,
cross the border if the fish do. They say they
merely go where they have to go to ensure
their livelihood, the resource base of which is
increasingly strained due to overfishing.

The issue of depletion of marine
resources is indeed pressing. But according
to the authorities it is a matter that needs
an official policy response and a formal
solution, rather than individual fishing boats
going out of bounds. Apparently, what is
needed is another kind of differentiation at
sea. From a policy note from the Tamil Nadu
Fisheries Department, I learned that "A sum
of Rupees 25 crore [ten million] has been
set apart for this purpose to add 500 new
mechanized boats or deep sea Tuna long
liners" (Policy Note 2011–2012). These new
boats are meant to encourage more people
in the many small fishing communities
along the coast to change to offshore fishing
and become day-labourers on larger mechanized vessels, instead of going for small-scale
fishing in their own boats.

In the policy note, there seems to be a
ring of both alarm and optimism in the face
of the distressing depletion of resources. The
Fisheries Department states:

> The vast fishery resources of both marine
> and inland waters have not yet been fully
> brought under production. The fishery
> resources in the inshore areas have been
> overexploited, whereas the offshore
> resources and deep sea resources are yet
> to be tapped to the optimum level.
> (Policy Note 2011–2012)

The solution to the problem of depletion, it
seems, is to encourage people to change the
way that the naval landscape is exploited.
What is necessary is a distinction between
inshore and offshore waters. If the costly tuna
live in a territory boundary that keeps it in
the deep sea, policy-makers and fishermen
might want to follow suit.

Although the waters of the Bay of Bengal
are perhaps visually unmarked, at least to
the eye of the inexpert visiting fieldworker,
and on the surface often gauged in terms of
hours of sailing, they are anything but an
undifferentiated expanse. National borders,
long-standing armed conflict, fish fewer and
further between, biological differentiation
and official economic incitements all emerge
and come ashore from the sea bordering the
village of Tharangambadi.

LIVING WITH ENVIRONMENTAL CHANGE

MAKING URBAN LANDSCAPES
PEOPLE, WATER, MATERIALS

In the urban neighbourhood of Primero de Junio, daily activities start early. From 5 a.m. women, old and young, dogs and some kids gather around the public water tap, with buckets, water containers, and wheelbarrows. The tap, *la pileta*, is a focal point and essential part of the neighbourhood landscape. As in other recent urbanizations, in Primero de Junio, the water flow ends in collective and public water taps, where settlers, *vecinos*, fetch the water, and from here carry it to their homes.

Primero de Junio was founded 20 years ago, practically on top of the city of Arequipa in southern Peru on the slope of the volcano Chachani, mainly by migrants from rural areas. Since the water has been passing and tapped by many urban dwellers when it reaches these heights, water pressure is low when it arrives in Primero de Junio; it is a rather small stream that comes out of the collective tap whenever the faucet is opened. Since they founded Primero de Junio, settlers have continuously been working on converting a piece of mountain slope into a liveable urban neighbourhood. Many hours have been spent in collective work sessions, so-called *faenas*: flattening terrain for construction of houses and roads, digging ditches and placing plastic tubes for running water, formulating petitions to authorities, among other things.

For people on the margins of the city, urban life is linked to hard work converting dry mountainous landscape into liveable space, and this process of accommodation requires material reordering as well as engagement in political dynamics. This mode of urbanization can be described through the term 'pressure', understood as a physical quality of water, as well as a particular socio-political engagement with local political authorities. The settlers in Primero de Junio tell the history of building their neighbourhood as a story of hardship, struggle and suffering. Again and again you hear complaints about the political authorities, for abandoning the "*pueblos*". Public services such as water, sanitation and asphalting of streets are obtained through good relations with people working in the local and regional governments – and through protests, marches – making demands on the governments or the mining company.

It takes physical pressure for the water to flow uphill, and it takes socio-political *pressure* on the political infrastructure for the neighbours to make the authorities respond to their demands for basic services. As one leader of AUPA, one of the largest organizations of urban dwellers, explains:

We work for the development of the marginal neighbourhoods. We organize the people, organize protests and public marches to make demands on the authorities, and make them finance water and sewage projects. There is a lot of internal fighting, but we have one common objective: to develop our neighbourhoods. If we don't push, it won't come out.[12]

Public water tap in urban neighbourhood in the making, on the slopes of the volcano Chachani.

LIVING WITH ENVIRONMENTAL CHANGE

Dwellers from the margins of the city marching in the centre of Arequipa to claim access to water and sewerage.

Isabel pushing her daily ration of water uphill.

Primero de Junio is one of many so-called *pueblos jóvenes* [young villages], within the city of Arequipa. According to statistics, more than 25 per cent of the urban population of close to one million are immigrants. Since the 1960s, an increasing migrant population has been adding to the city, transforming the irregular terrain around Arequipa into an urban landscape, developing new neighbourhoods with the necessities of water, electricity and other services. The city is expanding outwards and upwards, and most *pueblos jóvenes* are situated on volcano slopes or in very arid areas.

The topography in and around the city of Arequipa is characterized by verticality; three volcanoes embrace the city, pointing towards the high Andean ridge, making up a landscape of steep slopes and inclines. Populated settlements span between altitudes of 2,100 to 3,000 metres above sea level. This vertical and irregular landscape has implications for the flow of water, the construction of houses and for the development of social life.

The historical and present challenge of Arequipa, and especially of its growth, has been to get enough water to the city in order to expand the frontiers for agriculture, the population and industry. Apart from the obvious needs of the population, water is essential for the production of electricity, for agriculture, tourism, and the mining industry. The rainy season spans from December to March, the rest of the year is sunny and dry, which makes the capacity to store huge volumes of water pivotal. Water reaches the city via the Chili River that springs hundreds of kilometres away in the high Andes, above 4,400 metres of altitude. Arequipa's waters come from few sources. Rainwater is captured in the glaciers or swampy areas in the highlands, and is stored and regulated in one grand hydraulic system: five dams, rivers and canal connections in the highlands, from where water is regulated and released to reach its functional destinations in the city via the Chili River. In the city, water is used, after which it is again led into the river, to treatment plants, stored as oxidation ponds, or sinking into the subsoil where it continues travelling towards the Pacific Ocean. The urban metabolism[13] is thus highly dependent on ecology and hydrological processes far beyond the frontiers of the city, which complicates any strict separation of rural and urban life and landscape.

[12] Anand, N. 2011. Pressure: The PoliTechnics of Water Supply in Mumbai, *Cultural Anthropology*, 26(4): 542–561.

[13] Gandy, M. Rethinking urban metabolism: water, space and the modern city, *City: Analysis of Urban Trends, Culture, Theory, Policy, Action*, 8(3) (2004): 363–379.

Settlers in a marginal neighbourhood fixing water infrastructure in a collective work session.

Neighbourhood built by newcomers. Vertical topography shapes urban life in Arequipa.

In Primero de Junio, the water coming out of the tap is produced in the treatment plant, La Tomilla, situated about 5 kilometres down the Chachani volcano. From La Tomilla, water is pumped 300 metres of altitude up the volcano slope, travelling and being distributed via pipelines, reservoirs, and valves to many urban neighbourhoods and settlers. Some get water 24 hours a day, directly to their houses, but further uphill, water pressure drops, the pipes leading to homes get fewer, and in the most upper and recent urbanizations, water flow ends in collective and public water taps.

From Primero de Junio, looking uphill, you can see the construction of a new drinking water treatment plant, less than 1 kilometre away. Every morning, loads of cement, workers, water, and materials for construction are transported through the recently paved road of Primero de Junio, going to the construction site of the new treatment plant. With this monument emerging in the proximate landscape, hopes and expectations of a better water-situation are nourished among the neighbours of Primero de Junio. As Señora Isabel says: "We are waiting for La Tomilla 2 to be finished soon, so that water can flow directly to our homes, 24 hours a day." Señora Isabel is president of the Water Committee of Primero de Junio. Isabel's combined home and store is where neighbours pay for their monthly water service and where problems with the *pileta* or the water are reported. "Our main need is running water," Isabel states; "that is basic in order to be able to lead a life in dignity."

Verticality characterizes the Arequipan landscape; it shapes the direction and force of water flows as gravity pulls water down. At the same time, verticality also characterizes social relations within the city; living high on the volcano slope, on the margins of the urban centre, means living in a position of social disadvantage, since public services require pressure to move uphill.

DREAMS, WATER AND THE REMODELLING OF PLACE

In Greenland, the town of Maniitsoq finds itself located on an island with characteristic mountains, which are said to resemble a cake sprinkled with sugar. That is one explanation of its Danish name *Sukkertoppen* (Sugar Loaf Mountain). Historically, the location of Maniitsoq has made it a prosperous place where the marine environment for fishing and whaling influenced the dynamics of social life and the modelling of place. Today, the town is turning its attention to new water potentialities in the form of hydroelectricity and large-scale industries. It is not only a new dream but also a new landscape that has to be modelled.

The location made it the most dynamic fishing town in Greenland for decades, and people from other communities moved to Maniitsoq to partake in the fishing activities. In the words of a former factory production leader: "it was an adventure". Everyone in town tells stories about the fisheries booms and how fishing made the town what it is. Cod made the town rich, and in turn the richness of the sea furnished dreams of the good life. In the season, inhabitants worked in shifts at the factory and the fishing and processing activities were the nerve of community life. In the heyday of fishing in the 1970s and 1980s, the factory could employ 500–600 people on a daily basis. All-year access to an ice-free harbour combined with intensive remodelling by blasting the stony hills close to town turned the place into an expanding centre. The landscape had to be shaped to create the appropriate space for the fishing industry and the increasing population of the town. Economic and social dreams were carved out in the landscape to set the stage for their materialization.

Innovative social institutions were also modelled. As women pursued factory work, they lobbied hard politically to set up child-care institutions in order to have someone to look after their kids while they were working. This women's movement was central to the establishment of daytime nurseries all over Greenland. Furthermore, the richness of marine resources during the 1930s made investments in boats and hunting cabins possible, and people started to travel to the surrounding landscape to relax from work, to hunt musk oxen and caribou or to fish. Dreams about the good life fuelled by the felicitous riches of the sea thus manifested itself in social, economic and cultural activities expanding into the natural environment that more and more was included in the urban rhythms and identity strategies.

Large areas outside town, having until then served as hunting and fishing grounds for a group of occupational hunters and fishermen, were appropriated by the expanding population as a recreational landscape. During peak hours, the boat traffic back and forth to the ever-increasing number of cabins

Abandoned complexes constructed in the 1960s to boost urbanization in Maniitsoq.

LIVING WITH ENVIRONMENTAL CHANGE

turned the seascape into intense traffic corridors. The increasing population also accelerated these processes and put extra stress on the environment.

Since its establishment in 1782, the town has expanded and the population increased to 3,197 in 1991, where it peaked. In the 1950s and 1960s, urbanization and modernization strategies were actively implemented and as part of this process, large housing blocks were constructed in Maniitsoq in order to facilitate the concentration of the population. Also, the town's rich marine environment and perfect location were actively used by national planners in their design of a new urban landscape for Greenland more generally. Small places were to be closed down and the Greenlandic population to be concentrated in a few urban centres. For the Danish planners this would not only boost the efficiency of the welfare system, but also be the decisive step in bringing modernity to Greenland. Despite Maniitsoq's microscopic size compared to many towns in the world, it was certainly a place for big dreams. The town's dynamics not only depended on the environment, but turned the environment into a social landscape of a certain character. Furthermore, the social landscape was entangled in scaled-up ambitions by planners and firmly embedded in the creation of a national modern economy based on fishing.

However, the dreams were shattered when the fish stock collapsed. Apart from the crash in the fish stock, the fishing sector overheated due to overcapacity triggered by massive investments. Since the end of the 1980s, the sector has been undergoing a process of structural rationalization, which has resulted in the reduction of jobs and vessels as well as new ways of regulating the fisheries. Over the years, the town's population has decreased and many Maniitsormiut (inhabitants of Maniitsoq) are concerned that this decrease and the ensuing brain drain have brought the town to a critical point where it becomes difficult to maintain town dynamics. The stories told of Maniitsoq

elsewhere in Greenland have 'boring' or 'dead' as their leitmotif. Still, Maniitsormiut feel strongly about Maniitsoq and the prominent position it has had in the history of Greenland, even as they look at their town as 'an old woman in retirement'. Now, important businesses and institutions have closed down and moved to bigger towns in order to improve efficiency, it is argued. The big Royal Greenland fish factory has closed, and fishing is now pursued by only a few professionals who have restricted opportunities to sell their catch. The town has changed and turned into a shadow of itself. Maniitsoq is thus experiencing the boom and bust economy so often encountered in the Arctic.

Today, Maniitsormiut are devoted to the creation and construction of new contexts for thinking about their town, the surrounding landscape and its place in Greenland and the world. Due to new and thorough evaluations of the waterway accessibility of the island, the seafront potentialities for a large harbour complex, its closeness to water resources fit for hydroelectric power, and the access to freshwater, among other things, Maniitsoq has been chosen as a location for a planned construction of an aluminium smelter. It is going to be one of the biggest private investments in Denmark ever, and will require large-scale demolition of the

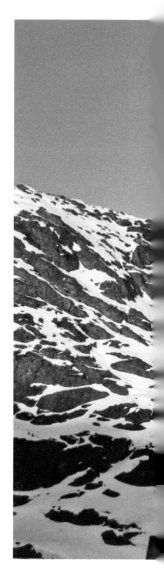

Few fishing vessels remain in Maniitsoq after the closure of the factory

An aluminum smelter is expected to transform the urban landscape of Maniitsoq.

Outsiders often imagine Maniitsoq as a place where life stands still.

rocky landscape, the construction of large-scale water dams and the establishment of a new part of town in order to house all the workers and their families. Maniitsormiuts' new ambitions made possible by the water affordances of the town's surroundings and driven by narratives of progress, wealth, global and national positioning have reawakened the town and initiated a new attitude to the national environment which now has to be remodelled and reshaped to fit the dream.

In the midst of all this, rumour has it that the cod has returned.

STRATEGIC THINKING
CHANGEABLE USAGES OF THE NIGERIAN LANDSCAPE

Farmers in the remote villages face increasing population pressure and difficult livelihood conditions.

Tropical dry lands are difficult to exploit for agricultural purposes; yet, people still live and survive in the desert fringe and cultivate crops that partly or entirely cover their daily need for food.

The cultivation potential in places such as the Sahelian region in West Africa is mainly influenced by the amount and distribution of rainfall. Through generations farmers have developed fine-tuned strategies for using different parts of the landscape under different rainfall regimes. In this way they have strived to get the best possible outcome given the rainfall conditions that prevail at a given point in time.

The remote and harsh environment around the small provincial town of Goudoumaria provides a compelling example of local people's ability to manoeuvre. The traditional land use systems in the region are 'typically Sahelian'. They consist of two, more or less, interconnected components: (1) subsistence peasants, permanently settled in villages, who mainly cultivate millet in the lower lying parts of the landscape (which they call *bas-fonds* in French) or in the dune landscape and supplement this activity with livestock rearing; and (2) migrating pastoralists passing through the region with their herds. The agriculturalists living in the villages are primarily Manga people, but some of the Peul pastoralists in the region have also become sedentary in recent times and have cultivated millet since the severe droughts of the 1970s.

Rainfall is scarce and it is highly variable in time and space in the Sahel. With an order of magnitude of around 300 mm per year as an average precipitation, the potential for rain-fed agriculture is confined to a very limited range of drought-tolerant crops (predominantly millet, sorghum, and cowpeas).

The landscape in south-eastern Niger is dominated by large dunes originating from periods that were drier than the present times. Depressions (*bas-fonds*) in the contemporary landscape originate from a hydrological network functioning some 20,000–40,000 years ago when the climate was wetter and the groundwater level was much higher. In subsequent drier periods, wind erosion deepened parts of the valley system and created approximately 200 small oases (called *cuvettes* in French). Hence, the landscape is mainly composed of these three landscape units: the dune, the *bas-fonds* and the *cuvettes*. The geomorphological history has significant implications for the suitability of the landscape units for present-day agriculture. Soils on the dunes are coarse and poor in organic matter while soils in the *bas-fonds* are superimposed upon clayey sand. Finally, the *cuvette* soils are advantaged by their proximity to the groundwater table.

The farmers are very conscious of their choice of field location. It is dynamic and strategic and reflects their deliberate intent to get the best possible outcome for their efforts on the basis of a deep-seated knowledge of the landscape. If they anticipate drier conditions than average, they will prioritize cultivation on the coarse sandy soils on the dunes. In fact, this is a wise choice. Soil scientists know that such soils contain more water, which is accessible for the plants, as compared to more loamy soils, if the total amount of soil water is limited. In years with more abundant rains, the local farmers will, on the other hand, give priority to fields

LIVING WITH ENVIRONMENTAL CHANGE

located in the *bas-fonds*. Their loamy soils give a higher yield if water is not in very short supply.

In other words, the field patterns are constantly shifting between the different landscape units, following the best possible judgement by the farmers when they anticipate the rainfall conditions in the coming agricultural season. Needless to say, the farmers' predictions are not always correct in the highly variable climate of the Sahel. It often happens that the experience from last year is extrapolated into the next season. After a dry year, farmers will be more eager to expand fields on the dune landscape, whereas the cultivation in the *bas-fonds* will be intensified after years of abundant rain. If their expectation is wrong, it will, of course, have adverse implications for their outcome. For example, a number of farmers have tried to expand their cultivation with sesame since a successful harvest in the rainy year of 2010. The following year was, however, dry, and the sesame harvest could not live up to the raised expectations.

The important additional agricultural potential provided by the *cuvettes* constitutes a unique feature for this specific region as compared to other similar dry lands in the Sahel. The *cuvettes* are used for the cultivation of cereals and vegetables. On a year-to-year scale, the dynamics of land use strategies are not as prominent as described for the dune and *bas-fonds* landscapes. But on a longer time scale, the *cuvette* fields have had very different importance for the local agricultural production. In the early 1900s, some villages were almost exclusively cultivating in the *cuvettes*, which were highly productive at that time. These fields satisfied most of

The poorly performing millet fields are mainly located in the valley system crossing through the dune landscape.

Small oases are a unique feature in the SE-Niger landscape

Small motor pumps enable irrigation and support intensification of the horticulture in the oases.

14 Reenberg, A., Maman, I. and Oksen, P. Twenty years of land use and livelihood changes in SE-Niger: obsolete and short-sighted adaptation to climatic and demographic pressures? *Journal of Arid Environments* 94 (2013): 47–58.

the local needs for cereals and vegetables at the time. Moreover, the *cuvette* was home to a very important production of date palms, which were a major source of export and cash income for the local people. Later in the century, the groundwater level lowered and the fields and the palms lost their productivity. Cultivation of cereals shifted to the surrounding landscape units and the *cuvettes* became mainly a place for horticulture, now supported by irrigation from local wells. Nowadays, the *cuvettes* are still an appreciated resource. Projects have introduced motor pumps as a means to accelerate the exploitation of groundwater resources to improve the intensive horticulture production. There is, however, a serious local concern about the durability of the groundwater resources. Local farmers consistently

report that the groundwater level is lowering, and that the long-term perspectives for the irrigated *cuvette* cultivation are gloomy.[14]

Even if small-scale farmers are able to read the landscape and adjust their practices to the ever-changing environment, they may be facing a major crisis about which they cannot do much. If the groundwater resources are constantly dwindling, their current livelihood strategies are not viable over a longer time perspective.

LANDSCAPES OF DROUGHTS AND FLOODS ON THE DESERT MARGINS

The Sahelian landscapes in Northern Burkina Faso consist mainly of two land use types: cultivated fields that provide food for the population, and grazing areas, which generate fodder for the livestock. Other land use types such as forested land and urban areas are not common in this area where people reside in small huts that are scattered throughout the landscape. This specific landscape of fields and pastures is most often associated with droughts and harsh conditions for humans and livestock.

When the Great Sahelian Droughts hit the region in the 1970s and the 1980s, dead cattle scattered throughout the landscape and sparse millet fields were a common sight at that time. Still, the Sahelian landscapes seem to invoke such images, and not entirely without merit.

The cultivated fields still look very poor, provide low yields, and only pearl millet, sorghum and cowpeas can be grown. Likewise, herders with their meagre livestock are seen in the landscape as they conglomerate around pastures hoping to find fodder although grazing resources are extremely sparse. The picture of a landscape dominated by droughts and sparse resources has indeed

persisted in the region since the Great Sahelian Droughts,[15] and villagers have to make a living on the sparse resources of the milieu they inhabit, even if the situation has improved somewhat since the 1970s and 1980s.

The Sahelian landscape is, however, increasingly being exposed to new climatic extremes. Many parts of the Sahel experienced, for example, extensive flooding in the 2000s as a result of unusually heavy rains. While it is the landscape of droughts featured by the sparse millet fields and the limited grazing resources, the flooding events are also readable in a landscape where they left a mark of severe destruction. In

Mare d'Yomboli in Northern Burkina Faso suffered from drought in 2009 due to a very bad rainy season.

LIVING WITH ENVIRONMENTAL CHANGE

A granary close to Mare d'Yomboli still standing despite severe flooding.

Granaries close to Mare d'Yomboli collapsed due to severe flooding in 2010.

Lack of water in the intermittent lake Mare d'Yomboli, Northern Burkina Faso

LANDSCAPE

the village of Yomboli, located in Northern Burkina Faso, a flooding event in August 2010 was especially conspicuous, when I visited the place in the last months of 2010. Fields were damaged and granaries had collapsed. Most of the ruined fields and granaries were located very close to Mare d'Yomboli, an intermittent lake, and with the heavy rains Mare d'Yomboli had exceeded its bounds; heavy rainfall and water from the lake flooded the landscape. This destruction meant that villagers lost most of their food stocks, both the stored food stocks and the crops they were about to harvest. As the planting season was in May and June, and the heavy rains began in August, re-planting was not an option.

While a landscape of droughts, low millet yields, sparse grazing resources and dead cattle was somehow a known landscape, a landscape with flooding events seemed incomprehensible for the villagers, despite the recent history of floods. This was reflected in the way villagers responded to the flooding events. They had earlier learned from agricultural extension officers who work for government departments with the aim of educating and assisting farmers that they should relocate some of their fields from a large sand dune to the areas close to Mare d'Yomboli. While millet cultivated on the large sand dune would be most resistant to droughts, this relocation of fields was a way of adapting to years with just adequate rainfall. The millet fields close to Mare d'Yomboli were assumed to be more productive in the years with adequate rainfall, but at the same time they also had the highest risk of production failure in very dry years. Having fields at both locations was thereby seen as a strategy to reduce crop failure. Villagers were also taught to build granaries close to the new fields by Mare d'Yomboli in order to save time on transport. With granaries located next to the new fields, they would avoid transporting the harvest back to the large sand dune where the granaries used to be. Considerations on the risk of flooding from Mare d'Yomboli were clearly

not incorporated into these new strategies, neither by the agricultural extension officers nor by the villagers.

The strong emphasis on droughts and sparse resources had, however, severe consequences in the village of Yomboli. With the fields and granaries being very close to Mare d'Yomboli, the villagers were partially accustomed to Mare d'Yomboli overflowing. Yet, rather than beginning to think about the risk of flooding, villagers continued to focus upon drought instead of flooding. They argued that they based their decisions on what they had learned from the agricultural extension officers as well as the memory of the severe droughts like the ones that hit the region in the 1970s and 1980s. When they were to rebuild their granaries, they therefore chose to build them at the exact same location – very close to Mare d'Yomboli, and the ruined fields by Mare d'Yomboli were re-established as well.

This made it clear that the villagers had always lived in a landscape of droughts and sparse resources, and despite the recent flooding events they continued to do so, or in other words "any landscape is composed not only of what lies before our eyes but what lies within our heads".[16] However, even though the area was hit by severe droughts in the past decades, and droughts therefore were a major concern, disregarding the possibility of new flooding events seems problematic. This is especially due to the uncertainty of the future climate projections for the Sahel, as there is no consensus among climate models as to whether extremely dry or extremely wet seasons are likely to be most common.

Taking the recent history of floods and the disagreement between climate models into account, one could argue that a landscape of both droughts and floods will constitute the Sahel in the future, and that villagers eventually will have to adjust to both.

[15] Tschakert, P., Sagoe, R., Ofori-Darko, G., and Codjoe, S. Floods in the Sahel: an analysis of anomalies, memory, and anticipatory learning, *Climatic Change*, 103(2010): 471–502.

[16] Meinig, D.W. The beholding eye: ten versions of the same scene, *Landscape Architecture*, 66 (1) (1976): 47–54.

A LANDSCAPE OF ICE

When joining a walrus hunting party and setting out on dog sledge one day in early May 2010, I was soon to relive my previous experiences of wayfaring in the Arctic landscape of north-west Greenland.

Once out on the sea ice, I was once again immersed in the distinct emotional topography of the North. The expansiveness of the world within which the sledge moved conveyed a sense of unlimited potential in a world without bounds. At the same time it reminded me of the insignificance of humans in this particular landscape, with no human-made structures within sight, apart from the sledge.

Wayfaring in a deep-frozen region is very much a matter of weaving a strand of movement into the apparent stillness of the world. The dogs and the sledges leave their unmistakable impressions on the ground – at least when the snow has newly fallen or the route is just opening up for passage due to changed ice conditions or other natural changes. With time, these impressions may turn into trails, for as long as the distant hunting ground is within reach and deemed worth the journey; or until the ice breaks up and destroys the trail, and with it the goal.

In the trip related here, our party set off at a time when the sea ice still allowed a passage, while the water had also opened up within a day's reach. This permitted potential access to walrus at the ice edge, which was now only about eight hours away. This was the actual time it took us to get there, but not one that could be pre-established, except in very general terms – between six and ten hours was the estimation when I asked beforehand. It was not so much a matter of uncertainty about the geographical distance; the hunters knew where they were going, but they could never know how the ice, snow, and wind would affect the pace of the dogs.

The decisive element in the conditions for our movement was the actual quality of the sea ice; one could argue that the ice itself became an actor in our progress. At a more comprehensive level, in the High Arctic communities, like the one I have come to know, the world itself is constituted with the ice, which is most often a strong presence under one's feet and on the horizon. The ice is a forceful argument in any story, any journey, and any vision of the future. With the changing climate, the constitutive power of the ice is degenerating. This goes for the sense of the Arctic in the general understanding, including the natural scientific views of the Arctic meltdown, and no less in the practical knowledge of people who have navigated the ice for generations. For

View from sledge en route.

The hunter on his sledge
embodies the icy landscape.

Hunters and dogs taking a
break during a seal-hunt in the
mighty landscape.

LIVING WITH ENVIRONMENTAL CHANGE

the hunters, the most important part of their landscape and their natural resources is increasingly inaccessible. They have always lived with great weather variability and shifting hunting luck, but in recent years, the magnitude of the changes and the unpredictability of the landscape transcend previous experiences. In the springtime, and more specifically at the time of the hunting expedition, in which I participated, the sea ice now changes more rapidly and more unpredictably than before. The landscape is increasingly susceptible to new forces of temperature and wind, and the boundary between the open water and the solid ice is much messier in both time and space.

The hunters knew that the closer we got to the ice edge, the more fragile the sea ice would be, and the more attentiveness would be demanded for the driving. While the sea ice was in some way a known territory, it was also a shifty partner in the progress of the party. *Knowing* the way certainly implied an astute "sensitivity to cues in the environment and a greater capacity to respond to these cues with judgement and precision".[17] Usually, I was told, the edge would have been much further away at this time of year, but over the past ten years the sea had opened up earlier and at a greater pace, and the hunting grounds for walrus had come within easier reach even from our village. The drawback was that access to the islands further away, where multitudes of birds were just arriving from the south to nest, had become more difficult.

Wayfaring by sledge in this specific landscape means immersing oneself in a world of ice, wind, and weather, and also of past and present opportunities. This makes any abstract time measure, such as hours, recede from consciousness, and progress becomes a matter of navigating and circum-navigating topographical obstacles. The goal was the hunt, not a particular point on the map. It was to take place at the ice edge, from where the hunters could reach the marine mammals in the open patch of the sea. As I sat there on the sledge, I realized

how much of the hunters' life is actually predicated by the ice, and how fine-grained their knowledge of the sea ice has to be for them to survive, and how eminent their reasoning about the elusive landscape is.[18] I became increasingly preoccupied with reading the driver 'over his shoulder', trying to second-guess the significance of the small topographical cues, that even I perceived, and which were to multiply with time. In other words, giving in to the experience of wayfaring and a sense of becoming part of the place, taught me that sledging is not so much a matter of moving *upon* the ground as making one's way *within* a comprehensive world of ice, weather, and wind.

An airborne view of the barren and icy landscape of the High Arctic.

Troubled passage.

Tracks made by sledges may
turn into real trails towards the
ice edge at particular times;
view towards Herbert Island.

In the region, where movement depends on dog sledges, the traces left stand out as lines in the snow. As footprints of human (and animal) movement they are far from permanent, however; the snow and the ice are likely to have either melted or been re-covered before the next movement. Yet, the cover is stable enough in certain periods for the ephemeral impression of the singular sledge to become one of many. A trail will emerge, as indicated above, but in a landscape of ice, these are as elusive as the ice itself.

On detailed topographical maps of northern Greenland, 'sledge roads' are sometimes featured. These are of a different kind than the trails, because they are always on land, where glaciers allow passage over headlands or peninsulas on sledge. By being roads, and not simply paths, they have a more permanent nature. One might even argue that they, like other roads, are engineered – if not intentionally by people of the present,

[17] Ingold, T. Footprints through the Weatherworld: walking, breathing, knowing, in *The Objects of Evidence: Anthropological Approaches to the Production of Knowledge.* Special issue of the *Journal of the Royal Anthropological Institute,* (2008): 121–139.

[18] Hastrup, K. Anticipation on thin ice: diagrammatic reasoning among Arctic hunters, in K. Hastrup and M. Skrydstrup (eds) *Anticipating Nature: The Social Life of Climate Models* (London: Routledge, 2013),pp. 77–99.

then incidentally through the long history of geological formation. The sledge roads follow the curves and openings between rocks and glaciers. They are used mainly though not exclusively, when the sea ice has become impassable, and the dog drivers have to choose an alternative route over land.

Roads are secondary to the paths, and with summer both will eventually become impassable; actually the passages across or along glaciers are increasingly closing down for all of the year due to rapid melt-off and surface destruction. Thus, even if footprints and sledge roads belong to different seasons and involve each their distinct temporalities, in the Arctic both features of the landscape are now increasingly ephemeral. Under the present siege of global summering, both geological and social times are changing. The perceived stillness of the world is shattering. If the ice is an argument, it certainly remains so even while withdrawing.

WALKING ALONG WATER

Grasslands known as the *puna*
traversed by the channel.

Steep slopes, white peaks and deep valleys make up the Andes. As phenomenologists of landscape have told us, different people have different landscapes.[19] By moving across the terrain, walking along, we might get a sense of how this has been carved out by the movement of wind and water, tectonics and people.

The steep slopes of the Peruvian Andes are criss-crossed with irrigation channels. Some have histories that can be traced back to the times of the Incas, others are of much more recent date. Be their histories as they may, irrigation channels are still absolutely vital for many families in the harsh climate of the highlands. In an area where the year is divided into a rainy and a dry season, irrigation channels secure a steady flow of water onto the fields of potatoes, wheat and a great variety of other tubers, cereals and legumes.

But irrigation channels are not givens in the landscape: they are human-made, contested ditches that allow waters to move across the landscape in defiance of its natural features. To understand how the water moves across – and inscribes itself into – the landscape, one way is to walk along the channel, to grasp the complexities, not only of the natural terrain but also of the social terrain that the water traverses.

It is part of a phenomenological understanding of the landscape that it is by being within it, and exploring it along with those people whose landscape we wish to understand, that the sense of the landscape emerges. Walking along with others is to share the bodily engagement, and incorporate their rhythms of movement; it sharpens the awareness of being in a landscape that is, by its very definition, a social production of the environment. As we walk along, we share the same social space, the same visual field, and we exchange impressions and experiences.[20] We see that the map is, indeed, not the territory.

One day I went uphill with Don Seferino. We drove by car, a taxi hired in the nearest small town, until we reached the shores of Lake Querococha. Behind the lake I could see the lowest parts of the glacier known as Yanamarey, a glacier that has been widely studied due to its relative accessibility and all too rapid retreat. This lake – and ultimately this glacier – are the source of water for the channel that brings water to the fields of Don Seferino and his fellow villagers. I had come up here with Don Seferino here so that we could walk back along the channel. Back in the village I had noticed that only little water came down from the lake, and now standing at its source I was hoping to understand why.

Don Seferino is a practical man, who earns his living not only from farming but mainly from performing basic veterinarian tasks. On this morning when there was still a

The intake constructed in 1996 bears the name of the then president Fujimori.

Walking past *puna* households that depend on the irrigation water for human consumption.

crust of ice on the silent waters in ponds and puddles, Don Seferino took out a razor blade and castrated a young donkey, charging around five US$ for the services that would help the family living there to keep their young *burro* from making too much trouble. After that, we walked down to the river and found the intake of the irrigation channel.

From there, we began to walk along the waters in the channel. Walking along conveys a tactile sense of the terrain, not only sharing the visual and auditory experiences with Don Seferino, but also the gentle gradient of the flow of water. Every now and then I would ask Don Seferino to explain to me how these water bodies had come into being. Only the first part of the channel was of an older date, and Don Seferino remembers

how it was to work the dry soils with pick-axes to make water reach the villages.

The first part of the channel runs along steep slopes, and following its course is an act of balancing, where Don Seferino and I must constantly cross the narrow waters of the channels in search of a foothold. But then the channel enters a curve, and the terrain flattens. From here it is a gentle gradient with ample space on each side of the channel. We can see the white peaks of the Cordillera Blanca to the East, but towards the West it is as if the vast highland grass area known as the *puna* merges with that on the opposite side of the valley. It is, as if there were no valley. That is what it is like to move about in the mountains: the landscape constantly changes, the horizon is never stable.

[19] Bender, B. Time and landscape, *Current Anthropology*, 43, Supplement: Repertoires of Timekeeping in Anthropology (Aug.–Oct.) (2002): S103–S112.

[20] Lee, J. and Ingold, T. Fieldwork on Foot: Perceiving, Routing, Socializing, in S. Coleman and P. Collins (eds) *Locating the Field: Space, Place and Context in Anthropology* (Oxford: Berg, 2006), pp. 67–85.

[21] Scott, J. *The Art of Not Being Governed: An Anarchist History of Upland Southeast Asia* (New Haven, CT: Yale University Press, 2009).

Moving across the Andes one senses that which James Scott calls the friction of the terrain.[21] A distance, which on the map may appear to be but a stone's throw away, may in reality require much effort and time. When one enquires into the distance, a measurement of kilometres or miles makes little sense. Instead, time is the appropriate answer; Don Seferino did not tell me how many kilometres we would have to walk, but for how long a time.

We reach places where people live only during part of the year. These families are newcomers to the area; only after the territorial re-orderings that followed the agrarian reforms in the 1970s did the land become accessible to them. They are using water from the channel without being legitimate users. The terrain is roughly the same as before the agrarian reform – even

before the conquest of the Spaniards – but the social configurations of the territories constantly shift. New boundaries are drawn that the water must cross, allowing some to take advantage of the flow of the water while excluding others.

Getting to know a flow of water is no easy task. As it moves across the terrain it traverses natural and social boundaries. Interviews, documents, meetings: all these political forms and artefacts are part of what I came to know as the channel. But it was from moving along the waters – here with Don Seferino – that I got a tactile, embodied sense of the landscape so intimately connected to the flow of water. The movement of the water is not only formed by the landscape; the opposite is equally true, water flows have a formative power in natural and social landscapes.

Don Seferino balancing on the concrete that lines the first part.

Don Seferino castrates a young donkey with a disposable razor blade.

LIVING WITH ENVIRONMENTAL CHANGE

OLD WATER, GARDENS AND PROPHETIC POWERS IN THE SAHEL

The gardens seen from the approaching side of the village.

Research into the relationship between social life and physical landscapes emphasizes the connectivity and inseparability of these two domains. Understanding social phenomena often depends upon understanding biophysical phenomena and vice versa. Maintaining a distinction between society and nature is therefore very difficult, if not impossible, and it has for some time now been argued that the social and the geographical are conflated in the experience of human beings.[22]

In the village of Biidi 2, located in the northernmost province of Burkina Faso, this conflation is clear as landscape features such as groundwater and gardens prop up the prophetic powers of the spirit of Modi Mawdo.

Biidi 2 is a small village with no sites of particular interest to outsiders, except the ruin of Modi Mawdo's mud brick hut and the lush gardens found nowhere else in this area. Modi Mawdo was a powerful Fulbe *Marabout* (Islamic religious leader), who left an unknown part of Mali some 130 years ago with a small group of slaves, the Rimaiibe, and blacksmiths, the Wahilbe, in search of better pastures. Walking south, they encountered another Fulbe *Marabout* who told Modi Mawdo about a place with 'old water' or 'a constant presence of water' which in Fulfulde, the language spoken by Modi Mawdo and his entourage, translate as *biidi*.

Despite the directions *biidi* was not easy to find. Modi Mawdo and his followers had to endure heat, sandstorms, cold nights and rely on the goodwill of others for food, water and shelter during their walk. After a couple of months the exhausted group finally found the site and Modi Mawdo immediately arranged for his slaves to construct huts for him and themselves; the village of Biidi 2 was established in this fashion. The settlers quickly took advantage of the groundwater and established gardens. Reached through small shallow wells found everywhere in the gardens a diverse array of fruit and vegetables watered with 'old' water were planted and the gardens have ever since constituted an important source of food and cash income for the villagers.

The presence of a reliable source of groundwater, and consequently, of lush gardens in the middle of the dry Sahelian landscape is nothing short of a miracle, according to the villagers, given the extremely dry northern Sahel, where readily available groundwater is not easy to find. What Modi Mawdo did gave him prophetic status as far away as northern Nigeria and Senegal and more and more visitors from such places arrive each year to visit the ruin of Modi Mawdo's mud hut. The ruin is by no means spectacular and hence the visitors do not come to marvel at its beauty, rather they go to the ruin because his spirit is said to reside there and it is this spirit the visitors hope to encounter.

Modi Mawdo's spirit, it is said, can make dreams come true and the pilgrims come to whisper their innermost desires, hoping Modi Mawdo will listen and help guide them to 'groundwater' as well. If finding a reliable water source is possible in northern Sahel, surely, the pilgrims hope and reason, sorting out quotidian marriage troubles, heartaches, sickness and failing crops is not too much to ask of Modi Mawdo's spirit.

That Modi Mawdo's spirit listens is testified to by various 'success stories'. Letters from previous pilgrims and other 'documentations' of his prophetic powers are often pulled out, relayed and discussed when pilgrims arrive in the village. The pilgrims themselves also offer success stories adding weight to the prophetic powers residing in the old mud hut. It is not uncommon to hear stories of healed uncles in Mali, well-married sisters in Niger, or bountiful harvests in northern Nigeria after a visit to the ruin.

Modi Mawdo's spirit apparently makes dreams come true and this is of course a major reason behind the increasing amount of visitors each year. Yet there is little doubt that Modi Mawdo's fame is also connected to the physical landscape of 'old' water and the gardens this makes possible. The villagers

Layya watering his aubergine plants with 'old' water.

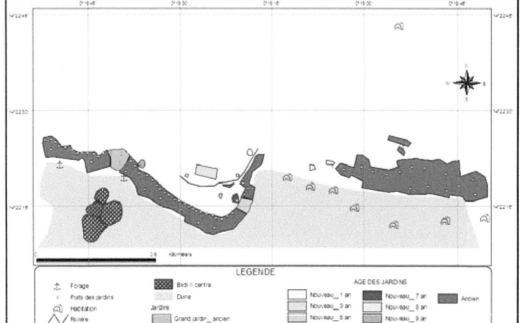

JARDINS DE BIIDI II

LEGENDE

The location of gardens in Biidi 2. The map also shows the wells, 'puits des jardins'.

The ruin of Modi Mawdo's
mud hut.

22 Hastrup. K. Social anthropology: towards a pragmatic
enlightenment? *Social Anthropology*, 13 (2005): 133–149;
Hirsch, E. and O'Hanlon, M.
(eds) *The Anthropology of
Landscape: Perspectives of
Place and Space* (Oxford: Oxford University Press, 1995).

of Biidi 2 often make this point when trying
to explain why people from faraway places
come to visit. The main caretaker of the
ruin, an old Rimaiibe man, put it like this:

> Modi Mawdo's powers are visible to all.
> They are unquestionable. When you
> turn off the road to Djibo and begin
> walking towards Biidi 2, you can see the
> gardens from 10 kilometres away. The
> pilgrims see green, they see big trees,
> they see, I think, hope in the middle of
> the dry sandy coloured *collade* (savan-
> nah). They see something they can't
> believe they are seeing. They are ready
> to believe in the powers of Modi Mawdo.
> When they go home, they tell their
> relatives about the wondrous sight of the
> gardens in Biidi 2.

Prophecy, in this case, consists in an expansion of the idea of potentiality of water in a
landscape dominated by drought.

CAN YOU SEE CLIMATE CHANGE IN A CHANGING ENVIRONMENT?

Two fisherwomen, Mama and Moana, a group of kids and me are heading to Koromiri, an islet in Muri lagoon on Rarotonga's eastern side. It is low tide and perfect for an excursion to the reef, when we take off in a new dugout canoe built by a group of men in the community.

During my fieldwork on environmental changes in this area, many people have pointed to these women for their intimate knowledge of the lagoon. They go out there whenever they can in order to harvest various sea-shells and edible seaweeds. With reef-shoes on, careful not to get stung by thorny sea urchins, we wade to the reef through shallow areas. When we reach the seaside of the fringing reef, the surf is impressive with high waves breaking into foam.

The reef looks grey and dead. Decades ago seaweed grew on it, and more corals were alive. According to the fisherwomen, it has never been a really colourful reef with many different corals and seaweeds. Nevertheless, marine biological reports have documented spells of coral bleaching, high nutrient levels, and extensive damage to the reef by both explosives and certain invasive species.

We notice new small coral heads, and we can see starfish, trochus, urchins, sea cucumbers and small schools of baby parrotfish. The lagoon fish are not edible. Their flesh is contaminated with a toxin stemming from coral, algae and seaweed. If consumed, it causes severe gastrointestinal and neurological symptoms known as the fish poisoning Ciguatera. It is widely discussed locally and in the expert literature whether the toxin is caused by pollution or fluctuates with long-term processes in the great ocean. We are laughingly told that the fish poisoning

may turn out to be a good thing; the fish stock may get time to recover from periods of overfishing

We collect trochus, an imported cone-shaped sea snail, and float them in a plastic canoe to the islet in order to open and clean them. The lazy method is to use a hammer, and the better one is to break a hole in one trochus by hammering the sharp end of another trochus into the side of it. Then you press the snail's entrails out through the hole, wash the shell in the seawater and blow out the snail. At a later stage, the snails are prepared for a community function, probably marinated with lemon and seasoned with herbs and greens.

Further down the beach, large turned-over ironwood trees with exposed roots bear witness to a swirl of cyclones that battered the island in 2005. According to aerial photos, the islet is slowly moving northward, so the erosion due to the cyclones and the storms is not necessarily resulting in a smaller island, but simply shifting the sand around.

The five cyclones shook the island and the islanders in several ways. Many islanders were indeed wondering whether the cyclones were caused by global warming. Assessments and reports from local and regional organizations working with disaster management, climate change, and environmental care certainly more than indicated that this was the case. In 2011, the situation

Muri village at the populated coastal plain in front of the rugged interior of Rarotonga rising to more than 600 metres.

LIVING WITH ENVIRONMENTAL CHANGE

changed once again. The general assessment by major regional scientific institutions now indicated that many Pacific islands would not experience more cyclones in the future, but that the cyclones generally would in all likelihood become more severe with higher wind intensities.[23]

Further up the beach there is a small clearing where large groups of tourists go picnicking after a cruise in a glass-bottomed boat. For people coming from overseas, it is a popular location for weddings too. On bright days, with flickering white sands, turquoise water, and waving coconut palms, many tourists claim that the lagoon looks like paradise. Some of the returning guests do, however, notice a declining water quality.

When we leave the islet and slowly approach the main island, smoke from the burning of leaves and garbage is rising at the back of the sailing club. About 2,000 people live in the Muri area, 15 establishments provide accommodation for tourists, and 300 pigs and 80 dogs add to the population[24] creating both a thriving community and a considerable amount of waste. Some of the liquid waste is entering the lagoon waters through streams and sewers.

Local residents and sailors often lament the deterioration of the lagoon: The water is not sparkling blue any more, the beach is eroding, the sand is getting murky, and during the hot summer, algae bloom is a returning problem. On the day of our little outing, however, the lagoon water seemed to be in a fairly good condition. I was told that this was due to the strong winds and high swells that flushed the whole area with fresh water from the ocean a few days earlier.

What were Mama and Moana's thoughts about climate change? Did they ascribe certain changes in the known landscape to climate in particular? They were not sure. They were sure, however, that the lagoon was changing all the time. They observed it every week. Sand spits were moving, certain stones exposed, vegetation and animal life waxed and waned. Stressing the constant changes in the landscape and in the ways islanders and tourists used the lagoon, they agreed with scientific assessments often stating that lagoons are highly dynamic environments.

Here, on a small island in a great ocean, everybody seems also to agree that there is no single, fixed and firm points of reference from which you can determine the ongoing changes. It takes multiple and meticulous observations to assemble even a rough overview. This is an ongoing process and the conclusions concerning the impact of global warming are not definitive yet. From

[23] Australian Bureau of Meteorology and Commonwealth Scientific and Industrial Research Organization (CSIRO) *Climate Change in the Pacific: Scientific Assessment and New Research, Country Report, Cook Islands* (2011).

[24] Hermann, T. *Muri Water and Sanitation Project: Final Completion Report* (Cook Islands: Hermann Consultants, 2011).

[25] SEAFRAME. *The South Pacific Sea Level and Climate Monitoring Project. Sea Level Data Summary Report, July 2010–June 2011.* Available at: http://www.bom.gov.au/pacificsealevel/index.shtml.

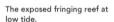
The exposed fringing reef at low tide.

advanced measurements it is known that the sea level is rising at a faster pace than a few decades ago, 4 mm a year, which is assessed to be a doubling compared to the previous decade,[25] but the consequences do not appear quite clear yet. Now, many more assessments have been undertaken, and the expectation is that in order to produce stable results, measurements must run over several years, often several decades.

On our trip, we had a great day. We were guided into new areas of the lagoon, shown dozens of species of marine life, and Mama and Moana shared delicious foods and detailed observations with us all along. More importantly, perhaps, they shared their

insight into a landscape with no definite landmarks. Thus, we did not 'see' climate change as if the landscape was an object, or a singular organism with definite markers of the changing climate. Many interacting movements are presently creating a surplus of reference points in sands, reefs, currents, marine animals, islets, and people. However, this may change with a rising sea level as a decisive driver.

Working with the trochus.

Café and sailing club in the late afternoon. Smoke from the burning of waste.

LIVING WITH ENVIRONMENTAL CHANGE

MENTAL
TOPOGRAPHIES

I am sitting at one of the outdoor tables at *Comme Ci,
Comme Ça*, one of the nicer places where it is possible
to get food and a cold beer in Bolgatanga, the regional
capital of the Upper East Region, Ghana.

Aidland has its own mental topographies, languages of discourse, lore and custom, and approaches to organizational knowledge and learning.[26]

I have just met Thomas, a well-respected local development practitioner. Bolgatanga is in many ways 'NGO country' – or a so-called *Aidland* – in the sense that development and humanitarian organizations play a very extensive and dominating role in this part of Ghana. The landscape is filled with obvious reminders of these organizations' presence such as the billboards that line the roads proclaiming various development projects and stating the missions and visions of local and international NGOs. Less obvious reminders include new varieties of (donated) seed, growing in geometrically shaped agricultural fields – measured out during NGO-led "farmer field schools."

Even more subtle reminders of the strong presence of the development sector is the development language that has been picked up by local development practitioners and has become prominent in the billboards cluttering the surrounding landscape, as well as in the 'mental topographies' of the local practitioners. I am meeting Thomas today

to talk to him about recent flooding that came with such severity and extremity that it is being linked to climate change. Models predict that it will happen again. The 'resilience' of the local population – their ability to bounce back with each new wave of flooding – is therefore apparently becoming a pressing concern. At least the concept of resilience, emanating from the development sector, is becoming increasingly incorporated into the local practitioners' mental topographies. Resilience is one of the topics I wish to discuss with Thomas.

Thomas tells me about how his organization, a local NGO, has worked closely with communities that were inundated by water during the flooding. When I ask Thomas about how he would define the concept of resilience, he states:

A situation where the community may be confronted with challenges and yet they are able to spring back, they are able to regenerate themselves. They are prepared in a manner that, "Yes, we know this can happen to us, but when this happens, we know what to do to continue to survive," that's how I understand it.

While the mental topographies of development aim for regularized order, pigs roaming freely serve as a reminder of a different local order onto which development models are grafted.

LIVING WITH ENVIRONMENTAL CHANGE

At NGO-led farmer field schools, farmers learn to measure out geometrically shaped fields.

In disaster management there has been a change in emphasis from reducing local vulnerability to building local resilience, which in some ways reflects an ongoing concern to make development policy and practice more participatory. The notion of vulnerability has been criticized for potentially reducing recipients to passive victims.[27] By focusing on the capacities of the local populations affected by disaster, the concept of resilience, by contrast, has the potential to acknowledge and incorporate local agency and this is often believed to be done best through participatory methods.[28] In other words, it could be argued that depending on which concepts are used, the local population is approached in different ways within disaster management. According to Thomas, however, new terms and old terms that originate in *Aidland*, should all be taken with a grain of salt. This becomes apparent when I ask Thomas whether resilience is a new term:

Well, personally, I have come across it for quite a long time. It has been in the

Billboards using development language and promoting NGOs are seen throughout the landscape. The billboards signal the strong presence of the development sector.

system, people who do the kind of work that I do, cannot fail to come across it. It's just that some of these technical jargons in development are used maybe for the sake of making yourself relevant, you know, to be able to get the needed attention and resources, because if you don't use them, you don't get the support. But as a matter of fact, *how they do it* is often questionable. For instance, many people are talking of participation. I am very sceptical about anybody talking about participation. Big international NGOs preach it, talk of people's rights. They say, "You must participate

26 Apthorpe, R. Coda: with Alice in Aidland: a seriously satirical allegory, in D. Mosse (ed.) *Adventures in Aidland: The Anthropology of Professionals in International Development* (Oxford: Berghahn Books, 2011), pp. 199–220 [p. 199].

27 Wisner, B., Blaikie, P., Cannon, T. and Davis, I. *At Risk: Natural Hazards, People's Vulnerability, and Disasters* (London: Routledge, 2004).

28 Editorial, *Participatory Learning and Action: Community-based Adaptation to Climate Change*, 60 (2009): 3–8.

29 Mosse, D. *Cultivating Development: An Ethnography of Aid Policy and Practice* (London: Pluto Press, 2005), pp. 4–5.

30 Bierschenk, T., Elwert, G. and Kohnert, D. The long-term effects of development aid: empirical studies in rural West Africa, *Economics*, 47(1) (1993): 83–111 [p. 83].

31 Mosse, *Cultivating Development*, 2005, p. 7.

in the development of whatever project that you are going to be involved in," and then they talk of participatory monitoring, participatory planning, participatory whatever. But when you go and you start to work with them, you soon realize that no, they come up with their own ideas ready-made. Then they get you into a meeting, they talk, talk, talk small. Show you a PowerPoint: "This is what you must do." Where is the participation?

The conversation I am having with Thomas mirrors similar discussions in the literature on international development. A widespread donor and development practitioner response to accusations of their domination of the local has been to embrace participatory methods. These methods have in turn been highly criticized, with critics contending that participatory policy

does not reverse or modify development's hegemony so much as provide more effective instruments with which to extend technocratic control or advance

external interests and agendas while further concealing the agency of outsiders, or the manipulations of more local elites, behind the beguiling rhetoric of 'people's control'.[29]

Seen in this light, Thomas is concerned that resilience may be yet another empty concept like 'participation'.

If participation is just by informing me and letting me know that this is it, then that for me is not participation. Participation means I must contribute to determining the agenda, to decide on what I want to do, and what I don't want to do. So it may be the same with 'resilience'. Because today climate change has become a big issue. Everywhere people are talking of climate change and people are definitely going to be using a word like resilience and say: "Our project is going to be contributing to community resilience", but if you ask, how is it happening, you won't find it.

Although the local people in northern Ghana are heavily influenced by international development policy and practice, they do not necessarily passively embrace development's mental topographies. There is no doubt truth in the critical "view that development aid is simply 'grafted' onto the essential structural characteristics of historical and contemporaneous African societies …"[30] One could turn this critique around, however, and argue instead that if the "local trees" are responsive to such grafting, this is often because the local population can see various possibilities in utilizing the fruit from the branches; "while 'beneficiaries' … may consent to dominant models – using the authorized scripts given them by projects – they make of them something quite different".[31] Thus, local mental topographies may be ripe with trees onto which international development concepts have been grafted. But their fruits are also consumed locally.

The agenda for a farmer field school meeting.

NOMADIC LANDSCAPES AND EPHEMERAL RESOURCES

Located on the fringe between the Saharan and the Sahelian climatic sector, arid south-eastern Mauritania is conditioned by a single rainy season marked by immense inter-annual variation. The annual precipitation is generally less than 250 mm, with many areas receiving below 100 mm. Due to the tropical trade winds, the dry season extends for approximately nine months between mid-October and mid-July, and the short rainy season runs from mid-July to mid-October. Lack of rain during the rainy season rapidly translates into a temporary degradation of pastures and thus a demand for movement on the part of the nomadic pastoralists inhabiting this landscape.

From an ecological viewpoint, large parts of the Sahel and Sahara can be distinguished as 'non-equilibrium' or 'disequilibrium' environments, characterized by extreme seasonal variations in the availability and location of natural resources such as pastures and water. Such areas are dynamic and influenced by change and fluidity, rather than by predictable variation. This inevitably calls for extraordinary flexibility and mobility by the nomadic pastoralists.

Mohamed Salem, a nomadic herdsman belonging to a faction of the Hamonat tribal confederation dispersed across the south-eastern part of Mauritania, was out herding his goats with his youngest son in the pastoral zone known as Teyarett. The pastures were all but entirely dried out, and all surface water had evaporated by now. It was February 2012, and under 'normal' conditions, water and pastures would still be available in this area. But this year was different. Rain had been absent the previous rainy season (*el khrif*), and it was getting hotter and the next dry season (*seyf*) was fast approaching. Mohamed was worried. That same evening, a lonely herdsman approached Mohamed Salem's tent. The man was out looking for some of his camels, who had been missing for several weeks. In his efforts to locate them, he had been all the way to *Timbedghra*, some 130 kilometres due east. He was told that animals bearing his mark had been sighted in this direction, and

Mohamed preparing the camels before taking them to pasture in the pastoral zone of Teyarett in Hodh el Gharbi. Mauritania, February 2012.

Mahmoud and Ishmael, two nomadic herdsmen from the Kunta tribe in the Tâgant region of central Mauritania, January 2004.

Ahmed, a nomadic herdsman, traversing the dunes of Ouarane in the Adrar region of Mauritania, April 2001.

now he was enquiring in the encampments around this area. Mohamed confirmed that he had seen a small group of camels with this distinct mark, and started to describe their appearance in remarkable detail.

Mohamed: One of them was dead, a female with a long, spotted neck. I saw them near M'deike some days ago. They looked tired.

Visitor: And what about 'Tamourt de Goungel'? Have you seen anything there? Is the water good there?

The man was referring to an area close by, renowned for its fertile soil and sweet groundwater.

Mohamed: Hundreds of animals are fighting over water there – but I haven't seen animals looking like the ones you describe. None bearing your mark. I tell you, there is nothing but trouble here these days … You should ask the others here in the camp whether they have seen anything. Their animals are pasturing to the southwest.

The two men continued to exchange information, up-dating each other with details about what was going on in the area. The main topic was the heightened pressure on the wells and how this was handled practically. Mohamed argued that in any case it would only get worse, and the only way to go about it was to respect each other. Discussions about the weather also featured prominently along with accounts of where and how people moved in the landscape. Because the lives of herders like Mohamed were predicated upon climate, pastures and water, these topics consistently emerged and were scrutinized endlessly. Only by sharing knowledge, debating possible future scenarios, and identifying the movements of herders and animals in the area could sustainable navigation and collective resource exploitation be ensured.

Mohamed: Usually, we spend the rainy season and the cold season here, pasturing in the 'Teyarett' [some 100 kilometres east] where pastures are plentiful. Last year we managed, but over the last five months it has become very dry. I have to take the camels to 'Zilt' [17 kilometres south] because that is the only place where there are still some pastures and not too many other herds.

Visitor: It is the same everywhere. Between here and Timbedghra everybody I have met complains that the pastures are much drier. It hasn't rained anywhere. Tell me, how is the situation at 'Hasi Ahmady'? [The nearest well] How is the water there?

Mohamed: The water is good, but too much waiting time. Too many herds. We will bring our animals tomorrow but it may take long before we can draw water. More people will be coming in the next months, for sure. They know there is water even at this time.

Among the nomadic pastoralists inhabiting south-eastern Mauritania, a question such as '*how is the water here?*' is standard inventory in most conversations. Questions about water, its quality, quantity, frequency and distribution are never mere environmental questions in the ecological sense, but reveal crucial information on the social and political features of a given landscape. By probing into water issues, the individual herder may obtain detailed insights into how water is managed and by whom in a given area at a specific point in time. Understanding these aspects are pivotal to the nomadic pastoralists, and through what might initially appear as simple conversations, the herders engage in a constant updating of complex information, which they subsequently process through a sort of modelling practice enabling them to make informed decisions about where, when and how to move. Anything but impulsive, the intricate trajectories of the various herders and groups are shaped through an elaborate calculation of human

Detail of map of the region of Hodh ech Chargui in south-eastern Mauritania.

32 Deleuze, G. and Guattari, F. *A Thousand Plateaus: Capitalism and Schizophrenia* (trans. B. Massumi) (London: Continuum, 2004).

33 Ingold, T. *The Perception of the Environment: Essays on Livelihood, Dwelling and Skill* (London: Routledge, 2000), p. 53.

34 Pedersen, M.A. At home away from homes: navigating the Taiga in Northern Mongolia, in P. Kirby (ed.) *Boundless Worlds: An Anthropological Approach to Movement* (Oxford: Berghahn Books, 2009), pp. 135–152.

35 Retaille, D. Concepts du nomadisme et nomadisation des concepts, in R. Knafou (ed.) *La planète 'nomade'* (Paris: Éditions Belin, 1998), pp. 37–57.

Nomadic pastoralists of the Hamonat tribe draw water at the well of Ain al-Argoub outside Oualata in Hodh ech Chargui region of Mauritania, May 2001.

and non-human elements, constantly repositioning themselves in relation to each other in time and space.

From their particular perspective, which consistently prioritizes the nomadic over the sedentary landscape, the philosophers Gilles Deleuze and Félix Guattari have conceptualized what they call '*espace nomade*' (nomadic space).[32] In the nomadic space, flows and distributions, the vectors, acquire predominance over points and centres, the singularities. This understanding corresponds with Tim Ingold's discussion of Pintupi perceptions of the Australian landscape, in which he argues that the landscape is "not so much a continuous surface as a topologically ordered network of places, each marked by some physical feature, and the paths connecting them".[33]

What appears from such investigations of what may be collectively called 'the nomadic landscape'[34] is a type of landscape that is organized in relation to centres within it, some of which are less stable than others,

rather than in relationship to boundaries and private landownership. This results in a fluid space, which never finds a final form, because of the many directions taken within it. The notion of a 'fluid' nomadic landscape is attractive to the analysis of social life in south-eastern Mauritania, inhabited and constructed by nomadic groups, which indeed operate through the distribution of animals in an open space or in an ecological environment.

Such an environment is characterized by an ephemeral topography, and by what has been called a 'space of circulation', pointing out how living in dry-lands characterized by scarcity of natural resources demands mobility, i.e. circulation.[35] In order to exploit the scarce and fleeting resources, water and pastures, the nomadic pastoralists must move, and this movement is inscribed within their socio-political organization.

LIVING WITH ENVIRONMENTAL CHANGE

MIRRORING

In Biidi 2, a village in Burkina Faso, and Arequipa, a city in Peru, climate change wisdom 'sits in places'.[36]

ICONS OF CLIMATE CHANGE
MIRRORING THE SAHEL AND THE ANDES

For people living there, as elsewhere, a place, be it a path on the savannah, large stones, shady meadows or, and as we shall explore here, volcanic mountains and watering holes, quite simply *is*. Places are natural and straightforward and they have always been so. The thought that such places might be complicated, interesting or even threatened does generally not cross people's minds until the places are transformed.

When this happens, a sense of physical and social dislocation occurs. People in the two locations mirrored below, these days feel somehow less at home in their world than they used to. The physical landscape no longer gives the same meaning to their pragmatic activities and their social, conceptual and perceptual understandings. Being *Arequipeños* is not as easy when Misti, the emblematic volcano of the city, is without snow. Nor is being *Fulani* if the herds can no longer find drinking water.

With respect to having 'a sense of place', or to feel at home in the world, changes to the landscapes and to particular places within them potentially matter a great deal not only for our material lives but also our social lives.[37] People use well-known landscapes and places as reference points when it comes to assessing the impact, pace, and truth of changes including climatic ones. In this text, we mirror Biidi 2 and Arequipa through such markers of climate change that present themselves in each context, as a way to compare how people experience change in climate over time and how these changes challenge particular identities tied to the places that are undergoing change.

A distance of approximately 8300 kilometres separates the two localities, Biidi 2 is located at latitude 14.0607° N and Arequipa at latitude 16.4176° S. The distance from each locality to the equator is similar, and both localities are placed in landscapes bordering a desert, Biidi 2 in the Sahel and Arequipa at the Northern limit of the Atacama Desert. It is therefore not surprising that in both places the lack of water and its observable consequences in the landscape create a sense of social and existential uncertainty.

Chili River flowing through landscape of cultivated fields. Volcanoes Misti and Chachani covered by clouds.

The river that runs just below the village of Biidi 2

LIVING WITH ENVIRONMENTAL CHANGE

Woman and boy watching the Chili River under the volcano Misti.

Cattle drinking from the sandy river at the end of the rainy season.

DARKENING PEAKS

In Arequipa, there seems to be a general agreement among people that the weather and the climate have changed. Most people point towards the emblematic volcano Misti when asked to explain and prove these changes; they lament that Misti hardly ever wears his white poncho any more. Misti used to be white to his feet all year long, but now only the very top is covered with snow, and this only during the rainy season.

The three volcanoes, Misti, Chachani and Picchupicchu, are crucial for life in the valley where Arequipa is placed, since they generate special hydrological conditions. Without these volcanoes, the Arequipa landscape would be all desert, like its surroundings. In this particular hydrological cycle, the volcanoes used to serve as natural water storage, gathering snow on their peaks during the rainy season, which would melt during the dry season, making water run through creeks and rivers, and filter into the soil and feed the aquifers. Now, with little storage of snow on the volcanoes, the cycle has shifted, and the dynamics of storage and availability have changed dramatically. Instead of melting water running freely from the peaks, dams have been built in the highlands for water storage. Water availability is prolonged, yet the concrete constructions in the highlands are too far away to see, and are not linked to the self-understanding of a courageous and tempered people.

Like other places in Peru and in tropical regions with mountain glaciers, the 'darkening peaks' around Arequipa act as both symbols and evidence of climatic changes.[38] Misti, Chachani and Picchupicchu stand out in the urban landscape and can be seen from almost everywhere in the city. Señor Misti is evoked in poems, songs, and demonstrations. For some he is a significant *Apu*, a holy mountain; for others, he is the fiancé of the female city of Arequipa. He is said to be the reason for the characteristic strong temper of the people of Arequipa: "not for nothing is one born at the feet of a volcano".

Five child mummies have been found in his crater, witnessing the respect with which the Incas engaged with the Apu. Misti marks the landscape as well as the history, identity and temper of *arequipeños*. Thus, the missing snow on Misti is linked with the feeling of a loss of identity among *arequipeños*, as well as an uncertainty in relation to future water availability.

When asking people in Arequipa about the changes in climate they have experienced, most people mention that the rain has changed over the past four decades. They say it rains less now and that less water is available as a consequence. Other changes mentioned are a growing unpredictability of the seasons, increasing temperatures (cold and warm), and sudden weather shifts. Winds are experienced to be more or less the same as in a remembered past, yet since many roads have become asphalted, less sand is carried by the wind, and changes of winds are thus associated with urbanization rather than climatic changes.

In contrast to the village of Biidi 2, discussed below, Arequipa is an urbanized landscape, the city is expanding, and the physical 'landscape' is continuously transformed. People who have lived there for several decades recall a very different city: fewer cars, less contamination, and more cultivated fields within and around the city. While the urban landscape keeps changing, the three volcanoes that embrace the city used to represent certain continuity. Yet, with their 'darkening peaks', the volcanoes, especially Misti, become indicators and proof of changes not necessarily linked to the growing city but to a globally changing climate.

Shallow watering hole for cattle.

Isabel and her neighbours fetching water from a public water tap.

LIVING WITH ENVIRONMENTAL CHANGE

Regulated flow of water streaming through the Chili River.

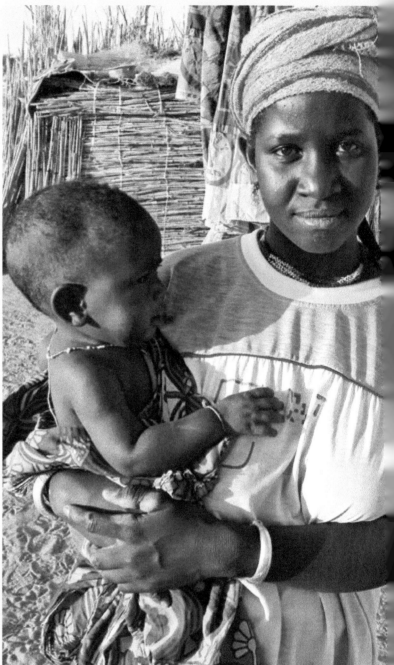
Fulbe living on the savannah get some of their drinking water from watering holes and rivers.

MOVING SANDS

Biidi 2 is not surrounded by majestic volcanoes like Arequipa – nor much else for that matter. The people living there have no dominant reference point, or marker of change in the landscape, to which they refer when trying to explain how the droughts have impacted their lives since they hit in the early 1970s. Yet the landscape is full of smaller 'markers' that serve well enough to demonstrate both to themselves and to strangers that something has changed.

The village is located on a dune system and surrounded by a flat savannah. On this the villagers have their fields and they graze their cattle. The cattle are watered from riverbeds or other indentions in the ground. But these are slowly but surely becoming less reliable sources of drinking water. Less rain has been falling since the early 1970s, but, and as is mentioned on numerous occasions, the less rain is not really the problem. Rather, it is the sand and the wind that cause trouble.

The wind and the problems associated with it are mentioned by farmers across the Sahel as a major climate change-related problem.[39] In Biidi 2, the wind is perceived to have become stronger during both the rainy and dry seasons and the storms to last longer. This is problematic for a number of reasons but the main problem is that the storms and strong winds pick up loose sand.

The loose sand is moved around and "ends there," says Mamadou while pointing towards a riverbed where his cattle are drinking water. Moving across the landscape during the storms, the sand eventually settles in indentions in the ground. This fills them up. When walking into the riverbed this becomes evident. Lots of loose sand is present and Mamadou explains how each year the riverbed becomes increasingly shallow. This has two consequences. First, evaporation of water into the air due to hot temperatures and sunlight quickens in shallow water pools. Second, Mamadou continues, less water collects here during the rainy season. Hence, "Our cattle have less water to drink during the long dry season."

Picking up a handful of loose sand and letting it run through his rough hands, Mamadou explains how he has lost cattle due to thirst. This puts him in a very precarious situation, as a large share of his income is dependent upon the sale of cattle at the market. The money earned via this sale is used to buy food. "I cannot produce enough millet to feed my family due to the poor rain," he continues, "and therefore I have to buy it."

The moving sand also challenges a central aspect of *Pulaaku* identity or 'being Fulani'. Being with the cattle on the savannah provides Fulani men and woman with freedom, solitude, and independence from the constraints of social life in the village. This is not only a personal desire, but also deemed necessary for the development of quintessential Fulani traits such as alertness, cunning, and endurance. To be and act Fulani, one must work and be with cattle on the savannah; ownership, knowledge, and love of cattle have always been used by Fulani as an ethnic marker setting them apart from their neighbouring groups.[40]

The diminishing watering holes, combined with ever increasing difficulties associated with transhumance (taking the cattle for relatively long treks to find pasture and water), makes it increasingly difficult to maintain the emphasis on such particular traits of 'Fulaniness' or *pulaade*. This is causing some anxiety among Fulani in Biidi 2 and as Mamdou put it, the moving sand in this way "makes our economic and cultural troubles clear".

LANDSCAPE AND SELF-PERCEPTION

By way of wrapping up, the two locations mirrored here remind us that social and geographical spaces are often conflated in experience. As Hastrup writes,[41] it is not possible to 'think away' the actual geographical location of social lives, as the materiality of the world and the actual space in which people dwell are not simply a background to but are integral parts of sociality. In Arequipa, landscape and identity are articulated in stories and understandings of the volcano Misti. If Misti changes, what does it mean to be *Arequipeño*? The loss of snow then is also a potential loss of a particularly grounded identity. In Biidi 2, the disappearance of watering holes due to loose sand initiates a similar process. The watering holes are used to water cattle, and cattle are important both financially and culturally in the village. Working with cattle is closely related to particular traits intimately connected to being Fulani. As in Arequipa, the changing landscape of northern Sahel challenges a particularly grounded sense of identity and place.

36 Basso, K.H. *Wisdom Sits in Places: Landscape and Language Among the Western Apache* (Albuquerque, NM: University of New Mexico Press, 1996).

37 Ingold, *Perception of the Environment*.

38 Orlove, B., Wiegandt, E. and Luckman, B.H. (eds) *Darkening Peaks: Glacier Retreat, Science, and Society* (Berkeley, CA: University of California Press, 2008).

39 Mertz, O., Mbow, C., Nielsen, J.Ø., Maiga, A., Diallo, D., Reenberg, A., and Diou, A. et al. Climate factors play a limited role for past adaptation strategies in West Africa, *Ecology and Society*, 15(4): Article 25 (2010). Available at: http://www.ecologyandsociety.org/vol15/iss4/art25/; Mertz, O., Mbow, C., Nielsen, J.Ø. et al. Adaptation strategies and climate vulnerability in the Sudano-Sahelian region of West Africa, *Atmospheric Science Letters*,12(1) (2011): 104–108.

40 Nielsen, J.Ø. and Reenberg, A. Cultural barriers to climate change adaptation: a case study from Northern Burkina Faso, *Global Environmental Change*, 20 (2010): 142–152.

41 Hastrup. K. Social anthropology: towards a pragmatic enlightenment? *Social Anthropology*, 13 (2005): 133–149.

TIME

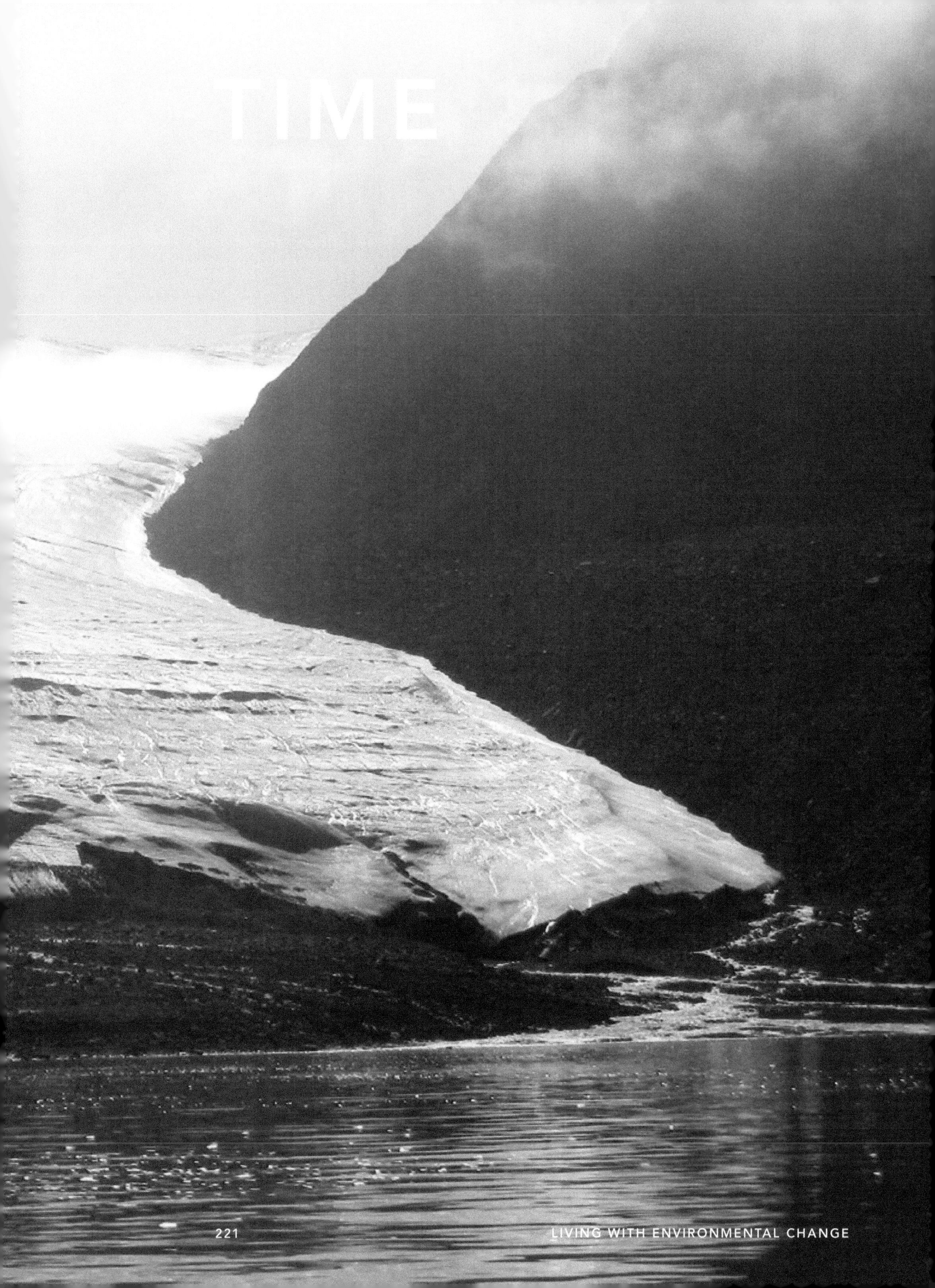

INTRODUCTION

The scientific notion of climate change is embedded in a long-term perspective based on measurements going back to former Ice Ages, and climate models making projections into the distant future. Most climate change scenarios are looking as far ahead as 2100, important data from ice sheets go as far back as 130,000 years, and glacial times are counted within millions of years. Only by considering a very extended time span is it possible to identify the changes and to determine their pace and nature.

Time takes on many shapes and qualities in changing environments.

In human history, such long-term perspectives are relatively new. The time span seems to have been stretched as an amazingly flexible elastic band. Not until the nineteenth century was the age of the Earth estimated to count millions of years. In modern scientific calculations the first living organisms date back several billion years, but at the same time it is nevertheless maintained by millions of people, often on a Biblical standing, that Earth is actually very young, about 6000 years.

Clearly, in a cultural perspective, whether the Earth is young or old, or the pace of time is fast or slow, is a relative question. More and more accurate time measurement devices have been developed, but experienced time unfolds within more flexible frames. People live in multiple time dimensions, and make up different past–present–future relations in and through their everyday activities.[1] In this part of the book, we concentrate on how seasonal rhythms, cosmologies, histories, collective and personal memories, and hopes are actually lived within multiple times.

When we embarked on our fieldwork in Asia, the Arctic, in West Africa, South America, and in the Pacific, we obviously crossed many time zones and settled down in new environments with shifting time sets. But not only was the time lag of two, six or 12 hours, the temporalities also changed during days of research. During one bout of fieldwork in the Arctic, it was dark all day and night, and completely opposite the next time, obviously changing everybody's life rhythm. It is part of fieldwork to observe and sense the different time sets and the shifting temporalities of the activities in which you participate and observe. Presently, 'climate change time' is entering the lived world, changing the established temporalities. Therefore, we will look into how time matters, not as something we can identify in the singular or as something-in-itself, but as qualities built into the experiences of a changing environment. In our research and particularly during fieldwork we have paid attention to how temporalities are intertwined with personal and collective experiences, and particular flows of knowledge and sentiments. Cosmologies and political visions are remoulded and redefined in accordance with new visions and anxieties for the future. Hopes are elastic too, both in terms of time and space: they may stretch out to the next few minutes, to the future of one's grandchildren, or include the ultimate fate of the entire human community. Thus, time is more than an abstract quantitative scale for measurement. Time is malleable, it takes on many shapes and qualities for people living in different and changing social and natural environments. In this sense, we may say that time is relative; it unfolds in the relations between living things and their environment.

To perceive the landscape of towns, hillsides and coasts may simultaneously be an act of remembrance and an anticipation of the future. Living in an environment is a question of timing, where the social patterning resonates with the different temporalities in the world.[2] Hunters of the Arctic must register the brief change of light and colour in the white landscape in order to identify the stray polar bear, whereas the harvest and distribution of fish from the Pacific Ocean and asparagus from Peru may organize people and transportation in networks over long periods of time. Nomads walk and camp according to the rhythm of the herds' need for water and green pastures, just as hunters and planters have to know their time. The tides

LIVING WITH ENVIRONMENTAL CHANGE

Even as a tool for measurement and comparison, time is not neutral; it depends on the scale and the way it is used.

orient fishing activities, and calendars are organized with returning events and orchestrate the pulse of collective events. Changing temperatures in soil and water speed up or slow down life processes.

Bearing in mind that people's time perceptions differ in various ways, depending on whether they make their rounds with a herd in the desert or sit in front of four computer screens in the stock market, the introduction to scenarios of climate change will for most people set up an unusually distant future horizon. Such an extension of time puts a pressure on the imagination of the changed landscapes and lifeworlds, and the introduction of the grand time scheme of climate change does not happen without redefinition, coordination and sometimes even clashes and confrontation. It may hurt to be confronted with a new kind of future and even with a new era, such as the Anthropocene. New futures evidently bump and slide into established temporalities, and change the destinations.

LINEAR TIME AND OTHER TIME DIMENSIONS

Linear time is the standard time for most people today. This is at least what we tend to think, and calendars, of which the Gregorian calendar is the most widely used, are organized according to the succession of hours and days. In the observations of a changing environment, time is instrumentalized through barometers, radiometers, boreholes, thermometers, and thousands of other instruments and methods by which change is determined at the appropriate time scales. Projections run within certain periods of time. 2050 scenarios are compared to 2100 scenarios. Monitors are put up all over the globe and the results are coordinated and discussed in scientific communities. Results from the melting glaciers are regularly adjusted; new findings of melting events in different eras are presented and thus contribute to new projections. When we have observed exemplars of time technologies physically in the field or in people's stories, we have paused, scratched a note, or documented it with a camera, and asked around more widely: What do you notice here? Does it fit well with the measurements? Sometimes the locals' observations are remarkably different from what the technological time machines measure; at other times a glance at a mountain top or on a reef can say exactly the same as data meticulously collected over decades.

The linear time frame may have become standard almost all over the world with the distribution of watches and the linear organization and coordination of societal practices. Nevertheless, we often bump or slide into other actualizations of duration.[3] Different durations may compete and curiously intermix and carry particular emotions: circular, fast, expanding, generational, optimistic, or awaiting. Different past–present–future relations are embedded in plans and strategies, and in myths and histories and the endless examples of narratives that embrace both myth and history.

Time *is* multiple. In the Pacific, 'island time' is often laughingly referred to when outsiders have lost patience with a time stretching into indeterminacy. Metropolises and peripheries

The future, even the far future, is not necessarily distant; it permeates the present in people's plans, strategies, fears, hopes and desires.

have different rhythms, and even at a personal scale most people do actualize different temporalities during the day – and night. Other experiences of time than the linear kind, where time's arrow points irreversibly forward, are enacted in everyday life and may even in some situation dominate, at least temporarily. The simple fact that we need watches in order to catch the train or make it to a meeting confirms that we sense other kinds of duration than the clock time. The ontology of time, whether there *is* a fixed, objective standard time or only a conglomerate of temporalities (or something in between), is still a long-standing discussion in the philosophy of time. Anthropologically, we note that studies from different locations in the world abound in temporalities, and that people experience them very realistically; the actualization of, say, the past in the present may be a quite ordinary occurrence.

Compared to the linear dimension of time, coming from the past and irreversibly pointing to a future ahead of you, Maori conceptions, to mention one example, follow other lines of direction. According to Jørgen Prytz-Johansen, in pre-colonial times, the Maori had no abstract word for time, and no technical word for year; they regularly placed the past in front of the human body and the future behind the present position. Parallel to many other cases found all over the world, years were not counted, whereas generations and other important periods were named and counted. Among Maori, says Prytz-Johansen, time was "qualitative", every day had "its own character, its individual stamp" and was created by actions. By repeating actions of the ancestors, one might call up the past.[4] Thus, time did not disappear. The Maori actualization of time was recursive rather than unidirectional. As Anne Salmond has put it: in the Maori case, time may be thought of as a spiral invoking the rhythms of the cosmos, returning to the source and alternating between opposed, yet interacting qualities and elements. "Winds, planets, the ocean, animals, plants and people – alternate between gift giving, amity and union, and quarrelling, enmity and exclusion, working towards equilibrium."[5]

Maybe Maori time is not so unfamiliar if we scratch a bit of the surface of our own watch time and think about speed and slowness, recursive rhythms and returning events in our lives. Seasons are incorporated in our rhythms of work and intervals of rest, and many activities resonate with the rhythm of light and darkness and weather conditions. It is not surprising that weather forecasts are so popular!

Qualitatively, diverse time dimensions are embedded in cultural practice throughout the world in the interactions unfolding between people and environments.[6] In some landscapes the paths of the ancestors are inscribed and valued, and occasionally re-enacted in celebrations and rituals. New grand-scale projects are designed in temporary models, negotiated and eventually dropped or implemented. Old ruins or barely visible signs of early settlements are excavated and preserved, others are flooded and forgotten. Access to certain areas is restricted in certain periods of time due to nature conservation, and fishing quotas and temporal bans put limits to fishing activities.

Curiously, temporalities are enveloped everywhere. Archaeologists carve their way downwards through layers of sedimentations and civilizations. Thus, in archaeological temporalities the 'oldest pasts' are usually found in the deepest layers. Tropical forests hide beneath the ice

In times of climate change, time changes too; moments, temporalities, intervals and lengths of times are reconfigured.

cap in Greenland, but incidentally the deep time may also turn out to be placed in the highest surface layers. Due to geological faults, older layers, and fossils of long-disappeared sea animals may be found in mountain tops, as noticed by herders in the high Andean mountains. Temporalities are thus at play everywhere, often incorporated and unnoticed in everyday living, and only brought to the attention when new circumstances reconfigure a certain practice. A new climate change scenario may redefine everything from national politics to local guidelines for water management.

Anthropologically speaking, we would claim too, that different temporalities whether linear, spiralling or layered are contemporary, and therefore also most likely mixed in diverse complex versions. The aim of this part of the book is not to untangle the different temporalities and present them in their singularity, but quite the contrary to present cases and situations where environmental and climatic changes, whether observed or imagined, reconfigure lived moments and conceptions of time.

A MEASURE OF TIME

People living in changing environments employ diverse means of measurement embedded in dissimilar time dimensions when trying to grasp on-going changes. Whether the geese have arrived weeks too early or not can be decided by consulting one's detailed and well-kept log book or a verbal almanac, and whether the rain falls too late may be determined by referring to one's intimate experiences in an environment or to exact meteorological measurements through decades. In both cases, discrepancies are often found, and they are not necessarily easy to mediate.

If change is a temporal phenomenon, climate change is absolutely so; and if time is a flexible and complex notion, then the ways of observing the changing environment are ever so. Types of measuring and evaluating time are constantly compared, discussed and contested. Quantitative measurements of sea level rise as 'millimetres per year' or of water flow in irrigation canals as 'litres per second' may or may not be in harmony with the fisherman's or planter's understanding. That physical conditions such as evaporation (making irrigation less effective) or storms (by rearranging coastal environments) influence the judgement, is perhaps straightforward to most, but questions of types of measuring, and thus of timing, are also often subtle parts of the judgement. Using one's boat as a measuring rod, comparing how deep the keel goes now compared to 20 years ago in order to judge the depth of the water does not necessarily confirm the absolute and objective measurements of a rising sea. In the meantime, tons of sand may have filled up a lagoon, making it shallower, and thus removed any firm point of reference.

In climate change discourses time is stretched from the far past to the far future; in between, people have many presents to deal with.

[1] Munn, N. The Cultural Anthropology of Time: A Critical Essay, *Annual Review of Anthropology*, 21 (1992): 93–123.

[2] Ingold, T. The Temporality of the Landscape, in T. Ingold, *The Perception of the Environment: Essays in Livelihood, Dwelling and Skill* (London: Routledge, 2000), pp. 189–208.

[3] Hodges, M. Rethinking time's arrow: Bergson, Deleuze and the anthropology of time, *Anthropological Theory*, 8 (2008): 399–429.

[4] Prytz-Johansen, J. The Maori and his religion in its non-ritualistic aspects, *Hau: Classics of Ethnographic Theory Series* ([1954] 2012). Available at: www.haujournal.org.

[5] Salmond, A. Ontological quarrels: Indigeneity, exclusion and citizenship in a relational world, *Anthropological Theory*, 12 (2012): 115–141.

[6] James, W. and Mills, D. Introduction: From Representations to Action in the Flow of Time, in W. James and D. Mills (eds) *The Qualities of Time. Anthropological Approaches* (Oxford: Berg, 2005), pp. 1–18.

As shown throughout this book, unstable amounts or cases of ill-timed water may be decisive for pastures, animals or drinking water resources. Moreover, it is shown how environmental changes also resonate with deeper bodily temporalities in various ways. When experiencing the Andean mountains on foot or the Arctic sea-ice on a sledge, even slight changes in the environment may collide with established rhythms and may change expectations of the future radically.

Even as a timely tool for measurement and comparison, time is not neutral. It depends on the scale and the way it is used. This goes for both the measurements of environmental changes and the measuring of people's actions. With the proliferation of climate change discussions, scientific results and methods, political initiatives, possible schedules for mitigation and adaptation initiatives are naturally discussed by many parties. New forums are created and new identities are enacted by the stakeholders. We now find an established catalogue of more or less positive and negative predicates within the climate change field such as alarmists, deniers, sceptics, eco-warriors, careless ignorants, frontline researchers, and innovative entrepreneurs. Implicitly, the predicates indicate different temporalities.

Given the many temporalities with which climate change time intermingles in metropolises and peripheries, and in the multiplicity of landscapes found on the planet, a standard climate change paradigm will take more than time to take root all over the place. Yet already, the scenarios of the far future are not only installing a point in the distant, faraway future. The far future also permeates the present in diverse plans, strategies, fears, hopes, and desires, at least implicitly.

GLACIAL TIME

In any landscape many times are at work, marking long-term histories of growth and depletion, more recent trajectories of movement and habitation, or new trails or canals made in response to environmental changes, to mention but a few examples. These times are at play simultaneously, and, depending on perspective, one or the other may take centre stage. In an Arctic landscape, the ice contributes to the scaling of time, in what seems to be a natural way. Glacial times may be constituted in different ways, and a good place to start is to go back to the nineteenth century, when a glacial theory was first proposed.

In 1837, the Swiss scientist Agassiz suggested that the entire northern hemisphere had once been covered in ice, of which the Alpine glaciers were remnants. At the same time, Swedish expeditions to Svalbard were able to ascertain that shellfish fossils found on mainland Scandinavia, still had living relatives in the icy ocean around the islands. On the strength of such empirical observations, the Ice Age was identified retrospectively. When Greenland was mapped in the early twentieth century, the Ice Age had become an established truth.

In 1916–18, a cartographic expedition was made to northern Greenland, where geologist Lauge Koch made important geo-morphological observations. He also made an interesting note on the Ice Age on his way North: "In Greenland, the ice has remained, one is still in the middle of the Ice Age, and travelling from South to North Greenland, is to experience the return of the Ice Age."[7]

Koch then guides the reader northwards and discusses the various landscapes in terms of their relative position in the history of an emerging ice age. Chapter by chapter, Koch takes new steps back in climate history, first experiencing the onset of the Ice Age, then its still firmer grip, until we reach it in full-blown form in the Thule region, where the ice covers almost everything. In this way, the ancient climate history was depicted in a contemporary space; cartography and the long story of the ice came together. When moving towards the pole, the traveller meets a distant past.

Since classical times, the poles were seen as lifeless points around which the Earth evolved; they constituted the *axis mundi*, which held the globe in place.[8] And they attracted explorers, who wanted to conquer the *terra incognita* covered by or consisting of ice, as old as the world itself, and one of the solids on its surface. Now, the solidity of the ice is increasingly cast into doubt. In northern Canada, Inuit observers have noted that, "the Earth is faster now".[9] By this poetic notion, they express their concerns about climate change, always more or less explicitly steeped in time. The frozen landscape is thawing at an increasing pace. Potentially, there will be no traces left of the Ice Age, although this seems almost impossible at present.

Glaciers are significant portents of this distant future, just as they became a sign of the past, when the Ice Age was invented, or acknowledged. Evidently, the Alps were

As the warming intensifies, new passages towards the Polar Sea open up – with both new threats and opportunities.

LIVING WITH ENVIRONMENTAL CHANGE

nearer at hand for European science, but an important contribution to knowledge about the untamed ice-tongues that licked the mountains actually came from Greenland, where Hinrich Rink studied the ice in the mid-nineteenth century. Rink's observations of both the icecap and the floating icebergs led him to conclude that glaciers were outlets from the icecap, under ever more pressure from each year's snow. He also identified the sub-glacial watercourses running under this ice, and

> was informed by the natives that this had always been a well-known fact to them. They say that the more abundant the supply of water, and the more violent its motion is in the streams of fresh water which takes the form of wells in the front of the glacier abutting the sea, the more effective will the glacier be in producing icebergs.[10]

Today the Greenlandic glaciers are more productive than ever in human memory, and just like people in Rink's time, the inhabitants of glacier-clad regions are closely observing their dynamics, because it affects their hunting grounds immensely, not to speak of the low-lying settlements and fishing places. The glaciers run off the slopes and burst into the sea at increasing pace, and their huge mass alters the mix between freshwater and seawater and changes the biotope in the process. Small wonder that the Earth may be perceived as faster under such conditions. Soot and micro-organisms colour the white tops, precipitating even more rapid meltdown. All of it contributes to a sense of a new beat of time – at best, irregular, at worst, destructive.

And like before, people living with the glaciers and listening to them hear nature's story about another time to come.[11] Accurate predictions cannot be made, neither by locals nor scientists, equally concerned about the future. It is worth remembering here that the observations we make on both past and future are always made here and now. Thus,

even though glacial time carries a heavy weight of ancient geological history and uncertain futures, the weight must be carried in the present.

Whenever we speak about climate, we invariably speak about time. Climate is an abstract notion based upon a certain pattern of weather and wind, established over a long time. Nowhere is this as conspicuous as in studies of ice-cores literally coming out of the depth of time. Drilling on the ice cap of Greenland has opened a window to c. 125.000 years of climate history; the ice core shows the yearly snowfall, and even though the lower layers are thinned out due to the pressure from new layers and the inherent plasticity of the ice, they are visible, and it is possible to study the composition and determine the shifting climates. One of the discoveries is that the climate of the Earth actually has shifted rather quickly from one period to the next, rather than evolving in a gradual and slow process.

The ice cores (also from Antarctica) provide archives that can be read by historians of climate. It takes a lot of technology to get at it, but once this is in place, the deep time of the weather on planet Earth can be unpacked. Meanwhile, the populations of the Arctic have to live with the present

A new world emerging? Icebergs coming out of the fog.

Glacier retreat is a sign of
changing times.

[7] Koch, L. Geologiske
iagttagelser, in K. Rasmussen, *Grønland langs Polhavet*
(Copenhagen; Gyldendal.
1919), pp. 553–576 [p. 565].

[8] Wilson, E.G. *The Spiritual
History of Ice. Romanticism,
Science, and the Imagination*
(New York: Palgrave Macmil-
lan, 2009).

[9] Krupnik, I. and Jolly, D. (eds)
*"The Earth is Faster Now":
Indigenous Observations of
Arctic Environmental Change*
(Fairbanks: Arcus, 2002).

[10] Rink, H. On the glaciers and
the origin of floating icebergs.
(Appendix I), in *Danish Greenland, its People and Products*
(London: Hurst, [1877] 1974),
p. 361.

[11] Cruikshank, J. *Do Glaciers
Listen? Local Knowledge,
Colonial Encounters, and Social
Imagination* (Vancouver, BC:
UBC Press, 2005).

uncertainty about the ice. It has become a persistent image of the Arctic environment that it will be among the first to disappear in a worst-case scenario of climate change. Of course, the ice-clad mountains will remain, but what has defined 'the Arctic' as a region may be irretrievably lost, and with it an age-old form of life.

Both the ice cores and the image of the canary in the mine testify to the possibility of sudden danger. In some sense, this has always been a fact of life in the North, at least implicitly. People have lived with great climate variability even within a human lifespan, and have known to seize the moment – any moment of promise. Now, in north-west Greenland, they look around and as someone said to me: "Well, if the sea opens up even more, then the traffic will

Buried in the stillness of a
deep-frozen world.

increase, and maybe we can get a harbour, so they have a last port of call before the Polar Sea right here." The future may have many things in store, even if the last vestiges of the latest ice age are disappearing, and the glacial time finally losing its grip, even at the poles.

LIVING WITH ENVIRONMENTAL CHANGE

SEASONS, TIMINGS, AND THE RHYTHMS OF LIFE

A grain field watered by the rain.

In the Andes, to plant a seed and wait for it to grow has always been a vulnerable and contingent act. In recent years, however, it is as if the intensity and durability of rain, wind, and temperature are changing, and peasants must deal with their environment in new ways.

As the year goes by in the Andes, time has many markers: the amount of water in the rivers and streams, the cloud cover that replaces the deep blue sky, the temperatures that rise and drop, the colours of the steep slopes that go from a yellowish brown to the brightest of green. The activities of the households, be they social, productive, or religious, follow the rhythms of the year. Sowing must be performed at exactly the right time so that the maturation of the crops coincides with the end of the rainy season. Festivities mark solstice, the coming and going of the rain, harvest and sowing. And the off-farm economic activities must fall in the seasons with less work in the field. In that way, the rhythm of life in the Andes is finely attuned to the rhythms of the seasons.[12]

Being an agriculturalist is fundamentally a matter of timing: it matters a lot when you choose to sow your fields, when you choose to harvest. In the altitudes, it becomes more complicated, as practices of irrigation, otherwise used to extend the cycles of agriculture, potentially are putting the crops in peril. A sudden drop in temperature can be devastating for the fragile sprouts on the thin soils. In Recuay, the majority therefore choose not to irrigate. "Here we wait for the rain," people will say.

But people also wait for the rain to stop again. As the rainy season comes to an end, the frequency of hailstorms increases. This kind of precipitation hits the crops and the economy hard. In a small village, the elderly

Doña Agrepina who makes a living as a travelling midwife and small-scale farmer narrated how she and her husband had misread the weather. Their horsebeans were ripe and plentiful, but still the elderly couple chose to leave them for a few more days to increase the yield even more. But bad luck struck, as hail fell and levelled the plants to the ground, causing the majority of the harvest to be lost.

Climate is an aggregation of weather phenomena. In that way, without time it would not make sense to talk of climate. In regional Spanish, *el clima* (or *la clima*, as the majority would say in accordance with the regional vernacular) is usually used to denote both weather *and* climate. There may be many explanations to this, but fundamentally it reflects a situation in which the coming and going of the seasons are perceived to be stable and predictable. This is not to say that the weather always follows the same pattern, as neither drought nor flooding are unknown, nor new phenomena. But there is a sense of 'normal' weather that is now being challenged.

What is climate if not a marker of regularity? The days, months and years in the Andes are marked by the shifting seasons, their peculiarity and temporal flow are deeply entangled with the ways in which the weather presents itself to the people as peasants, herders, merchants and migrant labourers. So the rhythms of the climate become attuned to other rhythms of life in

LIVING WITH ENVIRONMENTAL CHANGE

Preparing the potato fields with pickaxe and fertilizer purchased in the city of Huaraz.

The potato-fields must continuously be maintained throughout the agricultural cycle.

the mountains: religious celebrations, work, and even school. Indeed, the schools have often been highlighted as being out of tune with the flow of life in the Andes, born as they are out of the seasonality on the coast.

So the question then becomes: which rhythms to attune oneself to? Not that life in the Andes has ever been static, but the rhythms of life require one to read the future by knowing the past. Timing is central to living off the lands. With climate, it is as if the accumulated knowledge of the past and the imagined near and distant futures of the weather crystallize in the moment of the present. When the birds fly at certain heights, the clouds move across the cordillera, or when the fiesta of the Virgin of Mercy is held, people experience different signs in their natural and social environment

that indicate that the time is right. An act of timing, and of anticipating the most probable outcome of the movement of clouds beyond what even the most sensitive and elaborate meteorological models can predict, is, in a sense, a leap of faith. But from experience of reading the movements of the clouds, from knowing what it means that animals move in certain ways or flowers blossom at certain times, from the certainty of history and from the predictions circulated through the radio and other media of the weather to come, people have a sense of what to expect.[13] The rhythms of the seasons, the regularity of coming and going of the rain and the sun, the ability to read even the smallest of signs in the environment, make it no futile endeavour to sow even though planting seeds has always been imbued with uncertainty.

[12] Ingold, The Temporality of the Landscape.

[13] See Orlove, B., Roncoli, C., Kabugo, M. and Majugu, A. Indigenous climate knowledge in southern Uganda: the multiple components of a dynamic regional system, Climatic Change, 100(2) (2010): 243–265.

The weather in the Andes has always been, in a way, capricious. Droughts are not unheard of, and the people in Recuay could tell of years with hardly any rain. Also, they would tell me of years with way too much rain. Years, when the rivers overflow and crops rot in the fields. Years in which mudslides threaten to take away infrastructure and animals, even human lives. But recently there is a growing sense that things are not as they used to be, and that even the capriciousness of the climate has altered its temper.

People live with, and from, their climate. Because it is so deeply entangled with production and reproduction of the peasant household, agriculture and climate – sowing and weather – provide ways of understanding how the climate is both the here and now, and yet it points both backward and forward in time. As an accumulation of knowledge gained by oneself and the generations before, agricultural practices therefore entail timing with regards to the right moment of sowing or harvesting, and anticipation when it comes to planning ahead the diverse activities of the household.

Now it rains "whenever it wants to", people told me. The shifting patterns of precipitation, alternating directions of the winds, and new intensities of the temperatures each challenge the practices of timing that are otherwise embedded in the rural lives. To the peasants of Recuay, climate change is therefore not just quantitative: a matter of the amount of water, wind and degrees Celsius. It is qualitative, because it introduces a different sense of the environment in which the lives are embedded. A new climate is a new time, a new rhythm of life.

At harvest, bundles of wheat are carried to be threshed by the hooves of horses and donkeys.

A mixture of animal dung and synthetic fertilizer is applied to the potatoes.

LIVING WITH ENVIRONMENTAL CHANGE

FLEXIBLE
TRAJECTORIES
NOMADIC PASTORAL
MOBILITY PATTERNS

One of the defining characteristics of nomadic pastoral life and mobility is its fundamental relation to the changing seasons. Mobility *and* life are seasonal, governed by distinct temporal modalities which not only inform decisions of when, where and how to move with the animals, but also the way people interact, their tempo, mood and indeed their choice of clothing, food and the structural configuration of their tents.

As is the case with most nomadic pastoralist groups inhabiting the Sahelo-Saharan zone, the relatively fixed cyclic migration patterns of the nomadic pastoralists of south-eastern Mauritania are governed by a set of general indicators. Over the course of an annual cycle, the nomadic pastoralists move in a pendular pattern of variable amplitude, exploiting areas to the south during the dry season, progressively moving further north during the rainy season. Ideally, this annual migratory cycle is repeated along the same trajectories year after year, but variations in the emergence and availability of resources due to natural and political reconfigurations often necessitate alternative routes.[14]

The camp (*aïal*), which constitutes the centre of social life to the nomadic pastoralists, provides a temporary fixed recreational place, a fundamental social node, from which wanderings are performed up to the point when pastures are too far from camp to ensure adequate time for grazing, due to the time spent to reach them and return back within the day. Typically starting one hour before sunrise and continuing until sunset, the individual herders of the camp move with their animals in radiant circles from the centre towards the margin and back again. Depending on the season, herders alternate

between taking the animals to the pasture and taking them to drink at water holes. Furthermore, so as to be able to exploit different forms of pastures dispersed over a wide area and to minimize the risk of losing their entire herd in the case of severe droughts, the nomadic pastoralists diversify their herds and the pastures they frequent. Once the immediate area around the camp has been grazed, the nomadic pastoralists pack their belongings and tents, and move to a new area from which they continue this strategy.

Depending on the season, the quality of the pastures, the availability of water, as well as the size of the herds of the different households, they move camp anywhere between every third week and every second month, often splitting up into smaller groups or merging with larger groups depending on their shifting needs, i.e. those of the animals in terms of pasture zones. This changes continually, from season to season and from year to year. The different encampments live in close proximity with each other, sharing the same water holes and to a wide extent pastures. This means that herders of different conglomerations of families often meet each other, either while grazing the animals or giving them water at the communally accessible wells and watering holes.

Ahmed, a nomadic herdsman, traversing the dunes of Ouarane in the Adrar region of Mauritania, April 2001.

LIVING WITH ENVIRONMENTAL CHANGE

Within the different seasons of the year, the common mode of dispersion is a combination of pulsing and radiant trajectories exploiting pastures in all directions, with moments of concentration around water holes and wells during the dry season, and dispersal in the wet season to exploit areas otherwise inaccessible due to distance from water.[15] In short, throughout the year, a multitude of seasonal itineraries are effectuated, regionally and locally, regularly or ephemerally, which sketch out a complex rhythmic appropriation of pastures (*hatbä*), areas containing salt for the animals (*àmirsàl*), and a variety of water holes. However, prolonged years of drought in many areas have pushed large numbers of nomadic pastoralists to seek pastures further south, in areas which are more densely populated and thus, as more herds conglomerate, more pressure is put on the shrinking pasture zones and the limited water supplies.

A worrisome effect of prolonged droughts is that the migrations between North and South tend to become suspended as nomadic pastoralists hold their animals on the southern pastures for extended periods of the year. The vegetal cover is consequently not allowed to regenerate and socio-political controversies concerning access to the limited pastures and water holes tend to become more frequent. Arguably, prolonged suspension of the 'normal' migration pattern renders nomadic pastoralism *de facto* unsustainable.[16] Thus it is evident that mobility, the absolutely basic pastoral adjustment to scarcity, has become constrained and significantly reconfigured, as a result of the drying out of the natural environment in south-eastern Mauritania in the last decades.

While there seems to be ample evidence that the process of sedentarization observable

Ali, a nomadic herdsman from the Hamonat tribe complaining about the scarcity of pastures and water, Hodh ech Chargui, Mauritania, May 2006.

A nomadic household moving through the Tagant region in central Mauritania, January 2004.

Mahmoud and Ishmael, two nomadic herdsmen from the Kunta tribe in the Tagant region of central Mauritania, January 2004.

[14] Toupet, C. L'évolution de la nomadisation en Mauritanie sahélienne, in C. Bataillon (ed.) *Nomads et Nomadisme au Sahara* (Paris: UNESCO, 1963).

[15] Krader, L. The ecology of pastoral nomadism, *International Social Science Journal*, 11 (1959): 499–510.

[16] Nouaceur, Z. Disparités pluviométriques régionales, sécheresse et modification des équilibres de l'environnement mauritanien, *Revue de géographie de Lyon* 70(3–4) (1995): 239–245.

in Mauritania over the last five decades is more or less irreversible, significant numbers of nomadic pastoralists continue to practise a mobile livelihood. The first decade of the new millennium has been marked by increasing environmental pressure and political instability in the region; and among the nomadic pastoralists there is a growing concern about the future, as it becomes difficult to anticipate the turbulent convergence of these factors. While many hope to continue their mobile herding practices, circumstances are becoming increasingly tight and many families now depend upon income generated by family members working in the burgeoning urban centres. While the elderly nomads generally lament the situation, many youth dream of one day attending school, driving cars and having mobile phones.

As mobile livestock rearing becomes constrained, nomadic pastoral life is rendered even more hard and strenuous, compelling increasing numbers of people to settle down for longer periods of the year. Hence, the annual rhythm is fundamentally restructured and the nomadic pastoralists become even more dependent on the sedentary markets and economy. What has developed in Mauritania is something of a rural–urban continuum in which nomadism constitutes a contemporary nexus. In other words, large parts of the Mauritanian population remain mobile to a considerable extent – even those who inhabit the urban centres. The form of mobility, however, is no longer solely contingent upon the vagaries of the weather and the needs of the animals, but also on new economic opportunities developing from within the urban centres. If ever there was a boundary between nomadic and sedentary in Mauritania, it is at best blurred or indeed fluid today.

LIVING WITH ENVIRONMENTAL CHANGE

STILL LIFE ON THE SHORE

On the shore of the south-east Indian state of Tamil Nadu, a small piece of land is formally designated as cultural heritage to be preserved and cultivated in accordance with its own unique nature and history. The place is a Tamil fishing village called Tharangambadi, housing some 7,000 inhabitants. Like other settlements along the shore of India, the place was also once a European, in this case Danish, colonial trading post going by the name of Trankebar. In light of this past, the place is seen as historic.

From the early seventeenth century until the middle of the nineteenth century, a sequence of Danish kings and private shareholder companies were granted the right to use the settlement for trade in Indian produce such as textiles and spices, and to ship Asian goods from further east back home to Europe. The history of northern European interests in the village is very visible today, in that Tharangambadi is the hometown to a number of ancient colonial buildings, such as governors' and merchants' mansions, churches, residential houses and other buildings dating back to colonial times. Many of these are now renovated in the explicit interest of keeping

the shared history of the place alive and open to visitors, and the landscape around them is under plough as objects of various bio-conservations efforts.[17] Apparently, the presence in bygone colonial times of foreign traders now causes European and, in particular, Danish NGOs and institutions to assume a particular kind of perceived responsibility for preserving and beautifying Tharangambadi. It is, after all, a historic place.

Before the time of the Danish trading station, obviously, the place had a history of its own, just as time did not come to a halt when the Danes and other Europeans left, even if this is the assumption that cultural

The Danish Governor's
bungalow before restoration.

Reconstructed cultural
heritage in Tharangambadi.
The Danish Governor's
bungalow.

Fishing boats and cultural
heritage of Tharangambadi
sheltered from the encroaching
waves.

LIVING WITH ENVIRONMENTAL CHANGE

heritage work sometimes seems to be based on. Eager to preserve the old colonial structures and to argue for their historic value, heritage workers – whether delegates from the Danish National Museum, private Danish entrepreneurs or businessmen with corporate social responsibility – portray Tharangambadi as a pocket in time, which against all odds has maintained a uniquely calm ambience and managed to keep the homogenizing trends of modern lifestyle at bay. In information material describing the heritage projects, which are often combined with contemporary development ambitions of different kinds that are generally much appreciated locally – more so than restored antique buildings – Tharangambadi is sometimes described as a living museum, where 'one can experience a rich past, as well as a relaxing and rejuvenating nostalgic atmosphere', as one such publication documenting and promoting the ongoing renovation work in the village has it.[18] The village, in this particular cultural heritage vision, is a place at rest within its nature and at peace with its surroundings and in its seclusion from the grind of the modern, and apparently this nostalgic atmosphere demands protection for it to be kept intact and alive. While the Danish ancestors of today's heritage workers are mainly seen as present through the material vestiges of colonial rule that are found in the village, the present-day local Tamil inhabitants are often portrayed as living by admirable age-old cultural customs. Fishing practices, among other activities, is a particular artisanal lifestyle, implicitly presented as having a pace of its own, the pace of nature. Thus, whether addressing European or Tamil histories, inherent in much of the heritage work and heritage talk seems to be a kind of still life imagery of the village, which accordingly is seen to offer an oasis in the hectic routines of South Indian town and city life.

Nature, however, does not comply with such imaginary freezing of the moment captured in the notions of nostalgia and of being out of time. Regardless of the rulers' national origin or their cultural practices, the Bay of Bengal which lines Tharangambadi has moved steadily closer to the coastal settlement over the years. The beach has diminished rapidly, and a time when the stretch of sand was much wider than now is easily recalled by the villagers. The sea, too, the fishermen claim, is not what – or where – it

Eroding coastal land, eating the historic village of Tharangambadi if left unprotected.

used to be. Coastal erosion, forceful monsoons and intensified cyclone activity in the bay encroach on land, the inshore waters are depleted of marine resources, forcing fishing people to adjust their 'age-old customs', and the so-called rough season is seen as increasingly irregular. Global warming is often blamed, just as the Asian tsunami in 2004 that severely hit the region is seen as both a starting point and a consequence of bad times.

The changes of the coastline are evident. The Masalamani temple built to Shiva in 1305 is halfway submerged by the sea; several of the domes have broken off and are now lying in the water inundated and rocked by each wave. If no action is taken, this historic building, still sometimes used as a place of worship, will succumb.

Different initiatives are taken to keep the sea from eating away the ground of

[17] Hastrup, F. Qualifying coastal nature: bio-conservation projects in South East India, in K. Hastrup (ed.) *Anthropology and Nature* (London: Routledge, 2013), pp. 43–61.

[18] *Tranquebar – Land of the Singing Waves* (Bestseller Fund, 2010).

Tharangambadi. Seawalls of huge rocks and coastal shelter plantations have found their way into the project plans and practices of both the non-Indian heritage actors and local tourist authorities and now line the sea in an attempt to stop the pace of the ocean. Most fishing people, however, the protection of whose cultural practices is also quoted as one reason for intervening on the part of authorities and cultural heritage workers, have moved away and been resettled in a newly constructed village further inland. The local people have moved from the coast, the coast has moved closer, and heritage advocates have moved in to try to stop the movement and preserve Tharangambadi from losing its alleged nostalgic atmosphere. By protecting ancient structures and stopping the sea from doing its thing, heritage work strives in a way to synchronize Tharangambadi to itself, that is, to make it into what it was when Danes moved around as the ruling elite.

Curiously, it seems to require a particular intervention that among other things implies plants, rocks, water management, museum experts and lots of foreign capital, to make the nature of the village contemporary to itself.

Coastal protection and colonial heritage on the Tamil shore. The brick piers were on dry land when the fort in the background was built in 1620.

LIVING WITH ENVIRONMENTAL CHANGE

APPRAISING CHANGE
A QUESTION OF BASELINE

Contemporary environmental researchers have learned to appreciate the notion of coupled human–environmental systems.[19] Studying the dynamics of interaction between humans and their environment in coupled human–environmental systems can, on the one hand, be a useful intellectual activity helping to clarify the intricacies of temporal dynamics, cross-scale interactions, and complex adaptive action. It can, however, also have a more practical purpose as a way of assessing the sustainability, adaptive capacity, and functioning of a given human–environmental system.

One important aspect of improving our ability to manage for a desirable future development lies in understanding the long-term dynamics of human–environmental interaction. Knowing more about human responses to changing conditions in a long-term perspective can have a decisive bearing on the appraisal of present-day situations. The Sahelian region in West Africa provides an illustrative reminder of how important the choice of analytical baseline (or temporal point of departure and resolution) can be for the way in which change in human–environment relations is perceived.

Today the Sahel is, as a rule, featured as a desert fringe setting challenged by adverse climate changes and accelerating population pressure – conditions which lead to a vicious cycle of land degradation.[20] This description may certainly be true, inasmuch as the population has multiplied in the past 50 years coinciding with long periods of low rainfall. However, the assessment of the situation is significantly influenced by the temporal window applied by the observer.

Rainfall is a key resource for local livelihoods. Given the few rivers and deep groundwater levels in the Sahelian region, agriculture and pastoral production depend on adequate rainfall to sustain local populations. It is well known that the variability of rainfall is high in dry climate zones. Hence, the amount of rain varies from one rainy season to the other, as well as within the rainy season. This has important implications for the success of the harvest. Local

Depending on the direction you look, the environment may be appraised very differently. The two photos from Northern Burkina Faso are just looking east and west, respectively, from the same spot on the road.

LIVING WITH ENVIRONMENTAL CHANGE

people know this, and they have to some extent adapted to the situation in order to avoid the adverse implications of rainfall variability as much as possible. Yet, years of disasters have become part of the recent environmental history. The diagram provides a glaring illustration. We can see the extraordinarily abundant rains in the 1950–1960s and the good rains in the 1920–1940s, as well as the disastrous droughts in the 1970–1980s and the drought periods around 1910 and 1940.

It is interesting to reflect on the corresponding accentuation in the scholarly discourses of the drought events. At the time when the 1970s drought hit the Sahel, for example, it was frequently hypothesized that this event was part of a cyclic development: every 30 years a drought would occur, as it had previously been observed around 1910 and 1940. Later, when the drought in the 1970s persisted for decades, this discourse died out and became replaced with a notion of more permanent change towards drier conditions and human-induced environmental degradation. Later again, at the turn of the century, and with the event of some years with more rain, this new notion was also challenged by the discussion of a possible 'greening of the Sahel' in the scientific literature.[21] Hence, the entire notion of irreversible degradation caused by humans was challenged.

The huge attention to the drought catastrophe in the 1970s and 1980s was justified, people and animals in the region suffered and died and needed support from the global community. It was, however, not only the rain which deserved attention when looking for causal relationships. The temporal entrance point to the drought period was also quite unique; at the time when the Sahel experienced the unusually high rainfall coincided with independence of the nation states in the region. This co-development of the societal and environmental events created a great incentive to expand cultivation into marginal land, and the specific human–environment situation had, in turn, profound implications for the vulnerability of this land use system at the margin of the desert.

Seen in a much longer historical perspective, the twentieth century condition will appear as a dry spell in an oscillating system. In 10,000 BP (before present), the climatic situation was characterized by an intensified monsoon rainfall, and the landscape was dominated by lakes and open woodland. By 5,000 BP, a final collapse of the monsoon was experienced after periods of abrupt arid crises. The ultimate cause was a small, subtle change in Earth's orbit, leading to a change in the distribution of solar radiation on Earth's surface. Model simulations suggest that it was caused by an interaction

[19] Turner II, B.L., Lambin, E.F., and Reenberg, A. The emergence of land change science for global environmental change and sustainability, *PNAS* 104(52) (2007): 20666–20671.

[20] Reenberg, A. Insistent dryland narratives: portraits of knowledge about human-environmental interactions in Sahelian environment policy documents, *West African Journal of Applied Ecology*, 20(1) (2012): 97–111.

[21] de Menocal, P.B., Ortiz, J. Guilderson, T., Adkins, J., Sarnthein, M., Baker, L. and Yarusinski, M. Abrupt onset and termination of the African Humid Period: rapid climate response to gradual insolation forcing, *Quarterly Science Review*, 19 (2000): 347–361.

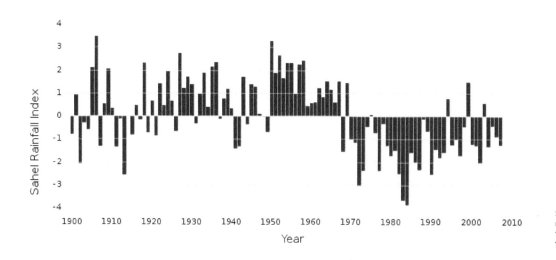

Sahelian precipitation in the rainy season (June–October) – the respective year's deviation from the mean value.

Drylands can sometimes seem very wet: the access road to Biidi-2 in Northern Burkina Faso in the rainy season.

Kids from Tintabora, Northern Burkina Faso.

between atmosphere, ocean, vegetation and sea-ice changes in widely separated parts of the planet. From this point in time, only, the agro-ecological conditions approached present day's conditions. Cattle herders migrated to the Sahel because pastoral land use by nomadic cultures was well suited to adapt to the spatially and temporally erratic resource base.

Historically, systemic resilience was then created through the diversification of livelihoods. The nomadic cultures that developed around pastoralism over the last 5,000 years became well adapted to the unpredictable resource base. The concatenation of societal and environmental events in the 1960s created, however, a large incentive to increase the number of settlements that, in turn, had profound implications for the vulnerability of the agricultural system in the face of successive droughts.

The example illustrates how appraisals of existing land systems or their dynamics may be flawed by insufficient attention to the selection of reference baselines and timescales.

247   LIVING WITH ENVIRONMENTAL CHANGE

LITRES PER SECOND
MEASURING THE
WATER FLOW

The flow of water is often measured in time related to volume, speed or a particular practice. In this chapter, I ask what motivates different methods for measurements and what are the implications of measuring the water flow in universal units of microscopic time? Can absolute and standardized measurements of volumetric flow rates be used as indications of climate change?

The Majes Canal is approximately 100 kilometres long and takes water through the Colca Valley to the arid lowlands.

In Colca Valley, relative measures are often preferred in the distribution of irrigation water, since two fields may measure the same in terms of area according to the metric system but have quite different water absorption rates. Relative measures like *topo* and *yuntada* are commonly used to calculate the size of fields and water tariffs: a *topo* refers to the amount of land that a team of men wielding a foot plough can prepare in one day, and a *yuntada* is the amount of land a team of oxen can plough in a day. These amounts vary by plot shape, slope, soil type, and distance from the village.[22] When irrigating their fields, the farmers of Colca Valley mostly use traditional methods based on gravity and furrows, and the water is measured in practised time: how many hours it

takes to flood a field. This time also depends on several factors, like the soil, slope, and the speed and volume of the water flow in the stream or canal. Both land and water are thus measured according to labour and movement in time, and the focus is on the accomplishment of a task: how long it takes for humans, animals or water to enable land to produce food.

However, relative measures are not very convenient in interregional trade, state building or science. Standardized units of measurement make scalable projects possible – be it of business or development – and units of size, volume and time have to a large degree been standardized in metres, hectares, litres, minutes and seconds. The amount of water going into the Majes Canal, which was built in the 1970s to take water from a highland dam to an irrigation project in the desert, is highly regulated. The canal goes through Colca Valley and there are today 26 valves providing irrigation water to the communities along the canal, and the rations are also strictly regulated. The water flow – or the volumetric flow rate (*caudal*) – is measured in litres per second or cubic metres per second. In the intake to the Majes Canal, there are electronic sensors to make exact measurements of the water volume on a daily basis. Once a month, a group of engineers led by the regional government do the 'regulation of the valves'. The engineers use a stick to measure the water that flows out of the canal valve and through a standard size triangular hydraulic channel outlet. Then they compare the centimetres of water to a chart to see how many litres per second the volume of the flow is. Sometimes, the engineers with years of experience, just need to take a look at the water flow to know the approximate volume. They call this *el ojímetro*; the 'eye-meter', which is a result of experienced measurements. If the measured flow is more than allowed, the engineers adjust the valve to attain the correct volume according to the regulations. The farmers in the communities seem to trust the methods for measuring the litres per second, yet the amounts can be contested and negotiated. The farmers pay a water tariff that is calculated according to the size of the land that they irrigate, and they also pay a state licence for the right to use a certain amount of water (in litres per second) from a specific source. These measurements and licences are part of the authorities' control of the water's movement and distribution, and they are justified as a necessary guarantee in case of future water scarcity.

Water measurements are, however, also performed in alternative ways, by other actors and for other purposes. Measurements create a sense of predictability and control, and the question is who has this control. In July 2011, a new commission of water users was created in Callalli, a community in

The water flow rate in the canal valves is measured through standardized hydraulic outlets.

The water flow is measured in litres per second.

the Colca highlands. Before they officially registered as an association, they conducted a complete registration of all the water resources in their territory. The Water Users' Organization in Colca Valley gave institutional, moral and educational support, and sent an engineer to teach a group of young men how to do the measurements and registration. He focused on two methods that did not require expensive or unavailable technology: 'the volumetric method' and the 'floating method'. For the first method, they needed a bucket (sized between 4 and 20 litres) and a stopwatch. For the second, they needed a small floating object (a cork), a measuring tape and a stopwatch. During the next month, they went out to every corner of the district to register every water source with the recorded litres per second. The motivation was to protect the water resources in their territory against intrusions of mining companies and to be able to have information about changes in the water sources due to climate change.

The engineer working for the
Water Users' Organization in
Colca Valley is the keeper of
the valve keys.

What do these measuring practices do to how people relate to water? Land is measured by the time it takes for men or oxen to move around a field with a plough. Water is measured by the time it takes to soak a field, or to fill a bucket, or the time it takes for an object to move between two lines. These are all highly relative measures, as they depend on topography, slope, speed of water flow, physical strength and personal skills. On the other hand, the introduction of absolute and standardized measurements of water contributes to the production of what Jamie Linton has called "modern water", which is not complicated by ecological, cultural, or social factors. "Modern water" is marked by an idea of universality, since all waters, in whatever environmental, social, and cultural circumstances they may occur, are reducible to this abstraction.[23] Meters express the social individuation that lead people to feel that their resource use takes place detached from the wider social and economic arrangement.[24] However, relative and standardized measures of time and water flow do not necessarily exclude each other, and in Colca both measurements are used. Today, in order to be able to make claims about decreasing water supplies in times of global warming, local communities need to engage in standardized measurements and thus in some ways make their scarce water "modern".

[22] Guillet, D. *Covering Ground: Communal Water Management and the State in the Peruvian Andes* (Ann Arbor, MI: University of Michigan Press, 1992).

[23] Linton, J. *What Is Water? The History of a Modern Abstraction* (Vancouver, BC: UBC Press, 2010).

[24] Strang, V. *The Meaning of Water* (Oxford: Berg, 2004).

LIVING WITH ENVIRONMENTAL CHANGE

NEW SCENARIOS AND UNSTABLE TEMPORALITIES

Matavera. Stony beach with scrub.

Climate projections for the Pacific Ocean show that in 2090, air temperatures will increase around 1.5–3.0 degrees Celsius. No doubt 2090 seems far away to most, if not all, Pacific islanders, yet in climate projection this is obviously a meaningful time frame. Plenty of time is needed to discern the temperature changes.

Numerous scenarios extending to 2030 or 2055 or even longer are colonizing future landscapes and lifeworlds. Being aware of the possible far-reaching consequences of global warming for small island states, it takes time for islanders to inhabit the new future. What are the implications of 1.5–3.0 degrees increase? How will it affect the weather conditions and everyday life? Will it predominantly change the seasons or result in more extremely hot days? Will water scarcity become a recurrent problem? Are some islands more exposed than others?

The numerous projections are stretching actual planning and the imagination of several decades beyond usual time horizons in national and personal contexts. New time frames are entering lifeworlds already occupied with a multiplicity of temporalities. Religious beliefs, ethical values, personal concerns and hopes, and different types of historical awareness all have their temporalities that are not necessarily easy to reconcile with climate change projections.

The Gregorian calendar structures to a large extent social life on the island of Rarotonga in the Cook Islands. The temporalities of schools, workplaces, and in the families are unfolding in the calendric wheel of the year; every year new pupils enter school, new taxes are paid, new passion fruits and new schools of mackerels are harvested. Seasons are generally divided into two: Summer from November to April, which is hotter, more humid with a higher rainfall than wintertime from May to October. Holidays, sports activities and celebrations have their moments, dates and extended periods of time throughout the year; and some activities have even a separate full-fledged calendar. *Te Tia* is such a version of the Gregorian calendar with suggested Bible readings for each day, used by ministers in the Cook Islands' Christian Church as a point of reference in worship in the congregation and by many people in their personal devotional life.

Yet, there are other calendars and other temporalities that flow simultaneously. One notable example is the lunar almanac calendar *Arapo* (lit. 'the path of the night'), formerly used extensively in fishing and gardening, and now also partly incorporated into the main calendar. The *Arapo* has a 13-month lunar year, well suited for its purposes, but notoriously difficult to synchronize with the seasons – and with the Gregorian calender in a strict and systematic way.[25] When used as an oral calendar, it was possible to make adjustments, but a written version poses many obstacles such as adding and extracting certain days and is dependent upon very accurate observations of the moon phases. These days, the Ministry of Agriculture publishes an adjusted version and gives advice to farmers about the monthly conditions for planting, and especially the older generations keep their personally inherited *Arapo* in mind when they go fishing for albacore in the open sea on a special night, forecast hot or stormy weather, or medicate themselves.

Global warming has been ascribed a role in the destabilization of the *Arapo*. In a speech in 2011, Prime Minister Henry Puna notes that agriculture in the Cook Islands "has suffered frequently from the effects of droughts while farmers have also observed changes in the timing of harvesting". He continues that "many attribute this to changes in the climate, and in particular rainfall", and that the *Arapo* had been used by "many of our farmers since the time of our ancestors ... passed down to successive generations", but that it now "with climate change seems to be out of phase".[26]

The *Arapo* exemplifies how different calendars build up certain temporalities in the social fabric. However, many more calendric temporalities are embedded in family life such as 21st birthday celebrations, the annual dance competitions, worship, community work days, and seasonal activities such as canoeing and picnics.

2035 or 2090 climate change scenarios may now become decisive factors in the actual plans and imaginative anticipations of how life will unfold. The reception is of course mixed. While large infrastructural projects are climate change proofed with reference to the scenarios, and some calendars as the *Arapo* seem to be losing a foothold, many others are so far veering in all directions. In some cases acute fear is raised

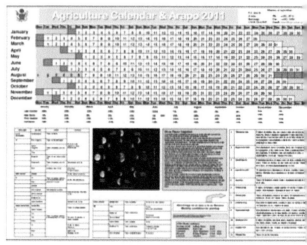

Arapo, issued by the Ministry of Agriculture.

that the low-lying atolls in the northern part of the Cook Islands will be uninhabitable due to the rising sea, droughts and freshwater scarcity. In other cases increased or unstable precipitation, increase in cyclone intensity or acidification of the ocean are feared to destabilize farming, fishing and the economically

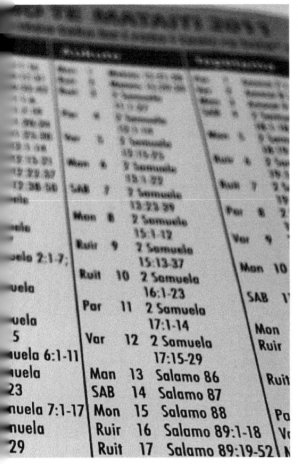

Te Tia, list of Bible readings for the year.

Arapo, sketched by Makiuti Tongia, Pacific Studies scholar, poet and former politician, and resident of Rarotonga.

crucial tourist industry. Consequently, the predictions, forecasts and prognoses have been many and the newsfeed fast about present and future climate change.

Presently, on Rarotonga, most people seem to react to the expert newsfeed by slowing down in a hesitant kind of waiting. "We have to wait and see what actually happens. Then we or our descendants will deal with it," is a very typical comment. For the natural science-minded kind of outlook, the pace is also often slowed down: "More detailed studies have to be made before the

prognoses are precise enough." For most people, the long-term scenarios are too open, too diffuse to act upon in any direct manner. Multiple calendars and temporalities are unstable and not yet recalibrated and reworked. It takes time to get a new future.

[25] MacCormack, G. *The Arapo and the Lunar Challenge* (Cook Islands Natural Heritage, n.d.).

[26] Puna, H. *The Cook Islands Herald*, November 10, 2011.

FACING REALITY
MANAGING/IMAGINING THE TIME LEFT ON AN ATOLL

Mangroves protect against erosion. President Anote Tong makes an appearance at a mangrove-planting project.

Because of erosion crop trees tumble into the ocean.

Scientific projections suggest that Kiribati will be uninhabitable by the year 2050. Coastal erosion, saltwater intrusion in freshwater resources, storm surges, and drought are considered some of the greatest threats to the country's future. Research has shown that rising sea levels could mean that up to half of the main island, South Tarawa, will be inundated by 2050.[27]

Needless to say, it is difficult to find anyone on these islands who does not have strong feelings about these predictions. Anote Tong, the President of Kiribati, has proposed one solution. He wants to relocate the population of Kiribati to other countries. This solution is not straightforward, neither emotionally nor practically. But according to Tong, this strategy demonstrates the kind of leadership required to manage the future awaiting Kiribati. He coined the phrase "relocating with dignity", that is, not as "climate refugees", but through training and education as skilled workers in neighbouring nations. As Tong explains, adaptation takes on a new meaning in Kiribati, where relocation is an adaptation strategy:

We have to face the reality that we will not be able to accommodate all the people on these islands. We have to consider migration beyond our shores as part of our adaptation strategy. As skilled people they will have better access to those labour markets, so that they can migrate with dignity. Not as climate refugees.[28]

A relocation programme extending over the next couple of decades encourages people to move slowly. Not abruptly, conjuring up images of an evacuation where there is limited infrastructure in the receiving countries. Tong promotes his relocation policy vigorously in the international debate where he advocates for new educational programmes abroad for I-Kiribati students.

In Kiribati, relocation strategies are not high on the political agenda. Such a relocation policy gives rise to feelings of uncertainty among the majority of the population, and scepticism among the population with higher education. Critical voices on the island suggest that conveying the message in the international media that Kiribati is hopeless does not demonstrate the political leadership needed to address the problem. Linda, a politically active film producer living on South Tarawa, shares her concerns about how relocation could unfold:

One of our concerns about the President is that he would willingly scatter some in Germany, some in California, some in New Zealand. I think he needs to be resisted on that thinking. There are places where we can go. I mean, North Western Australia, that have a similar climate. And if you are going to talk about migration as a solution you cannot simply take the people. What about our totems, and the bones of our loved ones? You are not just dealing with a living person, you are dealing with everything else.

While Linda tries to think creatively about how to practically relocate the population of Kiribati, the central concern expressed in this quote could be posed as a question to Tong and the world beyond these islands: Where will we go? Will we be scattered across the world or keep our national identity and history? And what will happen to all the artefacts that make us I-Kiribati?

One of the educational programmes in place for I-Kiribati students abroad is the Kiribati Australia Nursing Initiative (KANI) where I-Kiribati students receive a nursing degree at an Australian university. Upon finishing their degree they can stay and work in Australia, where there is a shortage of nurses, or return to Kiribati. About this programme, Tong says:

> What is happening with our young people being trained as nurses in Australia, that is actually part of the process [of relocation]. Whether it is deliberate or not, that is exactly the scheme I am talking about. It is possible. It is mutually beneficial. And it can be done.[29]

Tong is acting before the disaster sets in, long before 2050 when Kiribati is projected to be uninhabitable. As there is no imminent disaster yet, the programmes are mutually beneficial for the countries involved. The I-Kiribati students go abroad, not because the neighbouring countries have a responsibility to take them, but because they can be equipped with skills to fill gaps in labour markets. Thus, the link between labour migration and climate change remains implicit for the countries hosting I-Kiribati students. The difference between, on the one hand, preparing for climate change, and, on the other, working with regional labour markets, was confirmed

by a KANI representative who explained that KANI has nothing to do with climate change but only with labour mobility.

This is not the only way the political framework is being inconsistent with the experience of the people living in Kiribati. Another is expressed in the term 'climate refugee'. Currently the UN Refugee Convention does not recognize environmental harm, and hence the category of "climate refugee" has no legal weight. Still, the notion is invoked in the media and in non-governmental work. In 2012 New Zealand refused refugee status to a man from Kiribati who sought refuge in New Zealand due to climate change-related harm. On his application he stated that he was afraid for his children's future in Kiribati. However, as the I-Kiribati asylum seeker was not persecuted because of his race, religion, nationality, or political affiliation, his application for asylum status was denied.

Tong is working pragmatically to implement his relocation policy in this early stage as the neighbouring countries do not recognize climate change within the political framework, and he faces accusations of "giving up" rather than acting for the people of Kiribati. However, according to him, this is about being realistic and making demanding decisions:

> [Relocation] is deeply emotional. I can't imagine what it would be like because I won't be leaving. By the time the water comes I will be here. But the idea of relocating is something that the new generation will have to face. It is deeply emotional. But at the same time we have got to be harshly realistic ... *harshly* realistic. Being just emotional without common sense is not good leadership.[30]

Finding out what to do is not the only concern in climate change adaptation, *when* to do it is also crucial. Taking action too late and taking action too early are equally complex, and no doubt either strategy will invoke strong feelings.

[27] Campbell, J. *Climate Change, Vulnerability, and Adaptation Assessment for Kiribati: Technical Summary and Synthesis.* Report prepared for the World Bank by the Centre for International Global Change Institute (Waikato University, Hamilton, New Zealand, 2000); Storey, D. and Hunter, S. Kiribati: an environmental 'perfect storm', *Australian Geographer,* 41(2) (2010): 167–181.

[28] Excerpt from interview with Anote Tong from "Horizon – a vanishing nation, *Horisont,* Danish National Radio, 2009.

[29] Ibid.

[30] Ibid.

A man securing his possessions before the tide takes them out to sea.

People build seawalls from coral rocks to protect their land.

Even seawalls made from concrete cannot always protect houses against the ocean.

LIVING WITH ENVIRONMENTAL CHANGE

ANTICIPATING FUTURES AND THE RHYTHMS OF WATER

Rumours were circulating in town. Another workplace was expected to move away from Maniitsoq to Nuuk, the capital of Greenland, or to Sisimiut north of the town. More unemployment to be expected. Very often, people referred to Maniitsoq as 'an old retired lady', alive but slowly getting closer to a fatal point of no return.

Maniitsormiut (people from Maniitsoq) often talk vividly about the old days when the town was vibrant and dynamic due to the fishing industry. Previously, Maniitsoq was indeed the political and economic centre of Greenland where it was possible to establish the good life. The stories of earlier optimism and visionary town people cannot, however, hide the problems of today and the anxieties of a standstill in town.

Historically, the annual cycles of fish had a dominant imprint on the social cycles and rhythms of the town, and during hectic periods the factory was running all day long and even children were called in to help. The work-time was disciplined and all-day-shifts were used to optimize production. Old people in town recall the work ethics of people during the periods of intense production and processing. The fish not only influenced perceptions of the time cycles of days

The former mayor overlooks the area expected to host the new part of town if the factory is built.

and years, but also the long-term perspective on the future was imminent in the town's involvement in the fisheries. Like so many places in the Arctic, the town has experienced a boom and bust economy. Today, a small fish factory is maintained by a handful of men and most of the production has been moved elsewhere. The short- and long-term cycles of marine life have influenced the cycles of the town itself.

Understandably, the announcement of a potential large-scale factory to smelt aluminium was received as good news. In the beginning, the news was fragmented and people pieced them together in different ways. But no one was in doubt; such a factory could save the town from dying. To meet the requirements of the factory, experts said, the town had to double its population. Maniitsoq emerged as a potential powerful place again; not because of its strategic location to

LIVING WITH ENVIRONMENTAL CHANGE

Today, the fish factory in
Maniitsoq is a shadow of its
historical self.

A number of local citizen
groups worked to come up
with ideas to improve the
urban development to make it
match their dreams.

fish resources but due to its proximity to the biggest water reservoir in Greenland – the lake of Tasersiaq – which could serve as the basis of a large-scale hydro-electricity power plant providing cheap energy on a continuous basis which could make the factory operate 24 hours a day, 365 days a year, for approximately 70 years, which is its expected lifetime.

The shift from industrial fishing (a dependence on a marine waterscape) to a hydro-electric industrial aluminium production (an industrial waterscape) not only requires a new way of anticipating the good town life but is also a shift in time rhythm. The social and cultural dynamics linked to fishing and fish processing are quite different from those related to aluminium activities pursued and controlled by a transnational corporation. The explicit factory requirement of a stable and accessible workforce is going to influence the organization of everyday life

in, for example, highly scheduled work time and spare time. Furthermore, everyday life and the dynamics of town will be entangled in 'production time' which is influenced by factory requirements, fluctuating world prices of raw material and the demand for aluminium.

Locally, people started to organize citizen groups to rethink the future organization and potentials of town. Even though the many proposals originated in contemporary frustrations and wishes (like an indoor swimming pool, better conditions for pedestrians, etc.), they mobilized a new sense of time and anticipation. The potential factory forced people to think more ahead and to anticipate new futures. The future was considered new because they had to relate to the needs, expectations, and activities of a town population double the size of today. Therefore, part of the town's reorganization of resources and ambitions was related to ways to appear attractive and progressive in order to attract the new workforce. Maniitsoq did much to promote itself, to portray the town as an urban centre and as a dynamic place in the future, in short, as a proper site for investment and the good life. People creatively tried to establish a vision, to anticipate a story or a line of future development. By doing so they brought "the unprecedented into effect by way of imaginative power and thus expand[ed] the community's awareness of itself".[31] Special emphasis was on how to link local affordances (physical as well as cultural) and expectations to global requirements and national benefits. The local appropriation of the new factory and its water regime was thus closely linked to the creation of new time horizons, self-awareness building, anticipation of national dynamics and re-positioning in a global economy.

The astronomical investments required, the spatial and temporal consequences as well as the political expectations invested in the project add to the project's momentum. The planned construction and running of the factory embodied its own time perspective and its requirements for social organization and stability. This concept of 'technical momentum' is proposed by T.P. Hughes[32] in an attempt to bridge technological determinism and social constructivism and he suggests that the investment of money, effort, time and resources to develop, maintain and use technological systems can make it difficult if not impossible to change those systems when they are up and running. From his perspective, the technological system thus both shapes and is shaped by society.

The social-technical system centred on aluminium production and its controlled water regime disciplines time, people and water in profound ways quite different from former fishing-time and contemporary 'standstill-time'. People need to foresee futures with a totally different time rhythm. Furthermore, local expectations and aspirations have to be coordinated with, and are dependent on, national visions and long-term strategic planning. The synchronization of local time and national time horizons is also an arena for negotiations and enactments of different narratives about the good life and the proper attitude of what it entails to be a good citizen. Locally, they are therefore not only coping with contemporary change and predicaments but actively enacting social life through collective envisioning and negotiation of a new future.

Unemployment is a pressing issue.

[31] Hastrup, K. Performing the world: agency, anticipation and creativity, in E. Hallam and T. Ingold (eds) *Creativity and Cultural Improvisation* (Oxford: Berg, 2007), pp. 193–206 [p. 200].

[32] Hughes, T. P. Technological momentum, in D.G. Johnson and J.M. Wetmore (eds) *Technology and Society: Building Our Sociotechnical Future* (Cambridge, MA: The MIT Press, 2009), pp. 141–150.

LIVING WITH ENVIRONMENTAL CHANGE

SLOW VERSUS FAST CHANGES IN SAHELIAN LAND USE SYSTEMS

In the past few decades Sahelian land systems have been seen as threatened mainly by a rapidly rising population. Especially among policy-makers and NGOs has there been a tendency to take Sahelian field expansion as a given, a tendency which may be due to general narratives assuming that rural land use changes progress linearly and are primarily driven by population growth.

These simplistic explanations of the changes in Sahelian land use systems over time are based on the default assumption that farmers are subsistence farmers with a primary goal of producing food for the family. The field size is thus assumed to be a direct function of the family's food requirements, the available labour force and the crop yields. However, the deficiencies of such purely unidirectional perceptions of land use changes became apparent in the beginning of 2000, when researchers raised concerns about such general narratives of Sahelian land use changes, and their being mainly driven by population growth.[33]

Aiming to explore if the cultivated area really had expanded in order to supply a growing population, fieldwork was

Millet fields after harvest, Yomboli, Northern Burkina Faso.

conducted in 2010 in the village of Yomboli located in Northern Burkina Faso, on the desert margins of the Sahel. When trends in the size of the cultivated area are compared with population growth in a particular area, it should be acknowledged that the two elements operate at different time scales. While demographic changes most often operate at a rather long, at least generational, time scale, the size of the cultivated area may vary from year to year. In the attempt to estimate the population growth, it thus seemed reasonable to compare different points in time and thereby estimate a general trend. No official demographic statistics exist, for the case area, however, but the population had actually been counted during fieldwork in 1995[34] and now again in 2010. Based on these counts,

LIVING WITH ENVIRONMENTAL CHANGE

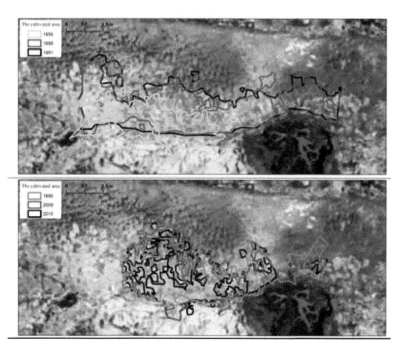

Changes in the cultivated area
during the period 1956–2010,
Yomboli.

an annual population growth rate of almost 2 per cent was estimated over those 15 years.

Turning to the changes in the size of the cultivated area, it would be misleading to include only two snapshots in time as was done for the population counting. That would not reveal anything about the dynamics in the intervening period. Instead, the quantification of land use changes rested on the use of aerial photos from 1955 and 1956, SPOT satellite images from 1988, 1989 and 1991 and GPS measurements carried out in the village of Yomboli in 1995 and 2010. The aim of this approach was to assess long-term changes as well as annual variations in the cultivated area.

As it turned out, people chose to cultivate a varying field size from year to year, depending on a wide range of factors such as the rain, crop prices and access to other income-providing activities. In Yomboli, substantial changes in the cultivated area were thus evident in the past few decades. The total field acreage more than doubled from 1956 to 1991, which corresponded to the immediate expectations of common responses to population growth and increased food requirements. More surprising was the reversed trend from 1991. The expansion of the fields stopped and total field acreage in 2010 was half of what it had been in 1991. During conversations with the people of Yomboli about this reversed trend, it did not take long before the diminishing role of agricultural production became apparent. It appeared that there was a strong focus on a cereal bank constructed in 1989 in the village by the Food and Agriculture Organization (FAO), which provided people with millet on credit or at highly subsidized prices. With this new possibility of buying millet in the village, people could not see the point in maintaining their large fields and continuing the physically demanding agricultural work. Rather, they began to regard non-agricultural activities as an optimal solution to the growing population and the low yields as these activities would provide them with an income to buy millet in the new cereal bank.

Moreover, there was a considerable difference in the size of the cultivated area from 2009 to 2010. Due to very dry conditions in

[33] Lambin, E.F., Geist, H.J., and Lepers, E. Dynamics of land-use and land-cover change in tropical regions, *Annual Review of Environmental Resources*, 28 (2003): 205–241.

[34] Reenberg, A., Nielsen, T.L., and Rasmussen, K. Field expansion and reallocation in the Sahel:land use pattern dynamics in a fluctuating biophysical and socio-economic environment, *Global Environmental Change*, 8 (1998): 309–327.

2009, many young men were forced to go on transhumance with their herds towards Mali and Niger in order to find pasture and water for the animals. The extremely dry conditions triggered a lengthening of both routes and duration of the transhumance. Normally, the men would be away for a couple of months, but then return around May when the rainy season as well as the agricultural work was about to begin. However, in 2010, the men stayed away for longer and did not return until August–September. Hence, there was a lack of labour in Yomboli, especially during the labour-intensive weeding in June, July and August. Despite good rain in 2010, the lack of labour thereby constrained the possibilities of field enlargements.

To return to the prevailing narrative of Sahelian land use systems that assumes close links between field expansion and population pressure, the above example shows that this unidirectional narrative may not conform well to reality. During the past 15 years, the food requirements had increased in Yomboli due to a growing population, but in the same period, the food production had decreased due to field abandonment, as people had moved away from being subsistence farmers. Population growth was thus clearly not the most important factor affecting the size of the cultivated area as fast-changing variables like credit possibilities offered by the millet bank and a sudden very dry year in 2009 constituted the main triggers of change in Yomboli. In that way, it became clear how processes that take place simultaneously, but have rather different time scales, may interact in a number of different ways, and how the link between field expansion and population growth has become very blurred.

Villagers buying millet from the cereal bank at low prices.

Millet for storage in the cereal bank.

LIVING WITH ENVIRONMENTAL CHANGE

Jonas Ø. Nielsen

THREE CALENDARS AND THE TEST OF TIME IN NORTHERN SAHEL

Ripples of sand in the dune. Often used as a metaphor to indicate the passing of time.

Among the Fulani living in northern Burkina Faso time depends upon which calendar is in use. Having three calendars, the Gregorian or Western calendar, the Hijri or Islamic calendar, and a traditional Fulani calendar, establishing when something took place or is going to take place is always a matter of discussion and clarification.

In general, official meetings with, for example, development project extension workers or at the town hall are always organized according to the Gregorian calendar. Religious events like Ramadan and the yearly pilgrimage to Mecca, the Hajj, are organized according to the Hijri calendar, and finally everyday subsistence activities like agriculture and herding are organized according to the Fulani calendar.

Unlike the Gregorian, which is a solar calendar, and the Islamic calendar, which is lunar, the Fulani calendar is organized according to annual climatic events. Like the Gregorian calendar, the Fulani calendar has four 'seasons': *Ndungu* (approximately June, July, August), *djamde* (approximately September, October, November), *dabundé* (approximately December, January, February) and *tjendu* (approximately March, April, May).

Ndungu comprises the wet months and correlates with the rainy season. *Djamde* is split in two periods. September and October are deemed 'humid hot' because of the moisture still in the air and because sporadic rain might still fall in September. November is a kind of in-between month. It is still a bit humid but the dry season is approaching quickly. It is also getting colder especially in the morning. *Dabundé* is a period of dry, 'cold' and windy weather and lasts until late February or early March when the last season, the *Tjendu*, starts. This is a period with extreme dry heat.

That climatic conditions and not the solar or lunar movements determine the annual calendar cycle among the Fulani makes talking about a fixed yearly calendar difficult. Correlating the Fulani calendar to the Gregorian one is hence very difficult. The 'new year' in the Fulani calendar starts with the first rain and not the 1st of January. The *Ndungu* or beginning of a new year is thus quite a variable point in time, because the first rain might fall early May or early June.

LIVING WITH ENVIRONMENTAL CHANGE

This does not necessarily push the other seasons as the rain might indeed stop in late August or early September, but sometimes rain falls until mid-October. Correlating dates is similarly difficult. Whereas the Gregorian calendar day changes at midnight, a Fulani day finishes when the sun sets.

When it comes to juxtaposing years, the challenge becomes even greater. Not only do the beginnings of the Fulani and the Gregorian year not correspond, but the Fulani years are also not numbered, but rather named in the Fulani calendar. It takes time and patience to align 'The year of the crickets' (2003), 'the year of the Malian immigrants' (1983–1984) or 'the year of the sun' (1973–1974) with the Gregorian calendar.

Northern Burkina Faso is, in other words, teeming with temporalities. Nevertheless, the Gregorian calendar is gaining ground. There are many reasons for this. The ever-encroaching state and its administrative procedures, the presence of Western-sponsored development projects, the establishment of schools running according to a nationally determined 'school year', and the increasing dependence upon wage labour organized in 24-hour shifts, weekdays and Gregorian months put 'Fulani time', as it is called locally, under pressure. But inter-seasonal and inter-annual weather variations are also to 'blame'.

Stories of a changing climate are rife in this region. Persistent drought periods hit the region in the early 1970s and 1980s and while the rain today is more abundant, it does not necessarily fall the right way and at the right times. The latter in particular creates problems for the Fulani calendar.

Based upon the changing seasons and to a large extent the predictability of these seasons, the Fulani calendar is becoming more and more obsolete in a time of increasing inter-seasonal and inter-annual rainfall variability. It makes little sense to organize the year according to climatic periods such as the rainy season if this does not arrive, or lasts only a month. A calendar, I was consistently told by the villagers, needs some kind

Hamidou, the traditional chief of the village, and a valuable source of information on time.

of yearly consistency to be an effective organizing tool. Moreover the Fulani calendar is closely correlated to subsistence activities and mainly agriculture, but as people are gradually abandoning agriculture and taking up other forms of work due to the poor and unpredictable rain, the Fulani calendar does not serve them well as a way to organize their daily work.

Yet it is still in use. Years are best remembered in the village by way of names. 'The year with a very cold *Dabundé*', or cold dry season, still makes more sense in the village than, in this case, 1997. The Fulani calendar captures the sensory experience of past life

Mamadou trying to draw a calendar in the sand. Moussa, my field assistant, is taking notes.

Harvest time. Moussa holding a millet stalk.

better than the Gregorian calendar. As such, the Fulani calendar is a calendar that – as it was put by Isa, an elderly Rimaiibe man – "describes what has been". Thinking of the current inter-seasonal variability and the socio-economic-political reality of life in the village, Isa's description of the Fulani calendar seems spot on.

LIVING WITH ENVIRONMENTAL CHANGE

'PACKAGES' WITH DISPARATE TIME HORIZONS

I am in the Upper East Region of Ghana in order to interview local Ghanaian development practitioners. In 2007, the area experienced major and unusual flooding, and there is general agreement, locally as well as globally, that there is a link to climate change. People in the area are therefore worried that flooding may become a recurrent problem. Before the 2007 floods many local and international organizations working in the area focused on the problem of drought, so I am interested in learning about how the new focus on climate change and flooding may have changed the way the local practitioners carry out and perceive their work.

Researchers put their hand into the relief package. You are compromising our identity, integrity. You are creating broken homes. You as a donor can pull out, but we are left.

(Albert, Ghanaian development practitioner)

Today, I have been lucky to meet two insightful local development practitioners, Albert and Dennis, at the same time. They come from two different organizations and they eagerly discuss the questions I raise. Albert is telling me about Cash for Food, a new system of distributing relief: "We determine the amount of cash a household will need for a month, we call on the households and give them the cash." The idea behind this system, which has been instituted by some donors after the floods in 2009, is that by giving

people cash, they are able to purchase their food in the area, thus supporting the local economy. These donors regard this as better than giving victims of flooding foods that are likely to have been imported. Albert and Dennis feel, however, that by introducing a new system, the donors are forcing them to start from scratch instead of allowing them to build on their considerable experience from the 2007 flooding: "Checks and balances improve with strategies that we have tried before and know, and now we are basically starting over."

Before the Cash for Food system, donors had enforced a different system. First, the local development practitioners were instructed to distribute immediate aid/food; then they were to hand out coupons that could be exchanged for essentials during the long-term recovery stage. This, Albert

The drying of mud bricks that will be used to rebuild a house destroyed by flooding.

Home destroyed by the flooding.

LIVING WITH ENVIRONMENTAL CHANGE

and Dennis feel, was more transparent. They worry that giving cash could create "broken homes" caused by disputes between household members about how to spend the money. Perhaps the household head could be tempted to spend it on *pito* – the local beer. Dennis agrees with the argument that, while the NGOs could have got more food for the same amount of money, if they had imported it all from the south of Ghana, they would not be supporting those local farmers whose agriculture was not affected by the floods. In this sense he can see that cash for food could be a good idea. He wonders, however: "What is the likelihood of the local market being able to have enough food to sell when there has been a disaster?"

Albert and Dennis feel that the reason the system of distributing aid is changing all the time is that "researchers" are using aid distribution as a way of testing different hypotheses. Instead of calling these relief packages, Albert and Dennis therefore refer to them as "research packages". They are both very upset by this. Albert further explains that in 2007 communities had seen that the relief package worked. Therefore, many communities rushed to the community meetings that they held concerning aid after the 2009 floods, because they felt it was worth the effort to show up based on their experiences in 2007. It was one of the biggest turnouts he had seen; normally it is hard to get the communities to meet. They are worried that with the new system, they will lose the trust that they had managed to build up with the communities. Albert then clarifies the difference between what he calls a relief package and a research package. In a research package, he explains, the end result does not matter, because it is about testing models, but in a relief package the end result is of vital importance to the people involved. Sometimes, they feel, it can be useful with research, but in general, Albert and Dennis argue, periods of emergency are a bad time to test models, i.e. to do a research package.

As a researcher myself, I am feeling a bit concerned about their frustration with researchers, but I realize that there is a real disconnect here concerning time horizons. Albert and Dennis have worked in this area for many years and plan to continue doing so for the rest of their careers. The large number of international organizations that came into the area because of the extent and severity of the 2007 floods "pulled out" as soon as the humanitarian crisis subsided. In terms of time horizons, the international disaster relief organizations have the shortest time horizons. The international organizations working with "development" issues have somewhat longer time horizons because their projects usually run over several years. Finally, the local "partner" organizations have the longest time horizons, being embedded in the societies receiving aid. These differences in time horizons can create tensions and misunderstandings between the organizations. Some of the local partner organizations, for example, find that they have to combine funding from several short-term projects supported by different international donors in order to create some continuity in the work they carry out in the communities. Even though they strive to fulfil the varying goals of the differently funded projects, this may cause some misunderstandings between donors and their local partners. The local partner organizations are often frustrated about the changing goals and conditions of implementation that come with the funding – it is difficult to establish good relations with a community when they have to keep changing the way they carry out their projects.

It is possible, however, that the time horizons of the different types of organizations may shift as a result of climate change. Organizations that used to work primarily with longer-term development issues are feeling the need to get involved with shorter-term relief work. They are experiencing difficulty talking to people about, for example, gender and corruption, when

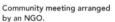
Community meeting arranged
by an NGO.

Private home rebuilt with
assistance from the Red Cross.

they have no homes and have lost all their food because of a major flooding disaster. Conversely, organizations that have primarily provided immediate relief aid are realizing that in order to prepare the local populations for the new and recurring natural disasters, they need to engage in longer-term projects. In general, climate change – having a much longer time horizon – is a challenge for organizations that are used to working

with time horizons where they can have measurable results within a few years. With climate change, organizations are preparing for the unknown – which will happen at an unknown time. This is especially the case in a place like West Africa where models predicting changes in rainfall point in disparate directions, some predicting more floods, others more droughts. In order to prepare for climate change international organizations could thus be pushed to change their time horizons. By engaging in an area for a longer period of time, there may be less short-term testing of various models and instead more continuity. Perhaps through longer-term engagements, the experiences of the local practitioners could even be recognized by donors and incorporated into the project design.

275

LIVING WITH ENVIRONMENTAL CHANGE

URBAN TALKS ABOUT CLIMATE AND WEATHER

On 9 May 2011, I joined two female social workers from the municipal district of Cayma on their monthly tour to marginal neighbourhoods, where provisions of powdered milk and cereals are distributed to mothers of young children. This distribution is part of a national Peruvian programme called *Vaso de Leche*, a glass of milk, which provides nutritional support to children of poor families. In Cayma, milk and cereal were distributed by two social workers, Bridget and Edith, and a driver, Señor Jacinto, in a big old yellow pick-up truck from 1971. The car belonged to the municipality of Cayma, to be used for official services only.

I joined the distribution party because I was looking for a neighbourhood, in which to study neighbourhood organization and access to drinking water. The four of us were sitting in the front seats of the municipal car. On this day we visited all marginal neighbourhoods in Cayma, which are mainly placed far up the slopes of the volcano Chachani. In each neighbourhood we stopped and delivered a measured amount of powdered milk and cereals in small bags to the neighbourhood president of *Vaso de Leche*. The day was opaque and rather windy; clouds of dust were periodically lifted from dirt roads, and blowing through the areas we were passing. The atmosphere in the car was cheerful. As we went along the milk route, the talk travelled along a variety of themes: Peruvian dishes, politics and upcoming presidential elections, social differences, neighbourhood development in Arequipa and the quality of

life in other countries of the world. During one of the stops, the conversation started turning around the weather.

Bridget: It is a strange day today [*el día está raro*], so many clouds around the volcanoes…

Jacinto: We are in May; weather is never like this in May. The clouds are charging, as if it is going to rain. Probably this year it will be raining already in August. Normally, the sky looks like this in September …

Astrid: And why would it be like this now?

Bridget: I wonder why the climate is changing … some say it's because the world is going to end in 2012 … but I don't believe in that.

We went on talking about the Mayan calendar and different end-of-the-world theories.

Wind blowing through a neighbourhood on the margins of the city.

LIVING WITH ENVIRONMENTAL CHANGE

The municipal yellow pick-up truck driving up to the district of Cayma to deliver milk to needy homes.

Social worker, Edith, delivering milk on a not-so-usual-weather day.

Bridget: I wonder what the end of the world will be like [*cómo será el fin del mundo*] … will it be a big atomic bomb? Or an enormous earthquake or natural disaster …? Somehow the impacts of these disasters are always limited; they don't bring the whole world to an end … Maybe it will be a world war. Yet it would take many years for it to arrive in Peru.

Jacinto: I once saw a movie in which the ocean eats the entire earth; no human being is left, and it looked terrible.

Astrid: I have heard many people in Arequipa say that the next world war will be because of water.

Bridget: Yeah, that's because fresh water will be used up. Here in Peru, for instance, the glaciers are disappearing, and that means we increasingly have less fresh water. All fresh water goes to the sea and becomes salt water.

Edith comes back to the car and joins the talk:

Edith: Don't say those things. Here in Peru we have many saints [*muchos santitos*] that protect us.

She looks to the sky:

But it is true; the weather [*el clima*] is very strange today …

In Spanish, as in other neo-Latin languages, the word for time – *tiempo* – also means weather. In Latin America, however, it is more common to talk about *el clima* – climate – when referring to the weather. This means that in a very practical manner, on an everyday level, the idea of a clear distinction between *weather* as the instantaneous, immediate state of the atmosphere, events of temperature, wind and rain elapsing and changing over time, and *climate* as a more general weather pattern taking place over a longer duration, is constantly ignored or mixed together as weather and climate are enacted as either *el clima* or *el tiempo*.

We keep driving upwards, the neighbourhoods around us become of more recent date. Precarious houses built in stone. Señor

Jacinto has worked in the municipality of Cayma for 20 years. He has seen many neighbourhoods arise, many of the upper settlements were founded 15 years ago but still don't have running water or a sewage system.

It seems Bridget has kept thinking about the weather, after a while she comments in a neutral tone:

> Arequipa used to be full of frogs. They are gone now. Some people say they are having an assembly in a secret place, planning how to take back the land that once was theirs.

It remains unclear whether Bridget actually thinks frogs will take over Arequipa or not; the point is that a future scenario is being produced, one in which the place of human life on earth will be significantly different.

The conversation in the yellow municipal pick-up took place in a particular and utmost quotidian here and now, in which the focus was all of a sudden pushed towards

the end of human history – the exact time of its occurrence being unknown – by clouds oddly gathering around the Arequipan volcanoes. The oddity of the phenomenon was due to seasonality rather than the occurrence itself: clouds embracing the volcanoes are known as signs of soon coming rain, which is a phenomenon seen in September and *not* in May. What to the person from outside seemed like a small alteration in weather patterns, triggered uncertainty of the near and far future among local Arequipans.

Further, it is interesting to note that several elements or reference points were drawn into and enacted in the conversation, together producing a plural temporality: Catholic saints, cinematic fiction, local meteorology, Mayan calendars, frogs, natural disasters and world wars were equally pulled into the talk, in order to make sense of and create some kind of response to the odd clouds being observed around the volcanoes. Each of these elements corresponds to a particular temporal and spatial logic, and each holds a different place in memory, imagination and expectations for the future.

The narrated conversation reveals how different temporalities, weather and climate become intertwined in particular ways when local theories are produced to make sense of odd changes observed in the sky. The conversation took place in a particular chronological time, framed by the distribution of milk in marginal neighbourhoods; yet, the times pulled into the conversation were plural, dispersed across different temporalities, where a singular and linear order of time seemed absent. This conversation was particularly rich in mixing a plurality of elements and temporalities to produce particular understandings of what is going on in the present and what will happen in the future. But generally, when people in Arequipa theorize about climatic and weather changes, they draw on a variety of elements in the near or faraway environment, and include plural temporalities, in the production of explanations and construction of possible future scenarios.

Clouds stroking the volcano Chachani. Not a normal sight in May.

LIVING WITH ENVIRONMENTAL CHANGE

MIRRORING

The notion of man-made climate change is introducing a characteristic sense of urgency.

TIMES OF CLIMATE CHANGE IN RELIGION AND ETHICS
MIRRORING THE ANDES AND THE PACIFIC

Concepts such as 'accelerated sea level rise', 'the melting of glaciers', 'tipping points', 'negative feed-back mechanisms' are dotting the news reports. Scientists urge politicians and populations to act now in order to avoid long-term changes. We have to do something *now* with the far future in mind.

Knowledge of many modes – sciences, policies and theologies – is now struggling to fill the gap between the urgent present and the long-term scenario of a changing climate by articulating visions for the present and the future. In Christianity, which is the largest religion in the Andean and the Pacific context, multiple time frames are envisioned all at once with notable differences from congregation to congregation. In some cases doomsday is regularly announced, in others the present responsibility towards one's neighbour and immediate environment is constantly addressed. These differences parallel major trends in Christian responses to climate change.[35] For some, climate change denotes a lost Eden, an imminent apocalypse, for others it is yet another occasion for mobilizing social and environmental justice.

Tunsho, or Pukaraju, set against the dark skies of the incipient rainy season.

Nadi Bay, Fiji.

END OF DAYS: ESCHATOLOGIES

The Andean and the Pacific landscapes are marked with signs that testify to the presence of Christianity. Churches abound, and even the tiniest of villages have their churches, chapels and altars. In the Andes, the Spanish brought Catholic Christianity, while the English Protestantism of the twentieth century gave light to a mix of congregations. Most places will not only have one, but at least two churches. In the everyday life, overlaps between congregations occur, and few are those who will fundamentally insist that one church excludes the other. Either way, the everyday is infused with Christian thought; even as it blends with other ways of knowing about the world, it provides a powerful foundation for understanding expected and unexpected turns of events.

Living in the tropical highlands, one has an easy view of the effects of climate change so elaborately documented by science, as formerly snow-capped peaks are turning into hard, solid and barren rock.[36] Being preoccupied with the end of the world, Andean

LIVING WITH ENVIRONMENTAL CHANGE

Christianity has no trouble incorporating the vanishing glaciers into a sequence of events that would also include killings, theft, war and violent deaths. 'It must be happening by permission of our divine', one old man says with a view to the mountains. 'How must his head be?', a woman asks rhetorically with reference to her heavenly Father as she goes through the 'deaths' and 'disgraces' of the contemporary world. Moral decay within humanity at large has led the Almighty to initiate the steps towards the final day, Judgement Day, where the good and righteous can go to a better place. The end of the world is therefore not the end of everything, but rather the chance of a new beginning. Don Elias tells me how heaven is certain for those who believe and live righteous lives. To him, the end of this world does not end all worlds.

The Gospel provides consolation in times of hardship for the mainly Pentecostal society of believers. And while some parts of Catholic Peru are becoming increasingly secular, the Word of the Bible weighs heavily in the Andes. A Christian model of climate change puts the present-day turn of events into a larger picture by naturalizing and moralizing about it. The old man continues, still looking towards the peaks of the mountains:

> He is stipulating the descent, the coming. Now, Judgment Day. It cannot be anything else … The world is moving forward; it is because there is a lot of disorder … Some don't believe in God, they are dedicated to stealing, to making themselves rich, cheating on the poor. There is no compassion: everybody must seek for himself. We are insulting God. We don't believe … everybody is dedicated to having more.
> [That is why] He is controlling and taking down the entire Cordillera … In my opinion, [Poccrac in twenty years] will be deserted.

A literalistic approach to biblical time frames is pronounced in pre-millennialist Christianities. Accordingly, the least optimistic scenarios of climate change projections feed well into certain 'last days' doctrines. In many Pacific churches, the importance of the Old Testament provides fertile soils for framing environmental changes in patterns of sin and redemption.[37] Notably, the projection of a rising sea level has highlighted the flood narrative in Genesis and God's promise not to flood the world again.

'If the world is flooded, and our islands are projected to sink, what happened to God's promise to Noah?' This question is reportedly often asked of church leaders in the Pacific when they work on 'raising awareness' of climate change in island communities. It calls for diverse answers. In some cases, the existence of global warming is denied and also that the rising seas are actually a kind of flood comparable to the biblical flood, in other cases, the trustworthiness of climate change scenarios are questioned.

Projections of climatic changes such as more severe cyclones may also call upon more intensified reactions of an apocalyptic character. In 2010, a letter was widely circulated in Fiji, entitled "A coming disaster (a message to all in Fiji)", warning that a great cyclone and tsunami would hit Fiji at a certain point of time a few months ahead. Signed by a pastor, the warning included numerous citations from the Bible and referred specifically to a number of signs and answers from God. It is explicitly stated that the intention was not to cause panic, but to give people a fair chance to prepare themselves with confidence in God's plans. The letter had a mixed reception among Christian Fijians. Some were reported to leave their homes for higher grounds, some kept children at home from school. Others could not hide a mischievous smile. Surely, they did not expect the Lord to take such action. According to the *Fiji Times*, the prophet was taken into custody for causing "unnecessary panic and anxiety".

Many islanders move on with a characteristic weaving between biblical and secular perspectives: "The meteorological officers, they will tell us if a tsunami is coming," one

San Yldefonso, guardian of herders, on the roadside with Mt. Huascaran hovering in the background.

Signpost at Suva Point, Fiji.

Rureq and the neighbouring peaks of the southern part of Peru's Cordillera Blanca.

lady voiced when discussing the coming and going of prophecies. "But", she added, "we do see many signs, for example, natural disasters, and climate change, indicating that we are getting closer to the end times."

The biblical cosmology is an important time machine in the imagination of the past, the present and the future. Yet, the different versions differ highly. Even in small places, the distribution of religion and science is uneven. This means that climate change is not only received differently by communities; it is also lived in manifold ways, stretching its ways into a meshwork of times of diverse and intermingling worldviews and cosmologies. Several flows of globalization interact, among them the spread of Christianities and versions of climate change.

NEXT DAYS: THE WORK IN PROGRESS AND PROTESTS

Some varieties of Christianity are explicitly engaged with the present ecological crises as both a natural, social and religious crisis. Some versions focus in particular at the personal and the community's responsibility. Notions of stewardship flourish. God told men and women to be responsible for the created world. The question is thus: how can Christians be good stewards and protect the land, the sea and all living creatures? The atmosphere and the oceans are thus included in prayers and exegesis.

Local theologies are now navigating in a new climate. The claim is that Christianity holds universal truths when made relevant and engaging for each generation and each congregation. Many advocates and preachers

LIVING WITH ENVIRONMENTAL CHANGE

In different forms, Christianity has long been part of the Andean landscape.

Cook Islands Christian Church, Avarua.

are attempting to renew and reform Christianity in new directions, an effort that may incorporate politics, economic theories and environmental issues in new variations. Eco-theologies are taking shape as climate theologies.

We would like to say a word about God's promise to Noah not to flood the Earth again. Some Christians view this covenant as a guarantee that they are not at risk of flooding from climate change. But the sea level is rising and threatening Pacific Islands with flooding from high tides and storm surges. This is not an act of God. It is a result of human economic and consumer activities that pollute the atmosphere and lead to climate change. Most of these polluting emissions come from highly industrialized countries. Our response to God's covenant should be to act in love toward God's creation and to reduce the pollution that

is contributing to climate change. By placing us on the Earth, God has given us both the right to use it and the responsibility to do so with care.

(Otin taai, 2004)[38]

In order to distinguish themselves, theologies of climate change are engaged in a critique of existing theologies. Spiritual, inwardly 'sin and redemption', and eschatologically oriented versions of Christianity are criticized for not taking the environment seriously. Literalist biblical beliefs are invited to respond to the covenant with God with a renewed respect for the changed and suffering creation. New environmental ethics is being shaped in the spaces between theologies and politics.[39]

Turning to the Andes again, in some cases, an ethics of the environment is successfully maturing and plans are made for securing e.g. water resources, recognizing that these are often inseparable from other pressures. In the Andes, water resources are

[35] Hulme, M. Four Meanings of Climate Change, in S. Skrimshire (ed.) *Future Ethics: Climate Change and Apocalyptic Imagination* (London: Continuum, 2010), pp. 37–58.

[36] See Mark, B.G., *et al.* Climate Change and Tropical Andean Glacier Recession: Evaluating Hydrologic Changes and Livelihood Vulnerability in the Cordillera Blanca, Peru, *Annals of the Association of American Geographers*, 100(4) (2010): 794–805.

[37] Ernst, M. New Forms of Christianity and the Dynamics of Religious Change in the Pacific islands, in M. Ernst et al. (eds) *The Pacific Islands: Society, Culture, Religion* (Suva, Fiji: Pacific Theological College, 2009).

[38] Otin taai (Sunrise) *Statement and Recommendations from the World's Council of Churches in the Pacific and WCC Member Churches in the Pacific, 6–11 March 2004* (Tarawa, Kiribati).

[39] Rubow, C. and Bird, C. (forthcoming) *Eco-theological Responses to Climate Change in Oceania*.

In 2010, a letter was widely circulated in Fiji warning that a great cyclone and tsunami would hit Fiji. Signed by a pastor, the warning included numerous citations from the Bible and referred specifically to a number of signs and answers from God. According to the Fiji Times, the prophet was taken into custody for causing 'unnecessary panic and anxiety'.

both the mining company and the government ministry were assuring the worried peasants that no harm would be inflicted on their lives, the experience of people living in a traditional mining region had taught them caution. A mine located at the very source of life for the entire valley was more than could be accepted.

The struggle against the mine that started on Parco Bridge in Cátac was therefore a moral struggle. It was a struggle to be taken into account, to be considered equal citizens in an unequal country. Values for an ethical life – Christian, Andean, international law – merged as the upset peasants argued against a particular use of the waters that were seen to be not only the source of life, but, indeed, life itself.

CLIMATE TIMES

A new environmental ethics is being formed as challenges to the very existence on Earth present themselves to people. Whereas the Christian eschatologies may bring certain forms of comfort by ordering the sequences of events into an easily recognizable past, present and future, and thus tapping otherwise dim prospects of the near future into a reassuring narrative of salvation, the emerging ethics tackles the future in different yet sometimes complementary ways. These are futures that can be rewritten by challenging the order of things of the present, insisting that things could be otherwise, be it in terms of theologies or politics, or somewhere in-between.

As matters of concern are articulated in different idioms, new horizons of action and engagement emerge. Climate change not only concerns the accumulation of past times, but offers a gaze into the future. Climate change is framed by particular temporalities; events are connected differently, and different possible futures come into being. How one interprets the past, engages the present and imagines the future are all intimately linked.

also put under threat by an entirely different global force: the unceasing mining for metals to sustain economic growth. An unequal distribution of water and harm come to stand as a symbol of the indifference of the government, of its valuation of money and material prosperity over the well-being of its citizens. Evoking an ethics of the environment, the deprivation of water resources in the Andes has increasingly proved capable of provoking popular unrest in order to defend the lives not only of this generation, but those of children and grandchildren.

During one such surge of protest an entire valley known as the Callejón den Huaylas was paralyzed during a week of intense struggle and direct confrontation between police forces and angry peasants upset by what could only be interpreted by them as utter disregard for their well-being and way of life. A mine was to be established in the headwaters of the main river, threatening to pollute and perhaps even dry up their valuable source of water and life. Although

BIBLIOGRAPHY

WATER

Allen, C. J. (1997) When pebbles move mountains: iconicity and symbolism in Quechua ritual. In R. Howard-Malverde (ed.) *Creating Context in Andean Cultures*. New York: Oxford University Press.

Aron fra Kangeq and Thisted, K. (1999) *"Således skriver jeg, Aron", samlede fortællinger og illustrationer af Aron fra Kangeq (1822–1869)*, vols I–II. Nuuk: Atuakkiorfik.

Barnes, J. (2012) Pumping possibility: agricultural expansion through desert reclamation in Egypt. *Social Studies of Science*, 42 (4): 517–538.

Bonte, P. (1975) Pasteurs et nomades: l'exemple de la Mauritanie. In P. Bonte, J. Copans, S. Lallemand, C. Messiant, C. Raynaut, and J. Swift (eds) *Sécheresses et Famines du Sahel*, vol. 2: *Paysans et Nomades*. Paris: Maspero.

Carey, M. (2010) *In the Shadow of Melting Glaciers: Climate Change and Andean Society*. New York: Oxford University Press.

Carey, M., Huggel, C., Bury, J., Portocarrero, C. and Haeberli, W. (2012) An integrated socio-environmental framework for glacier hazard management and climate change adaptation: lessons from Lake 513, Cordillera Blanca, Peru. *Climatic Change*, 112 (3–4): 733–767.

Carse, A. (2012) Nature as infrastructure: making and managing the Panama Canal watershed. *Social Studies of Science*, 42(4): 539–563.

Christensen, J. H., et al. (2007) Regional climate projections. In S. Solomon, *et al.* (eds) *Climate Change 2007: The Physical Science Basis: Contribution of Working Group 1 to the Fourth Assessment Report of the Intergovernmental Panel on Climate Change*. Cambridge: Cambridge University Press, pp. 847–940.

da Vinci, L. (2008) *Notebooks*. Selected by I. A. Richter; edited with an introduction and notes by T.Wells; preface by M. Kemp. Oxford: Oxford University Press.

de Bruijn, M. and van Dijk, H. (2005) *Arid Ways: Cultural Understandings of Insecurity in Fulbe Society, Central Mali*. Amsterdam: Thela Publishers.

Gulløv, H.C. (ed.) (2004) *Grønlands forhistorie*. Copenhagen: Gyldendal.

Grigg, R.W. (1982) Darwin Point: a threshold for atoll formation. *Coral Reefs*, 1(1): 29–34.

Heide-Jørgensen, M.P., Hansen, R.G., Westdal K., Reeves, R.R. and Mosbech A. (2013) Narwhals and seismic exploration: is seismic noise increasing the risk of ice entrapments? *Biological Conservation*, 158: 50–54.

Helmreich, S. (2001) Nature/culture/seawater. *American Anthropologist*, 113(1): 132–144.

Hulme, M. (2001) Climatic perspectives on Sahelian desiccation: 1973–1998. *Global Environmental Change*, 11: 19–29.

Kallis, G. (2008) Droughts. *Annual Review of Environment and Resources*, 33: 85–118.

Knudsen, P. K. and Andreasen, C. (2009) *Cultural Historical Significance of Areas Tasersiaq and Tarsartuup Tasersua in West Greenland and Suggestions for Salvage Archaeology and Documentation in Case of Damming Lakes*. Nuuk: Nunatta Katersugaasivia Allagaateqarfialu. [In Danish].

Latour, B. (2005) *Reassembling the Social*. Oxford: Oxford University Press.

Linton, J. (2010) *What Is Water? The History of a Modern Abstraction*. Vancouver, BC: University of British Columbia Press.

Lyberth, K. (2010) *Siumut's landstingsgruppes kommentar til Redegørelse om aluminiumprojektet med udgangspunkt i de nu gennemførte undersøgelser, herunder den strategiske miljøvurdering* (SMV) Nuuk: Inatsisartut.

Maidment, D.R. (ed.) (1993) *Handbook of Hydrology.* New York: McGraw-Hill.

Nielsen, J.Ø. and Reenberg, A. (2010) Temporality and the problem of singling out rain as a driver of change in a small West African village. *Journal of Arid Environments,* 74: 464–474.

Nunn, P. (2007) *Climate, Environment and Society in the Pacific During the Last Millennium.* Amsterdam: Elsevier.

Nunn, P., Hunter-Anderson, R., Carson, M. T., Thomas, F., Ulm, S. and Rowland, M.J. (2007) Times of plenty, times of less: last-millennium societal disruption in the Pacific basin. *Human Ecology,* 35: 385–401.

Nunn, P. and Mimura, N. (2007) Promoting sustainability on vulnerable island coasts: a case study of the smaller Pacific islands. In L. McFadden and R.J. Nicholas (eds) *Managing Coastal Vulnerability.* Oxford: Elsevier.

Rasmussen, L.V. and Reenberg, A. (2012) Land use rationales in desert fringe agriculture. *Applied Geography,* 34: 595–605.

Reenberg, A. and Fog, B. (1995) The spatial pattern and dynamics of a Sahelian agro-ecosystem - land use systems analysis combining household survey with georelated information. *GeoJournal,* 37(4): 489–499.

Strang, V. (2006) Turning water into wine, beef and vegetables: material transformations along the Brisbane River, *Transforming Cultures, eJournal,* 1(2): 9–19.

Qujaakitsoq, U. (1990) Hunting regulations in Thule: a few salient features from the municipality of Qaanaaq. *North Atlantic Studies,* 2(1–2).

UNICEF and World Health Organization (2012) *Progress on Drinking Water and Sanitation: 2012 Update.* Geneva: WHO.

White, G.F., Bradley, D.J. and White, A.U. (1972) *Drawers of Water: Domestic Water Use in East Africa.* Chicago: University of Chicago Press.

White, I. and Falkland, T. (2010) Management of freshwater lenses on small Pacific islands. *Hydrogeology Journal,* 18: 227–246.

Wisner, B., Blaikie, P., Cannon, T. and Davis, I. (2004) *At Risk: Natural Hazards, People's Vulnerability, and Disasters.* London: Routledge.

TECHNOLOGY

Adriansen, H.K. and Nielson, T.T.(2005) The geography of pastoral mobility: a spatio-temporal analysis of GPS data from Sahelian Senegal. *Geo Journal,* 64: 177–188.

Allen, M.S. (1998) Holocene sea-level change on Aitutaki, Cook Islands: landscape change and human response. *Journal of Coastal Research,* 14: 10–22.

Bierschenk, T., Elwert, G. and Kohnert, D. (1991) The long-term effects of development aid: empirical studies in rural West Africa. *GIGA German Institute of Global and Area Studies/Institute of African Affairs.* MPRA Paper No. 4217.

Choplin, A. (2009) *Nouakchott: Au carrefour de la Mauritanie et du monde.* Paris: Karthala.

de Laet, M. and Mol, A. (2000) The Zimbabwe Bush Pump: Mechanics of a Fluid Technology. *Social Studies of Science,* 30(2): 225–263.

Feenberg, A.(1991) *Critical Theory of Technology.* New York: Oxford University Press.

Fleming, J.R. (2010) *Fixing the Sky: The Checkered History of Weather and Climate Control.* New York: Columbia University Press.

Ford, M. (2012) Shoreline changes on an urban atoll in the Central Pacific Ocean: Majuro Atoll, Marshall Islands. *Journal of Coastal Research*, 28(1): 11–22.

Gandy, M. (2004) Rethinking urban metabolism: water, space and the modern city. *City*, 8(3): 363–379.

Gardner, R. (2009) Trees as technology: planting shelterbelts on the Great Plains, *History and Technology: An International Journal*, 25(4): 325–341.

Graham, S. and Marvin, S. (2001) *Splintering Urbanism: Networked Infrastructure, Technological Mobilities and the Urban Condition.* London: Routledge.

Hastrup, F. (2011) *Weathering the World: Recovery in the Wake of the Tsunami in a Tamil Fishing Village.* Oxford: Berghahn Books.

Hastrup, K. and Skrydstrup, M. (eds) (2013) *The Social Life of Climate Change Models.* New York: Routledge.

Hughes, T.P. (2009) Technological momentum. In D.G. Johnson and J.M. Wetmore (eds), *Technology and Society: Building Our Sociotechnical Future.* Cambridge, MA: The MIT Press. pp. 141–150.

Ingold, T. (2011) Walking the plank. In T. Ingold, *Being Alive: Essays on Movement, Knowledge and Description.* London: Routledge, pp. 51–62.

Juul, K. (1996) Post drought migration and technological innovations among Fulani herders in Senegal: the triumph of the tube! *IIED Drylands Programme Issue Paper*, No. 64.

Latour, B. (1993) *We Have Never Been Modern.* Cambridge, MA: Harvard University Press.

Leach, M. and Mearns, R. (1996) Environmental change and policy: challenging received wisdom in Africa. In M. Leach and R. Mearns (eds) *The Lie of the Land: Challenging Received Wisdom on the African Environment.* Oxford: James Currey, pp. 1–33.

Linton, J. (2010) *What Is Water? The History of a Modern Abstraction.* Vancouver, BC: University of British Columbia Press.

Mauss, M. ([1935] 1973) Techniques of the body. *Economy and Society*, 2(1): 70–88.

Moriwaki, H. *et al.* (2006) Holocene changes in sea level and coastal environments on Rarotonga, Cook Islands, South Pacific Ocean. *The Holocene*, 16(6): 839–848.

Naalakkersuisut (2010) *White Paper on the Aluminium Project Based on Recent Completed Studies, Including the Strategic Environmental Assessment (SEA).* Nuuk: Greenland Self Rule.

Nielsen, J.Ø, D'Haen, S. and Reenberg, A. (2012) Adaptation to climate change as a development project: a case study from Northern Burkina Faso. *Climate and Development*, 4(1): 16–25.

Programa Subsectorial de Irrigaciones, available at: www.psi.gob.pe.

Rasmussen, K. (1932) *Den store slæderejse.* Copenhagen: Gyldendal.

Ross, J. (1819) *Voyage of Discovery, Made under the Orders of Admiralty, in His Majesty's Ships Isabelle and Alexander, for the Purpose of Exploring Baffin's Bay, and Inquiring into the Probability of a North-West Passage.* London: John Murray.

Salomon, F. and Niño-Murcia, M. (2011) *The Lettered Mountain: A Peruvian Village's Way with Writing.* Durham, NC: Duke University Press.

Scott, J. (1998) *Seeing Like a State. How Certain Schemes to Improve the Human Condition Have Failed.* New Haven, CT: Yale University Press

SEAFRAME. *The South Pacific Sea Level and Climate Monitoring Project. Sea Level Data Summary Report, July 2010–June 2011.* Available at: http://www.bom.gov.au/pacificsealevel/index.shtml.

Tsing, A. (2012) On nonscalability: the living world is not amenable to precision-nested scales. *Common Knowledge*, 18(3): 505–524.

Umeyama, M. (2012) Shore protection against sea level rise and tropical cyclones in small islands states. *Natural Hazards Review*, 13: 106–116.

White, I. and Falkland, T. (2010) Management of freshwater lenses on small Pacific islands. *Hydrogeology Journal*, 18(1): 227–246.

Winner, L. (2009) Do artifacts have politics? In D.G. Johnson and J.M. Wetmore (eds) *Technology and Society. Building Our Sociotechnical Future.* Cambridge, MA: The MIT Press, pp. 209–226.

LANDSCAPE

Allen, C. J. (1988) *The Hold Life Has: Coca and Cultural Identity in an Andean Community.* Washington, DC: Smithsonian Institution Press.

Anand, N. (2011) PRESSURE: the politechnics of water supply in Mumbai. *Cultural Anthropology*, 26(4): 542–564.

Apthorpe, R. (2011) Coda: with Alice in Aidland: a seriously satirical allegory. In D. Mosse (ed.) *Adventures in Aidland: The Anthropology of Professionals in International Development.* Oxford: Berghahn Books, pp. 199–220.

Australian Bureau of Meteorology and Commonwealth Scientific and Industrial Research Organization (CSIRO) (2011) *Climate Change in the Pacific: Scientific Assessment and New Research. Country Report. Cook Islands.*

Basso, K.H. (1996) *Wisdom Sits in Places. Landscape and Language among the Western Apache.* Albuquerque, NM: University of New Mexico Press.

Bates, B.C., Kundzewicz, Z.W., Wu, S. and Palutikof, J.P. (eds) (2008) *Climate Change and Water.* Technical Paper of the Intergovernmental Panel on Climate Change. Geneva: IPCC Secretariat.

Bender, B. (2002) Time and landscape. *Current Anthropology. 43, Supplement: Repertoires of Timekeeping in Anthropology (Aug.–Oct.)*: S103–S112

Benediktsson, K. and Lund, K.A. (eds) (2010) *Conversations with Landscape.* Farnham: Ashgate.

Bierschenk, T., Elwert, G. and Kohnert, D. (1993) The long-term effects of development aid: empirical studies in rural West Africa. *Economics*, 47(1): 83–111.

Bourdieu, P. (1990) *The Logic of Practice.* Cambridge: Polity Press

Brody, H. (1987) *Living Arctic.* London: Faber and Faber.

Deleuze, G. and Guattari, F. (2004) *A Thousand Plateaus. Capitalism and Schizophrenia* (trans. B. Massumi. London: Continuum.

Editorial (2009) *Participatory Learning and Action: Community-based Adaptation to Climate Change*, 60: 3–8.

Gandy, M. (2004) Rethinking urban metabolism: water, space and the modern city. *City*, 8(3): 363–379.

Gelles, P.H. (2000) *Water and Power in Highland Peru: The Cultural Politics of Irrigation and Development.* New Brunswick, NJ: Rutgers University Press.

Gose, P. (1994) *Deathly Waters and Hungry Mountains: Agrarian Ritual and Class Formation in an Andean Town.* Toronto: University of Toronto Press.

Hastrup. K. (2005) Social anthropology: towards a pragmatic enlightenment? *Social Anthropology*, 13: 133–149.

Hastrup, K. (2013) Anticipation on thin ice: diagrammatic reasoning among Arctic hunters. In K. Hastrup and M. Skrydstrup (eds) *The Social Life of Climate Change Models: Anticipating Nature*. London: Routledge, pp. 77–99.

Hermann, T. (2011) *Muri Water and Sanitation Project. Final Completion Report*. Cook Islands: Hermann Consultants.

Hirsch, E. and O'Hanlon, M. (eds) (1995) *The Anthropology of Landscape: Perspectives of Place and Space*. Oxford: Oxford University Press.

Ingold, T. (2000) *The Perception of the Environment: Essays on Livelihood, Dwelling and Skill*. London: Routledge.

Ingold, T. (2008a) Anthropology is *not* ethnography. Radcliffe-Brown Lecture in Social Anthropology 2007. *Proceedings of the British Academy*, 154: 69–92.

Ingold, T. (2008b) Footprints through the Weatherworld: walking, breathing, knowing. In *The Objects of Evidence: Anthropological Approaches to the Production of Knowledge*. Special issue of the *Journal of the Royal Anthropological Institute*, pp. 121–139.

James, W. (2003) *The Ceremonial Animal*. Oxford: Blackwell.

Lee, J. and Ingold, T. (2006) Fieldwork on foot: perceiving, routing, socializing. In S. Coleman and P. Collins (eds) *Locating the Field: Space, Place and Context in Anthropology*. Oxford: Berg, pp. 67–85.

Massey, D. (2005) *For Space*. London: Sage.

Meinig, D.W. (1976) The eholding eye: ten versions of the same scene. *Landscape Architecture*, 66(1): 47–54.

Mertz, O., Mbow, C., Nielsen, J.Ø., Maiga, A., Diallo, D., Reenberg, A., Diouf, A. *et al.* (2010) Climate factors play a limited role for past adaptation strategies in West Africa. *Ecology and Society*, 15(4): Article 25. Available at: http://www.ecologyandsociety.org/vol15/iss4/art25/.

Mertz, O., Mbow, C., Nielsen, J.Ø. *et al.* (2011) Adaptation strategies and climate vulnerability in the Sudano-Sahelian region of West Africa. *Atmospheric Science Letters*, 12(1):104–108.

Mosse, D. (2005) *Cultivating Development: An Ethnography of Aid Policy and Practice*. London: Pluto Press.

Nielsen, J.Ø. and Reenberg, A. (2010) Cultural barriers to climate change adaptation: a case study from Northern Burkina Faso. *Global Environmental Change*, 20: 142–152.

Orlove, B., Wiegandt, E. and Luckman, B.H. (eds) (2008) *Darkening Peaks: Glacier Retreat, Science, and Society*. Berkeley, CA: University of California Press.

Pedersen, M.A. (2009) At home away from homes: navigating the Taiga in Northern Mongolia. In P. Kirby (ed.) *Boundless Worlds: An Anthropological Approach to Movement*. Oxford: Berghahn Books. pp. 135–152.

Reenberg, A., Maman, I. and Oksen, P. (2013) Twenty years of land use and livelihood changes in SE-Niger: obsolete and short-sighted adaptation to climatic and demographic pressures? *Journal of Arid Environments*, 94: 47–58.

Retaille, D. (1998) Concepts du nomadisme et nomadisation des concepts. In R. Knafou (ed.) *La planète 'nomade'*. Paris: Éditions Belin, pp. 37–57.

Schama, S. (1995) *Landscape and Memory*. New York: Alfred A. Knopf.

Scott, J. (2009) *The Art of Not Being Governed: An Anarchist History of Upland Southeast Asia*. New Haven, CT: Yale University Press.

SEAFRAME. *The South Pacific Sea Level and Climate Monitoring Project. Sea Level Data Summary Report, July 2010–June 2011*. Available at: http://www.bom.gov.au/pacificsealevel/index.shtml.

Talu, A. (1979) *Kiribati: Aspects of History*. Suva: *Fiji Times and Herald Ltd*.

Tschakert, P., Sagoe, R., Ofori-Darko, G. and Codjoe, S. (2010) Floods in the Sahel: an analysis of anomalies, memory, and anticipatory learning. *Climatic Change*, 103: 471–502.

Tuan, Y.-F. (1990) *Topophilia: A Study of Environmental Perception, Attitudes, and Values*. New York Columbia University Press.

Vuille, M., Francou, B., Wagnon, P., Juen, I., Kaser, G., Mark, B.G. and Bradley, R.S. (2008) Climate change and tropical Andean glaciers: past, present and future. *Earth-Science Reviews*, 89 pp.

Wisner, B., Blaikie, P., Cannon, T. and Davis, I. (2004) *At Risk: Natural Hazards, People's Vulnerability, and Disasters*. London: Routledge.

TIME

Campbell, J. (2000) *Climate Change, Vulnerability, and Adaptation Assessment for Kiribati: Technical Summary and Synthesis*. Report prepared for the World Bank by the Centre for International Global Change Institute. Waikato University, Hamilton, New Zealand.

Cruikshank, J. (2005) *Do Glaciers Listen? Local Knowledge, Colonial Encounters, and Social Imagination*. Vancouver, BC: UBC Press.

de Menocal, P.B., Ortiz, J. Guilderson, T., Adkins, J., Sarnthein, M., Baker, L. and Yarusinski, M. (2000) Abrupt onset and termination of the African Humid Period: rapid climate response to gradual insolation forcing. *Quarterly Science Review*, 19: 347–361.

Ernst, M. (2009) New forms of Christianity and the dynamics of religious change in the Pacific islands. In M. Ernst *et al.* (eds) *The Pacific Islands. Society, Culture, Religion*. Suva, Fiji: Pacific Theological College.

Guillet, D. (1992) *Covering Ground. Communal Water Management and the State in the Peruvian Andes*. Ann Arbor. MI: University of Michigan Press.

Hastrup, F. (2013) Qualifying coastal nature. bio-conservation projects in South East India. In K. Hastrup (ed.) *Anthropology and Nature*. London: Routledge, pp. 43–61.

Hastrup, K. (2007) Performing the world: agency, anticipation and creativity. In E. Hallam and T. Ingold (eds) *Creativity and Cultural Improvisation*. Oxford: Berg, pp. 193–206.

Hodges, M. (2008) Rethinking time's arrow: Bergson, Deleuze and the anthropology of time. *Anthropological Theory*, 8: 399–429.

Hughes, T.P. (2009) Technological momentum. In D.G. Johnson and J.M. Wetmore (eds) *Technology and Society: Building Our Sociotechnical Future*. Cambridge, MA: The MIT Press, pp. 141–150.

Hulme, M. (2010) Four meanings of climate change. In S. Skrimshire, (ed.) *Future Ethics: Climate Change and Apocalyptic Imagination*. London: Continuum, pp. 37–58.

Ingold, T. (2000) The temporality of the landscape. In T. Ingold, *The Perception of the Environment: Essays in Livelihood, Dwelling and Skill*. London: Routledge, pp. 189–208.

James, W. and Mills, D. (2005) Introduction: from representations to action in the flow of time. In W. James and D. Mills (eds) *The Qualities of Time: Anthropological Approaches*. Oxford: Berg, pp. 1–18.

Koch, L. (1919) Geologiske iagttagelser. In K. Rasmussen, *Grønland langs Polhavet*. Copenhagen: Gyldendal, pp. 553–576.

Krader, L. (1959) The ecology of pastoral nomadism. *International Social Science Journal*, 11: 499–510.

Krupnik, I. and Jolly, D. (eds) (2002) *"The Earth is Faster Now": Indigenous Observations of Arctic Environmental Change*. Fairbanks: Arcus.

Lambin, E.F., Geist, H. J. and Lepers, E. (2003) Dynamics of land-use and land-cover change in tropical regions. *Annual Review of Environmental Resources*, 28: 205–241.

Linton, J. (2010) *What Is Water? The History of a Modern Abstraction*. Vancouver, BC: UBC Press.

MacCormack, G. (n.d.) *The Arapo and the Lunar Challenge*. Cook Islands: Natural Heritage.

Mark, B. G., *et al.* (2010) Climate change and tropical Andean glacier recession: evaluating hydrologic changes and livelihood vulnerability in the Cordillera Blanca, Peru. *Annals of the Association of American Geographers*, 100(4): 794–805.

Munn, N. (1992) The cultural anthropology of time: a critical essay. *Annual Review of Anthropology*, 21: 93–123.

Nouaceur, Z. (1995) Disparités pluviométriques régionales, sécheresse et modification des équilibres de l'environnement mauritanien. *Revue de géographie de Lyon*, 70(3–4): 239–245.

Orlove, B., Roncoli, C., Kabugo, M. and Majugu, A. (2010) Indigenous climate knowledge in southern Uganda: the multiple components of a dynamic regional system. *Climatic Change*, 100(2): 243–265.

Otin taai (Sunrise) (2004) *Statement and Recommendations from the World's Council of Churches in the Pacific and WCC Member Churches in the Pacific*, 6–11 March, Tarawa, Kiribati.

Prytz-Johansen, J. ([1954] 2012) The Maori and his religion in its non-ritualistic aspects. *Hau. Classics of Ethnographic Theory Series*. Available at: www.haujournal.org.

Puna, H. (2011) *The Cook Islands Herald*, November 10.

Reenberg, A. (2012) Insistent dryland narratives: portraits of knowledge about human–environmental interactions in Sahelian environment policy documents. *West African Journal of Applied Ecology*, 20(1): 97–111.

Reenberg, A., Nielsen, T.L. and Rasmussen, K. (1998) Field expansion and reallocation in the Sahel: land use pattern dynamics in a fluctuating biophysical and socio-economic environment. *Global Environmental Change*, 8: 309–327.

Rink, H. ([1877] 1974) On the glaciers and the origin of floating icebergs. (Appendix I), in *Danish Greenland, its People and Products*. London: Hurst.

Rubow, C. and Bird, C. (forthcoming) *Eco-theological Responses to Climate Change in Oceania*.

Salmond, A. (2012) Ontological quarrels: indigeneity, exclusion and citizenship in a relational world. *Anthropological Theory*, 12: 115–141.

Storey, D. and Hunter, S. (2010) Kiribati: an environmental 'perfect storm'. *Australian Geographer*, 41(2):167–181.

Strang, V. (2004) *The Meaning of Water*. Oxford: Berg.

Toupet, C. (1963) L'évolution de la nomadisation en Mauritanie sahélienne. In C. Bataillon (ed.) *Nomads et Nomadisme au Sahara*. Paris: UNESCO.

Tranquebar: Land of the Singing Waves, Bestseller Fund, 2010.

Turner II, B.L., Lambin, E.F. and Reenberg, A. (2007) The emergence of land change science for global environmental change and sustainability. *PNAS*, 104(52): 20666–20671.

Wilson, E.G. (2009) *The Spiritual History of Ice. Romanticism, Science, and the Imagination*. New York: Palgrave Macmillan.

FURTHER READING

GENERAL

Adger, N.W., Lorenzoni, I. and O'Brien, K. (eds) (2009) *Adapting to Climate Change: Thresholds, Values, Governance*. Cambridge: Cambridge University Press.

Bankoff, G., Frerks G. and Hilhorst, D. (eds) (2004) *Mapping Vulnerability: Disasters, Development and People*. London: Earthscan.

Brichet, N. and Hastrup, F. (2011) Figurer uden grund. Museumsansamlinger og globale klimaforandringer. *Tidsskriftet Antropologi*, 64: 119–135.

Chapin III, F.S., Kofinas, G.P. and Folke, C. (eds) (2009) *Principles of Ecosystem Stewardship: Resilience-Based Natural Resource Management in a Changing World*. New York: Springer Verlag.

Fleming, J.R. (2010) *Fixing the Sky: The Checkered History of Weather and Climate Control*. New York: Columbia University Press.

Giddens, A. (2009) *The Politics of Climate Change*. Cambridge: Polity Press.

Graedel, T.E. and van der Voet, E. (2008) *Linkages of Sustainability*. Strüngmann Forum Reports: Cambridge, MA: MIT Press.

Graham, S. and Marvin, S. (2001) *Splintering Urbanism: Networked Infrastructures, Technological Mobilities and the Urban Condition*. London: Routledge.

Hastrup, F. and Rubow, C. (2011) I omegnen af COPenhagen. *Tidsskriftet Antropologi*, 64: 61–69.

Hastrup, K. (ed.) (2009) *The Question of Resilience. Social Responses to Climate Change*, Copenhagen: The Royal Danish Academy of Sciences and Letters.

Hastrup, K. (2013a) Anthropological Contributions to the Study of Climate: Past, Present, Future. *WIREs Climate Change* 2013; doi: 10.1002/wcc.219.

Hastrup, K. (2013b) Water and the Configuration of Social Worlds: An Anthropological Perspective. *Journal of Water Resources and Policy* (JWARP) 5: 59–66.

Hastrup, K. (2013c) Nature: anthropology on the edge. In K. Hastrup (ed.) *Anthropology and Nature*. London: Routledge, pp. 1–26.

Hastrup, K. (2013d) Anticipating Nature: The Productive Uncertainty of Climate Models. In K. Hastrup, and M. Skrydstrup (eds) *The Social Life of Climate Change Models: Anticipating Nature*. London: Routledge, pp. 1–29.

Hastrup, K. (ed.) (2013e) *Anthropology and Nature*. London: Routledge.

Hastrup, K. and Olwig, K.F. (eds) (2012) *Climate Change and Human Mobility. Global Challenges to the Social Sciences*, Cambridge: Cambridge University Press.

Hastrup, K. and Skrydstrup. M. (eds) (2013) *The Social Life of Climate Change Models: Anticipating Nature*, London: Routledge.

Hulme, M. (2009) *Why We Disagree about Climate Change*. Cambridge: Cambridge University Press.

Ingold, T. (1986) *The Appropriation of Nature: Essays on Human Ecology and Social Relations*. Manchester: Manchester University Press.

Kaika, M. (2005) *City of Flows: Modernity, Nature, and the City*. London: Routledge.

Kane, S. C. (2012) *Where Rivers Meet the Sea: The Political Ecology of Water*. Philadelphia, PA: Temple University Press.

Kopnina, H. and Shoreman-Ouimet, E. (eds) (2011) *Environmental Anthropology Today*. London: Routledge.

Law, J. (2004) *After Method. Mess in Social Science Research*. New York: Routledge.

Leach, M. and Mearns, R. (eds) (1996) *The Lie of the Land: Challenging Received Wisdom on the African Environment*. Oxford: James Currey.

Mearns, R. and Norton, A. (2010) *Social Dimensions of Climate Change: Equity and Vulnerability in a Warming World*. Washington, DC: The World Bank.

Mehta, L. (ed.) (2011) *The Limits to Scarcity: Contesting the Politics of Allocation*. London: Earthscan.

Nielsen, J.Ø. and Reenberg, A. (2012) Exploring causal relations: the societal effects of climate change. *Danish Journal of Geography*, 112(2): 89–92.

Nielsen, J.Ø. and Sejersen, F. (2012) Earth System Science, the IPCC and the problem of downward causation in human geographies of Global Climate Change. *Danish Journal of Geography*, 112(2):194–202.

Nielsen, J.Ø., Olwig, M.F., Rubow, C., Patt, A. and Christoplos, I. (2012) Causal narratives and policy in a warming world, *Danish Journal of Geography*, 112(2): 208–209.

Nuttall, M. and Crate, S.A. (eds) (2009) *Anthropology and Climate Change: From Encounters to Actions*. Walnut Creek: CA Left Coast Press.

Oliver-Smith, A. and Hoffman, S. (eds) (1999) *The Angry Earth: Disaster in Anthropological Perspective*. New York: Routledge.

Olwig, M.F. (2009) Climate Change = Discourse Change? Development and Relief Organizations' Use of the Concept of Resilience. In K. Hastrup (ed.) *The Question of Resilience: Social Responses to Climate Change*. Copenhagen: The Royal Danish Academy of Sciences and Letters, pp. 314–335.

Olwig, M.F. (2012) Multi-sited resilience: the mutual construction of 'local' and 'global' understandings and practices of adaptation and innovation. *Applied Geography*, 33:112–118.

Olwig, M.F. (2013) Beyond translation: reconceptualizing the role of local practitioners and the development 'interface'. *European Journal of Development Research*, 25(3): 428–444.

Olwig, M.F., Sørensen, M.K., Rasmussen, M.S., Danielsen, F. Selvam, V., Hansen, L.B et al. (2007) Using remote sensing to assess the protective role of coastal woody vegetation against tsunami waves. *International Journal of Remote Sensing*, 28(13,14): 3153–3169.

Ong, A. and Collier, S. (eds) (2005) *Global Assemblages: Technology, Politics and Ethics as Anthropological Problems*. Oxford: Blackwell Publishing.

Parry, M.L., Canziani, O.F., Palutikof, J.P., Linden, P.J. v. d., and Hanson, C.E. (eds) (2007) *Climate Change 2007: Impacts, Adaptation and Vulnerability: Contribution of Working Group II to the Fourth Assessment Report of the Intergovernmental Panel on Climate Change*. Cambridge: Cambridge University Press.

Prigogine, I. and Stengers, I. (1984) *Order out of Chaos: Man's New Dialogue with Nature*. London: Heinemann.

Reenberg, A. (2009) Land system science: handling complex series of natural and socio-economic processes. *Journal of Land Use Science*, 4(1–2): 1–4.

Rodima-Taylor, D., Olwig, M.F. and Chhetri, N. (2012a) Adaptation as innovation, innovation as adaptation: an institutional approach to climate change. *Applied Geography*, 33: 107–111.

Rodima-Taylor, D., Olwig, M.F. and Chhetri, N. (eds) (2012b) Special issue: resilience, adaptation, and innovation: applied geographies of climate change. *Applied Geography*, 33: 107–167.

Sejersen, F., Hastrup, K., Brooks, N., Widgren, M., Rasmussen, L.V. and Rasmussen, M.B. (2012) Environmental history and the understanding of causal relations. *Danish Journal of Geography*, 112(2): 203–205.

LIVING WITH ENVIRONMENTAL CHANGE

Seto, K.C., de Groot, R., Bringezu, S., Erb, K., Graedel, T., Ramankutty, N., *et al.* (2010) Stocks, flows, and prospects. In T. Graedel and E. van der Voet (eds) *Linkages of Sustainability*, Strüngmann Forum Report, vol. 4. Cambridge, MA: MIT Press, pp. 71–96.

Seto, K.C. and Reenberg, A. (eds) (2014) *Rethinking Global Land Use in an Urban Era: Strüngmann Forum Report.* Cambridge, MA: MIT Press.

Sörlin, S. and Warde, P. (eds) (2010) *Nature's End: History and the Environment.* New York: Palgrave-Macmillan.

Strang, V. (2004) *The Meaning of Water.* Oxford: Berg.

Strauss, S. and Orlove, B.S. (eds) (2003) *Weather, Climate, Culture.* Oxford: Berg.

Swyngedouw, E. (2004) *Social Power and the Urbanization of Water: Flows of Power.* Oxford: Oxford University Press.

Vayda, A. P. (2009) *Explaining Human Actions and Environmental Changes.* Lanham, MD: Altamira Press.

Wisner, B., Blaikie, P., Cannon, T., and Davis I. (2004) *At Risk: Natural Hazards, People's Vulnerability and Disasters.* 2nd edn. London: Routledge.

THE ARCTIC

ACIA (2005) *Arctic Climate Impact Assessment.* Cambridge: Cambridge University Press.

AHDR (2004) *Arctic Human Development Report.* Akureyri: Stefansson Arctic Institute.

AMAP (2011) *Snow, Ice, Water and Permafrost in the Arctic (SWIPA).* Oslo: Arctic Monitoring and Assessment Programme, Arctic Council.

Brody, H. (1987) *Living Arctic: Hunters in the Canadian North.* London: Faber and Faber.

Hastrup, K. (2009a) The nomadic landscape. People in a changing Arctic environment. *Danish Journal of Geography*, 109(2):181–189.

Hastrup, K. (2009b) Arctic Hunters: Climate Variability and Social Flexibility. In K. Hastrup (ed.) *The Question of Resilience: Social Responses to Climate Change.* Copenhagen: The Royal Danish Academy of Science and Letters, pp. 245–270.

Hastrup, K. (2013a) Scales of attention in fieldwork: global connections and local concerns in the Arctic. *Ethnography*, 14(2): 145–164.

Hastrup, K. (2013b) Anticipation on Thin Ice: Diagrammatic Reasoning among Arctic Hunters. In K. Hastrup and M. Skrydstrup (eds) *The Social Life of Climate Change Models: Anticipating Nature.* London: Routledge, pp. 77–99.

Hastrup, K. (2013c) The ice as argument. topographical mementos in the High Arctic. *Cambridge Anthropology*, 31(1): 52–68.

Hastrup, K. (2013d) Of Maps and Men: Making Places and Peoples in the Arctic. In K. Hastrup (ed.) *Anthropology and Nature.* London: Routledge, pp. 211–232.

Keskitalo, E.C.H. (2004) *Negotiating the Arctic: The Construction of an International Region.* New York: Routledge.

Koivurova, T., Keskitalo, E.C.H. and Bankes, N. (eds) (2009) *Climate Governance in the Arctic.* New York: Springer.

Krupnik, I., Aporta, C., Gearhead, S., Laidler, G.J., and Holm, L.K. (eds) (2010) *SIKU: Knowing Our Ice: Documenting Inuit Sea-Ice Knowledge and Use.* London: Springer.

Nuttall, M. (1992) *Arctic Homeland: Kinship, Community and Development in Northwest Greenland.* Toronto: University of Toronto Press.

Nuttall, M. (2010) *Pipeline Dreams: People, Environment, and the Arctic Frontier.* Copenhagen: IWGIA/ Document 126.

Sejersen, F. (2007) Entrepreneurs in Greenland. In L.P. Dana and R.B. Anderson (eds) *International Handbook of Research on Indigenous Entrepreneurship.* Cheltenham: Edward Elgar Publishing, pp. 201–210.

Sejersen, F. (2009) Resilience, human agency and climate change adaptation strategies in the Arctic. In K. Hastrup (ed.) *The Question of Resilience. Social Responses to Climate Change.* Copenhagen: The Royal Danish Academy of Sciences and Letters, pp. 218–244.

Sejersen, F. (2010) Urbanization, landscape appropriation, and climate change in Greenland. *Acta Borealia,* 27(2): 167–188.

Sejersen, F. (2012) Mobility, Climate Change and Social Dynamics in the Arctic: The Creation of New Horizons of Expectation and the Role of the Community. In K. Hastrup and K.F. Olwig (eds) *Climate Change and Human Mobility: Global Challenges to the Social Sciences.* Cambridge: Cambridge University Press, pp. 225–254.

Vitebsky, P. (2005) *The Reindeer People: Living with Animals and Spirits in Siberia.* New York: Houghton Mifflin Company.

HIGHLANDS AND GLACIERS

Andersen, A.O. (2013) Water is life: entangled topographies and politics of water in Arequipa, Peru. PhD thesis. Department of Anthropology, University of Copenhagen.

Carey, M. (2010) *In the Shadow of Melting Glaciers: Climate Change and Andean Society.* Oxford: Oxford University Press.

Cruikshank, J. (2005) *Do Glaciers Listen? Local Knowledge, Colonial Encounters, and Social Imagination.* Vancouver, BC: UBC Press; Seattle: University of Washington Press.

Gelles, P. (2000) *Water and Power in Highland Peru: The Cultural Politics of Irrigation and Development.* New Brunswick, NJ: Rutgers University Press.

Orlove, B. (2002) *Lines in the Water: Nature and Culture in Lake Titicaca.* Berkeley, CA: University of California Press.

Orlove, B., Wiegandt, E. and Luckman, B H. (eds) (2008). *Darkening Peaks: Glacier Retreat, Science, and Society.* Berkeley, CA: University of California Press.

Rasmussen, M.B. (2009) Andean Meltdown: Comments on 'The Declaration of Recuay'. In K. Hastrup (ed.) *The Question of Resilience: Social Responses to Climate Change.* Copenhagen: The Royal Danish Academy of Sciences and Letters, pp. 197–217.

Rasmussen, M.B. (2011) La historia de un canal: Cambio Climático y Politicas del Agua en la Sierra Peruana., *Huaraz,* 3. Documento de Trabajo, Instituto de la Montana.

Rasmussen, M.B. (2012a) *Prisms of Water: Abandonment and the Art of Being Governed in the Peruvian Andes.* PhD-Series No. 73, 2012. Department of Anthropology, University of Copenhagen.

Rasmussen, M.B. (2012b) Greening the economy: articulation and the problem of governance in the Andes. *Mountain Research and Development,* 32(2): 149–157.

Stensrud, A.B. (2010) Los peregrinos urbanos en Qoyllurit'i y el juego mimético de miniaturas. *Anthropologica*, 28: 39–66.

Stensrud, A.B. (2011) 'Todo en la vida se paga': Negotiating life in Cusco, Peru. PhD dissertation, Faculty of Social Sciences, University of Oslo

Stensrud, A.B. (2013) Commodifying water in times of global warming. *NACLA Report on the Americas*, 46(1).

Stevens, S.F. (1993) *Claiming the High Ground: Sherpas, Subsistence and Environmental Change in the Highest Himalayas*. Berkeley, CA: University of California Press.

Trawick, P. (2003) *The Struggle for Water in Peru: Comedy and Tragedy in the Andean Commons*. Stanford, CA: Stanford University Press.

Wiegandt, E. (2008) *Mountains: Sources of Water, Sources of Knowledge. Advances in Global Research*, Vol. 31. Dordrecht: Springer.

THE PACIFIC AND TROPICAL COASTLANDS

Barnett, J. (2001) *The Meaning of Environmental Security: Ecological Politics and Policy in the New Security Era*. London: Zed Books.

Barnett, J. and Campbell, J. (2010) *Climate Change and Small Island States: Power, Knowledge and the South Pacific*. London: Earthscan.

Connell, J. (2013) *Islands at Risk? Environments, Economies, and Contemporary Change*. Cheltenham: Edward Elgar Publishing Limited.

Danielsen, F., Sørensen, M.K., Olwig, M.F., Selvam, V., Parish, F., Burgess, N.D., et al. (2005) The Asian tsunami: a protective role for coastal vegetation. *Science*, 310: 643.

Hastrup, F. (2009) A sense of direction: responsibility and the span of disaster in a Tamil coastal village. In K. Hastrup (ed.) *The Question of Resilience: Social Responses to Climate Change*. Copenhagen: The Royal Danish Academy of Sciences and Letters, pp.114–131.

Hastrup, F. (2010) Materializations of disaster: recovering lost plots in a tsunami-affected village in South India. In M. Bille, F. Hastrup, and T.F. Sørensen (eds) *An Anthropology of Absence: Materializations of Transcendence and Loss*. New York: Springer Publishers, pp. 99–112.

Hastrup, F. (2011a) *Weathering the World: Recovery in the Wake of the Tsunami in a Tamil Fishing Village*. Oxford: Berghahn Books.

Hastrup, F. (2011b) Shady plantations: theorizing coastal shelter in Tamil Nadu, *Anthropological Theory*, 11(4): 425–439.

Hastrup, F. (2013a) Certain Figures: Modelling Nature Among Environmental Experts in Coastal Tamil Nadu. In K. Hastrup and M. Skrydstrup (eds) *The Social Life of Climate Change Models: Anticipating Nature*, London: Routledge, pp. 45–56.

Hastrup, F. (2013b) Qualifying Coastal Nature: Bio-conservation Projects in Southeast India. In K. Hastrup (ed.) *Anthropology and Nature*. London: Routledge, pp. 43–61.

Hoeppe, G. (2007) *Conversations on the Beach:. Fishermen's Knowledge, Metaphor and Environmental Change in South India*. New York: Berghahn.

Hviding, E. and Bayliss-Smith, T. (2000) *Islands of Rainforest, Agroforestry, Logging and Eco-Tourism in Solomon Islands*. Aldershot: Ashgate.

Nunn, P. (1999) *Environmental Change in the Pacific Basin: Chronologies, Causes, Consequences.* Chichester: Wiley.

Nunn, P. (2007) *Climate, Environment and Society in the Pacific during the Last Millennium.* Amsterdam: Elsevier.

Robertson, M.L.B Connecting worlds of water: an ethnography of environments in Tarawa, Kiribati. PhD thesis. Department of Anthropology, University of Copenhagen (forthcoming).

Robertson, M.L.B. (in press) Crafting certainty in liquid worlds: encountering climate change in Kiribati. *Versita.*

Robertson, M.L.B. and Rubow, C. (2013) Engaged World-making: Movements of Sand, Sea, and People at Two Pacific Islands. In K. Hastrup (ed.) *Anthropology and Nature.* London: Routledge, pp. 62–78.

Rubow, C. (2009) The metaphysical aspects of resilience: South Pacific responses to climate change. In K. Hastrup. (ed.) *The Question of Resilience: Social Responses to Climate Change.* Copenhagen: The Royal Danish Academy of Sciences and Letters, pp. 88–113.

Rubow, C. (2012a) Enacting Cyclones: The Mixed Response to Climate Change in the Cook Islands. In K. Hastrup and M. Skrydstrup, M. (eds) *The Social Life of Climate Change Models: Anticipating Nature.* London: Routledge, pp. 57–76.

Rubow, C. (2012b) Klimaforandringernes metafysik: verden som natur, omgivelser og ophav. *Tidsskriftet Antropologi,* 64: 101–117.

Rubow, C. (2013) Laguneteologiseringer i Sydhavet. *Kritisk forum for praktisk teologi,* 132: 74–84.

Rubow, C. (in press) Whoosh: Cyclones as cultural natural whirls. A case from the South Pacific. *Versita.*

Schneider, K. (2012) *Saltwater Sociality: A Melanesian Island Ethnography.* New York: Berghahn Books.

Strang, V. (1997) *Uncommon Ground: Cultural Landscapes and Environmental Values.* Oxford: Berg.

Subramanian, A. (2009) *Shorelines: Space and Rights in South India.* Stanford, CA: Stanford University Press.

Waddel, E., Naidu, V. and Hau'ofa, E. (1993) *A New Oceania: Rediscovering our Sea of Islands.* Fiji: The University of the South Pacific, School of Social and Economic Development.

AFRICAN DRYLANDS

Batterbury, S. and Warren, A. (2001) Viewpoint. The African Sahel 25 years after the great drought. *Global Environmental Change,* 11: 1–8.

Claude, J., Grouzis, M., Milleville, P., Fauck, R., Chevallier, P., Langlois, M. *et al.* (1991) *Un espace sahelien: la mare d'Oursi, Burkina Faso.* Paris: Orstrom.

Cordell, D.D., Gregory, J.W., and Piché, V. (1996) *Hoe and Wage: A Social History of Circular Migration Systems in West Africa.* Boulder, CO: Westview Press.

De Bruijn, M. and Dijk, H.V. (1995) *Arid Ways: Cultural Understandings of Insecurity in the Sahel.* Amsterdam: Thela Publishers.

Dietz, A.J., Ruben, R. and Verhagen, A. (2004) *The Impacts of Climate Change on Drylands: With Focus on West Africa.* Dordrecht: Kluwer Academic Publishers.

Mortimore, M. (1998) *Roots in the African Dusts: Sustaining the Drylands.* Cambridge: Cambridge University Press.

Mortimore, M. (2009) *Dryland Opportunities: A New Paradigm for People, Ecosystems and Development.* London and Nairobi: IUCN, Gland, IIED, UNDP/DDC.

Nielsen, J.Ø. (2009) Drought and Marriage: Exploring the Interconnection Between Climate Variability and Social Change Through a Livelihood Perspective. In K. Hastrup (ed.) *The Question of Resilience: Social Responses to Climate Change.* Copenhagen: The Royal Danish Society of Arts and Letters, pp. 159–177.

Nielsen, J.Ø. (2010) The outburst: climate change, gender relation and situational analysis. *Social Analysis*, 54(3): 110–123.

Nielsen, J-Ø. and D'Haen, S. (in press). Asking about climate change: reflections on methodology in qualitative climate change research published in global environmental change since 2000. *Global Environmental Change.*

Nielsen, J.Ø., D'Haen, S. and Reenberg, A. (2012) Adaptation to climate change is a development project: a case study from northern Burkina Faso. *Climate and Development*, 4(1): 16–25.

Nielsen, J.Ø. and Reenberg, A. (2010a) Cultural barriers to climate change adaptation: a case study from Northern Burkina Faso. *Global Environmental Change*, 20: 142–152.

Nielsen, J.Ø. and Reenberg, A. (2010b) Temporality and the problem with singling out climate as a current driver of change in a small West African village. *Journal of Arid Environments*, 74: 464–474.

Nielsen, J.Ø. and Vigh, H. (2012) Adaptive lives: navigating the global food crisis in a changing climate. *Global Environmental Change*, 22(3): 659–669.

OECD (2009) *Regional Atlas of West Africa.* Paris: OECD.

Olwig, M.F. and Gough, K.V. (2013) Basket weaving and social weaving: young Ghanaian artisans' mobilization of 'social capital' through mobility. *Geoforum*, 45: 168–177.

Proud, S.R., Fensholt, R., Rasmussen, L.V. and Sandholt, I. (2011) Rapid response flood detection using the MSG geostationary satellite. *International Journal of Applied Earth Observation and Geoinformation*, 13(4): 536–544,

Proud, S.R. and Rasmussen, L.V. (2011) The influence of seasonal rainfall upon Sahel vegetation. *Remote Sensing Letters*, 2(3): 241–249.

Rain, D. (1999) *Eaters of the Dry Season: Circular Labor Migration in the West African Sahel.* Boulder, CO: Westview Press.

Rasmussen, L.V., Rasmussen, K., Birch-Thomsen, T., Kristensen, S.B.P. and Traoré, O. (2012) The effect of cassava-based bioethanol production on above-ground stocks: a case study from Southern Mali. *Energy Policy*, 41: 575–583.

Rasmussen, L.V., Rasmussen, K. and Bruun, T.B. (2012) Impacts of Jatropha-based biodiesel production on above and below-ground carbon stocks: a case study from Mozambique. *Energy Policy*, 51: 728–736.

Rasmussen, L.V., Rasmussen, K., Reenberg, A. and Proud, S.R. (2012) A system dynamics approach to land use changes in agro-pastoral systems on the desert margins of Sahel. *Agricultural Systems*, 10: 56–64.

Rasmussen, L.V. and Reenberg, A. (2012a) Land use rationales in desert fringe agriculture. *Applied Geography*, 34: 595–605.

Rasmussen, L.V. and Reenberg, A. (2012b) Collapse and recovery in Sahelian agro-pastoral systems: rethinking trajectories of change. *Ecology and Society*, 17(14).

Rasmussen, L.V. and Reenberg, A. (2013) Multiple outcomes of cultivation in the Sahel: a call for a multifunctional view of farmers' incentives. *International Journal of Agricultural Sustainability* 12(3).

Raynaut, C. (1997) *Societies and Nature in the Sahel*. London and Stockholm: Routledge/Stockholm Environment Institute.

Reenberg, A. (2009) Embedded Flexibility in Coupled Human-environmental Systems in the Sahel: Talking about Resilience. In K. Hastrup (ed.) *The Question of Resilience. Social Implications of Environmental Changes*. Copenhagen: The Royal Danish Academy of Sciences and Letters, pp. 132–158.

Reenberg, A. (2012) Insistent dryland narratives: portraits of knowledge about human-environmental interactions in Sahelian environment policy documents. *West African Journal of Applied Ecology*, 20(1): 97–111.

Reenberg, A., Maman, I. and Oksen, P. (2013) Twenty years of land use and livelihood changes in SE-Niger: obsolete and short-sighted adaptation to climatic and demographic pressures? *Journal of Arid Environments*, 94: 47–58.

Reenberg, A., Oksen, P. and Svendsen, J. (2003) Land use changes vis-à-vis agricultural potential in southeastern Burkina Faso: the field expansion paradox. *Danish Journal of Geography*, 103(2): 57–64.

Reenberg, A., Rasmussen, L.V. and Nielsen, J.Ø. (2012) Causal relations and land use transformation in the Sahel: conceptual lenses for processes, temporal totality and inertia. *Danish Journal of Geography*, 112(2): 159–173.

Thébaud, B. (2002) *Foncier pastoral et gestion de l'espace au Sahel*. Paris: Khartala.

VanVliet, N., Reenberg, A. and Rasmussen, L.V. (2013) Scientific documentation of cropland changes in the Sahel: a half empty box of knowledge to support policy? *Journal of Arid Environments*, 95: 1–13.

Vium, C. (2009) Nomad_Scapes: Mobility and Wayfinding as Resilience Among Nomadic Pastoralists in the Islamic Republic of Mauritania. In K. Hastrup (ed.) *The Question of Resilience: Local Responses to Climate Change*. Copenhagen: The Royal Danish Academy of Sciences and Letters, pp.178–196.

T - #0323 - 160425 - C320 - 276/216/17 [19] - CB - 9780415746670 - Gloss Lamination